The Upper Room
Disciplines
2000

The Upper Room
Disciplines
2000

UPPER
ROOM BOOKS
NASHVILLE

Contents

CONTENTS

CONTENTS

CONTENTS

CONTENTS

CONTENTS

Foreword

Welcome to *Disciplines 2000* and twelve months of reading the Bible devotionally. *Disciplines* is designed to help you establish a daily pattern of reading the Bible, praying with scripture, and listening to God. Each week a respected spiritual leader/writer explores particular scripture lessons and breaks open the Word for us.

How do we read the Bible devotionally? One ancient practice of Christian devotion that can guide our use of *Disciplines* is the Benedictine tradition of *lectio divina* (or *lectio*), which means "sacred reading." Simply put, *lectio* is listening to God through prayerful reading of scripture. I commend it to you for your spiritual practice for several reasons.

First, *lectio* reminds us that the ultimate purpose of reading the Bible devotionally is encounter with God who seeks our transformation in the Word. Second, *lectio* holds together devotional reading and intellectual inquiry. Solid reflection on the background and meaning of a biblical text prepares the way for prayerful encounter with God. The daily reflections in *Disciplines* help us engage the scripture with our minds so we can enter into it with our hearts. *Lectio* instructs us to slow down, to select small portions of scripture we can carry within us through the day, and to prepare for a fresh word from the most familiar passages.

Third, *lectio* reorients personal prayer to the word of God. When our prayer life depends on spontaneous outpourings of the heart, our time with God eventually degenerates into me-centered preoccupation with personal needs and wishes. Prayer means nothing else but the readiness and willingness to receive and appropriate the Word.

Fourth, *lectio* serves as a guide for group reflection and prayer, as well as individual devotion. With the aid of *Disciplines*, group *lectio* enriches people who regularly gather for biblical reflection and listening to God that does not depend on a teacher or scholarly preparation.

Finally, *lectio divina* is a way of life, not just a method for "doing our devotions." The traditional four movements of *lectio divina* describe the process by which we enter into the Word and allow it to transform us in Christ.

The first movement is *lectio*, or reading. We prepare ourselves for God by taking time to quiet our bodies and minds. We open our Bible expecting God's word to address us, and we read with openness of heart and readiness to respond.

The second movement is *meditatio*, or reflection. We engage the text with our minds. We ponder someone else's thoughts on the text in *Disciplines*. We search for relevant meanings, applications, and insights. We involve ourselves imaginatively in the text. We write thoughts in our journal. We commit to memory short phrases that speak to us so that we can savor them throughout the day. We seek to hear what God wants to communicate to us today.

The third movement is *oratio*, or response. We move from thinking about God to conversing with God. Reflection on the scripture gives way to and guides the exchanges of a living relationship. Thought turns to prayer as we address God personally. Dialogue ensues as we respond in all honesty to what we feel God is saying to us and listen to God's response. Intimacy deepens as we pour out our love for God in adoration and intercession and experience the gift of a renewed spirit.

The fourth movement is *contemplatio*, or rest. In *contemplatio*, we move from conversation with God to communion with God. We relax our efforts to actively meditate and pray. We let God be God in us. Our sole desire is to be one with our Lord, to live our lives today as love is leading us. Being transformed in the Word, we come to say with Saint Paul, "I have been crucified with Christ; and it is no longer I who live, but it is Christ who lives in me."

—*Stephen D. Bryant*
World Editor of The Upper Room

God's Word Runs Swiftly

January 1–2, 2000 • *Michael E. Williams**

SATURDAY, JANUARY 1 • Read Ecclesiastes 3:1-13

Many people make resolutions on the first day of a new year, but what do you resolve on the first day of a new year? We are beginning a new decade, a new century, and find ourselves poised on the threshold of a new millennium. You and I already may have made our resolutions, many of which we will break before the week is out.

I want to consider a different question: What would your prayers be for Christians across the world as we navigate this important transition? Let me share a few of mine.

First, I pray that we as Christians approach the twenty-first century more determined to live out God's commandments to love God and our neighbor than to make everyone believe exactly the way we do. Second, I pray that Christians would include as neighbors every part of God's creation. Third, I pray that Christians would talk less and do more to respond in love to violence, poverty, hunger, homelessness, loneliness, and hurt. Fourth, I pray that Christians would look for Christ in other cultures and traditions. This practice may protect us from turning Jesus into an idol that simply mirrors ourselves.

I believe that if we, as followers of Jesus, will follow his example in these ways, we will transform our world and this new millennium into a place and time where God's love reigns. What are your prayers on this day?

PRAYER: Dear God, make me over into the image of your love. Help me live out my calling from you as fully as Jesus lived his. Help me make the world a place filled with your love. Amen.

---

*Pastor of Blakemore United Methodist Church, Nashville, Tennessee; General Editor of *The Storyteller's Companion to the Bible.*

SUNDAY, JANUARY 2 • Read Revelation 21:1-6a

Toward the end of Revelation, John receives a vision of God's future plan for the faithful. Throughout most of his vision, John offers a word of encouragement to followers of Jesus who are experiencing persecution. He does not claim to be an apostle or to hold any special position in the church. John's only authority for writing to Christians who are suffering for their faith comes from his having suffered too. He writes from exile on the island of Patmos.

The one word of hope that echoes throughout John's vision is that the future belongs to God. God's future promises the end of death and pain. The coming of the city of God will exhibit the festivity of a marriage feast. Those who have wept will have their tears wiped by the very hand of God.

As we begin a new year, those of us who have acquired many things and who hold positions of power in the church and the world may not hear John's warning that this world will pass away as particularly good news. Still those around the world who struggle to live from day to day and who suffer for their faith hear with open ears and hearts the good news of God's new heaven and new earth.

PRAYER: God, you wipe away all tears and invite me into a new creation. Help me hear with joy your promises for the future. Amen.

New Beginnings

January 3–9, 2000 • Larry M. Goodpaster*

MONDAY, JANUARY 3 • Read Psalm 29:1-2

Today is the first Monday of the first month of the first year beginning with the number 20. We will leave it to the philosophers and those persons with time on their hands to debate whether the twenty-first century has now officially begun or if we must wait another year. The Bible does not concern itself with such matters but rather views each day as a time and a call to radical faithfulness and trust in God.

We begin our reflections on new beginnings at that very point. The psalmist's words call us to attention, invite us to worship, and stir us to imagine the glory and strength of God. The approach of a new year, regardless of the century in which it is counted, encourages us to refocus. The psalmist affirms that we are to experience all of life and all of our days in the context of the sacredness of time. Standing at this unique moment in history, we are to refocus our attention toward God.

Many people start a new year with resolutions. This year, let us resolve to make a new beginning by opening our hearts and souls to the Creator and Redeemer of time and life, past and future. Let us resolve to live out that new beginning in creative openness to the movement of God's spirit.

Let us resolve to worship God in the holy splendor of transformed and redeemed lives.

PRAYER: Holy God, your name and your presence are holy. I give you glory and honor as the One who makes each day a new beginning. Let it be so in this moment. Amen.

---

*Senior Pastor, First United Methodist Church, Tupelo, Mississippi.

TUESDAY, JANUARY 4 • Read Genesis 1:1-5

Recent scholarship raises important questions about the most accurate translation of the opening lines of today's scripture. I grew up having memorized, "In the beginning, God created"—and that was enough. In many ways, it still is. We will never know the how or the what. It is enough to know the why of creation, which the opening celebration of the scripture affirms. An alternate reading suggests that the opening verse reads, "In the beginning, when God began to create," which is rich with its own imagery and power. It suggests that creation and re-creation continue and that we are part of that exciting new beginning with every new day, every new life, and every new glimpse of hope and peace.

At the start of it all, when it all came together—or was blown apart in order to be reconnected—there was God. The gift of creation was twofold: order and light. From the chaos, the void, and the deep came order and life. New beginnings always imply a new sense of order and direction for our living. Out of what seems to be deep turmoil and confusion comes the hope of newness in God's graceful reordering and reshaping of our lives.

At the same time, new beginnings throw fresh, bright light on previous darkness and doubt. Suddenly we see again and discover a whole new world and a new way of walking. The Creator of all beginnings, of all time, extends the ordering word to bring light to our lives in this new day, new year, new century.

PRAYER: Creator God, recreate within me a sense of excitement and passion for what you have done in all creation. Bring order to and shed light on the darkness of my soul, through the One who is the Light of the world. Amen.

WEDNESDAY, JANUARY 5 • **Read Psalm 29:3-11**

Assumptions often get us into trouble. Many people assume that a new beginning simply means a continuation of what was with a few minor adjustments and additions here and there—like exercising without changing eating habits and assuming that we will somehow lose weight; like making New Year's resolutions about priorities and involvements and then assuming they will happen with no discipline on our part.

The psalmist vividly describes the dawning of a new day: God's presence and power as the beginning of a new creation. For that new beginning to occur, an ending of the old must come. Thus, in graphic terms, the psalmist talks about God's breaking down cedars, shaking the wilderness, and stripping the forests. This manifestation of power is not to bring about the end of the world as we know it; rather, it demonstrates the majesty of God's ability to create new possibilities out of the old. Our only response in the face of such work is to shout, "Glory!"

Many of us have witnessed the rebirth of life following devastating storms—both those of nature and those of personal experience. The twentieth century began with great hopes, dreams, and goals. Despite the marvelous advances in technology and medicine and social science, the century draws to a close with a limp in the midst of a storm of confusion and despair. But hope still exists for a new beginning through the God who sits enthroned above it all.

This day, may we look for demonstrations, both great and small, of God's creative presence and power. When we observe God in the midst of life, we will glimpse a new beginning that offers strength and the blessing of peace.

PRAYER: God of grace, in the beauty of creation and in the power of storms, may I continually turn to you as the one who rules over all and whose compassion is ever directed toward me. Amen.

THURSDAY, JANUARY 6 • Read Matthew 2:1-12; Isaiah 60:1-6

EPIPHANY OF THE LORD

We interrupt our reflections on new beginnings to observe and celebrate the Day of Epiphany. Today's readings include the familiar story of wise men from the East who make a journey, follow a star, respond to their instincts, and ask questions. Their story makes this a day to discover in fresh, new ways the unfolding and the unveiling of the great good news of God's love in Christ Jesus.

Today the question that seems to permeate these brief twelve verses haunts me: Where is he? The wise men ask it. In his own way, King Herod asks it. While they know the location, the chief priests and scribes are not sure—this could not be the time and place, could it? The answer to the question, of course, surprises them, the world, and us. He is not where anyone expected. He is not in royal palaces on comfortable beds, not in designated holy places and sacred spaces. He is in Bethlehem—small town, every town. He is among shepherds and peasants and those on the margins. He is there in the midst of life even in its arrogance and pride, its self-confident answers, and its suspicions and prejudices. He is there to shine the light of God's love among us all.

For that reason we can sing with Isaiah, "Arise, shine; for your light has come....Lift up your eyes and look around." The answer to the question guides us into this new year. Perhaps Epiphany has not been an interruption after all but a revelation. He is among us still, and it really is a new beginning.

PRAYER: Revealing God, open my eyes that I may see again the glory of your light revealed to me and for me in the presence of the One born in Bethlehem but living for all time. Amen.

FRIDAY, JANUARY 7 • **Read Acts 19:1-7**

It is like starting all over again. We have experienced the thrill of new starts and restarts, of cracks in the door and cracks in history—where God's recreating power is set loose once more.

Paul finds his visit to Ephesus full of surprises. A group of believers is already there. These believers know of Jesus, and have, in their own ways, chosen to follow him. However, they lack the experience and the power of coming authentically alive through God's spirit moving into them. This story elevates limited knowledge to status quo and tells of believers who live a less than flourishing life. As Paul opens the windows of their souls to the reality of the Holy Spirit, they suddenly catch fire—a Pentecost experience in another place and time. And for the believers, it is like a new beginning.

We often settle for less than full exposure to God's power; we content ourselves with where we are, what we know, and how we have learned in the past. Sometimes we are better at quenching fires than encouraging the spread of them for fear something might happen. This text invites us into a new explosion of God's spirit, which ignites a new beginning in ministry and service.

The new beginning leads us to share the good news of Christ Jesus both in spoken word and lived deeds. It inspires us to new depths of faith and new avenues of reaching out. Before we know it, Pentecost happens all over again—as it did at Ephesus. If God keeps doing this, what will the world come to? A new beginning for a new year?

PRAYER: Empowering God, energize me again with the flame of your Holy Spirit. May I feel again the renewing power of your spirit flowing through me and sending me out with words and deeds of grace and love. Amen.

SATURDAY, JANUARY 8 • Read Mark 1:4-11

John the Baptizer keeps popping up in all the seasons of our church calendar. And each time he pokes his head into our lives, something of God happens again. In Advent, we meet him as a forerunner, a new Elijah, preparing the way, announcing that something amazing is about to happen: God is about to act in a revolutionary new way. People must prepare or miss it. Now, in the season of Epiphany, we meet him as a prophet—one who speaks a word for God, from God, to a nation of people desperate for a fresh, lively experience of God. He points beyond himself to the One who acts to create, recreate, redeem, and transform.

What happens out in the wilderness has never before occurred. John's proclamation and the response of the people have stirred up quite a scene, as people from the whole Judean countryside and all the people of Jerusalem go out to him. Certainly this text contains some poetic license and preacher-counting, but the symbolism is vivid. People tired of what they have been receiving in their religious rituals and practices, as well as those who probably don't have a religious bone in their bodies, are going to the wilderness to find hope in the preaching of a rugged man and the water of a river. God's very presence is breaking into their lives, and their hungers and hurts find satisfaction. And it is like a new beginning for them.

Perhaps a new beginning will come for us outside the boundaries of the expected and the accepted. Perhaps a journey to the wilderness—or at least away from the trappings of religiosity and the distractions of the culture—will open our hearts and ears to God's word for our day. Listen.

PRAYER: Speaking and renewing God, stir up in me a hunger for the word that will heal and help, and direct me to the place where I will hear again your message of hope and renewal. Amen.

Mark goes straight to the point, taking little time for explanation and even less time for debate. Jesus comes and is baptized. That's it. No word as to why Mark believes the baptism necessary; no hesitation about the symbolism of perfection coming for repentance; no insights into the amount of water John uses. As they say, timing is everything. After growing up and working around Nazareth, Jesus knows it's now time: time to expand the boundaries and time to engage in ministry for all people. It is beginning.

A new world, a new time, a new century stretches before us. No one knows what may be ahead, but this much we know: God is preparing the way already for those who choose to follow. Some will get stuck in wondering about why Jesus went to the Jordan for this service of baptism; others will invest energy in questions that, while fascinating, miss the point. Who will listen for the voice of God in the midst of the noise of the world, the beat of the crowd's feet?

Mark does not tell us who heard the voice (the impression is it was only Jesus). But what Mark does remind us of is that after years of laboring in his hometown with the skills and artistry of his parents, Jesus is called by the wilderness voice and the voice of God. When we hear those voices, it will be like a new beginning as we walk in new paths and into new experiences. But it will also be like an adventure in grace, for who knows where the voice will take us. We only know that as we listen, the voice of God still invites us to new beginnings and new ministry.

PRAYER: Inviting God, here I am. Help me hear and respond to your voice and follow in the way, wherever it takes me. Amen.

Searched and Known

January 10–16, 2000 • Dorothy Watson Tatem*

MONDAY, JANUARY 10 • Read 1 Samuel 3:1-20

The unexpected voice

We all have a perception of how knowledge is to come to us. One expects the teacher to impart to the student, the doctor to the patient, the broker to the investor, the trainer to the trainee. The expert teaching the novice seems to be part of the natural order.

Yet one perceives that God often has chosen another process. Eli is the high priest. Samuel is the novitiate, and a boy at that. God has not spoken to Israel for many years. One might expect that when the word from the Lord comes again, it will come to the high priest, Eli. But the divine word comes to a mere child—Samuel.

God's order differs greatly from our expectations. Abram hears from God, not his father Terah. Joseph, rather than one of his older brothers, becomes the second in authority in Egypt. God calls Moses, not Aaron, to lead Israel out of Egypt. God chooses Gideon, the weakest of his family from the weakest clan in Manasseh, to save Israel from the Midianites; and a woman Jael brings down the mighty Canaanite warrior Sisera.

God, after a long silence, again speaks to Israel through a mere boy-apprentice; and the long-awaited message concerns his high priest. Eli wisely discerns God's speaking through an unexpected source. The priest eagerly hears all that God says, though it brings words of severe judgment.

SUGGESTION FOR MEDITATION: **In what areas of your life are you willing to hear God's word from an unexpected voice? Having heard, do you willingly accept the message?**

---

*Director, Office of Resourcing for the Eastern Pennsylvania Conference of The United Methodist Church, Valley Forge, Pennsylvania.

TUESDAY, JANUARY 11 • **Read Psalm 139:1-6**

More than a number

Our social security numbers, our Orwellian identification, empower us. These personal digits allow us to apply for employment and be identified by the government for tax purposes. We can open bank accounts, apply for credit cards, negotiate mortgages, and claim an identity for health care. Portions of our numbers empower us to unlock the doors of buildings. Our social security numbers in many ways define us.

We also can bemoan the impersonal nature of the number; however, this is the way of technology. While we acknowledge that we are infinitely more profound than our social security numbers can ever reveal, sometimes we forget this truth.

The Lord shares with us the intimacy of the divine knowledge of our being. In intimacy, one knows beyond the overt behaviors. Intimacy accepts the faults and applauds the gifts. Intimacy gives us the space to be whoever we are. Intimacy is knowing and simultaneously accepting.

God knows us and accepts us even when we cannot accept ourselves. In this being known, we can come to know and to accept who we are. In this being known we can become more fully who we are meant to be.

A number may appear to give us power, but the power resides in the number, not us. If the numerical designation is erased or stolen, our identity seems to disappear. This is not so with God's knowledge of us. God knows *us* intimately. God's knowledge of us imbues us with power, a power given through uniqueness and belovedness. The loss of a number does not devalue our significance; our identity as a child of God remains.

PRAYER: **Creator God, when the numbers that define me are stripped away, may I find myself in your presence as a loved and known child of yours. Amen.**

WEDNESDAY, JANUARY 12 • Read Psalm 139:1-6

In the darkness

Sometimes in the pitch darkness in which our souls find themselves, we cry out with a strangled voice, and the agonizing sound seems to seek out the edges of eternity. The voice frantically races toward the far recesses of the eternal, searching for something to bring a gentle, caressing touch to the soul. The voice of our spirit dashes here and there in our inner being, pausing only for microseconds in hope of hearing a responding utterance that will speak of solution or resolution of our present dilemma. Within, we run screaming like a person to whom order and quiet are foreign concepts. One by one, we reject possible confidants. We shriek within, because we cannot find or do not trust anyone to know the horrors that drive us into such frenzy. We feel utterly alone and powerless. All the while we seem to run like mad persons in a graveyard at a moonless midnight hour.

Does someone mention God? Do the mind and heart whisper, "Tell God"?

Because we have no other hope, we surrender to the suggestion. We go to the altar within and sob out the trouble until we are bone-weary with the telling and the weeping. We become silent. Seconds pass. Sometimes hours and days pass. The only response from the eternal corridors is silence—unbroken soundlessness.

Then, when we least expect, out of the void—a thought, a phone call, an insight—something comes to us out of the abyss of pain. We glimpse hope, a modicum of understanding, a whisper of peace, a fleeting sense of direction. Nothing is clear, but God has given enough—enough knowing for this moment, this day.

PRAYER: Dear God, in my frenzy and fear, hem me in "behind and before…lay your hand upon me," that I may have the assurance of your presence today. Amen.

THURSDAY, JANUARY 13 • Read Psalm 139:13-18

Still amazed

Like the psalmist of thousands of years gone by, we marvel at the child in the womb. Even our sophisticated technologies, like ultrasound, have not rendered as ordinary the development of life.

This weaving together of the human form in the womb awes the psalmist beyond rationality. The phrase "curiously wrought" (v. 15, KJV) is literally the image of embroidery with reference to the veins and arteries. The author expresses utter amazement at the divine creative initiative and power. The consideration of humanity in miniature overwhelms him with reverence and praise. The psalmist cannot begin to fathom the mind of God. God's innumerable thoughts lie beyond humankind's persistent, consistent, and probing endeavors.

Each of us is the product of the mind and creativity of God. Does not the Creator know the created better than anyone? To be so intricately constructed is to be intimately known. We are not unknown and alone. God is with us in the totality of our lives, for we are divinely created.

Persons readily use the designation "low self-esteem" to describe a lack of self-confidence or self-worth. Usually confident individuals may experience this low state of being during times of failure or hardship. Yet today's psalm verses explicitly refute any perception of a deficiency in human worth. Humankind is full of the wonder of God's creative activity. We are not cosmic accidents but the purposeful results of God's creativity.

Let us hold tenaciously to the reality that we are quintessential works of art created by our God!

PRAYER: **Creating God, who created all things and called them good, make me mindful of my place in your wonderful plan. May I never downplay the wonder of life! Amen.**

FRIDAY, JANUARY 14 • Read John 1:43-51

Relegated to insignificance

I sat at the table with students, businesspersons, and educators listening attentively to the engaging speaker, the classic example of the "good" orator. His logical and well-substantiated presentation employed vivid images. He interjected humor at precisely the appropriate moment in order to keep the audience alert, entertained, and informed.

Then the speaker offered an illustration about people in despair: He cited residents of north Philadelphia (in Pennsylvania). There it was again—that dastardly view that one would find nothing of worth in this geographical area. He did not qualify his statement; his comment enshrouded all of north Philadelphia. He left no room for the existence of families in that area who aspired to everything that a family in the suburbs desires. He made no reference to the many homeowners, the hard workers, the caring neighbors, and the diligent students. The speaker assumed that surely no person from that deplorable locale could possibly be sitting in the room. At the close of the presentation, I raised my hand and said simply, "I am from north Philadelphia."

In Jesus' time, the government housed the despised Roman garrisons just outside Nazareth, a town of about 1,500 to 2,000 persons. One traveled by the town on the way to somewhere else. Nathanael's mind-set in this passage that nothing good can come out of Nazareth almost causes him to miss Jesus. But Nathanael accepts Philip's invitation to "come and see."

Many have missed Jesus because the Savior did not come as they desired. How many times have we refused to "come and see" because of birthplace, race, gender, social status?

SUGGESTION FOR MEDITATION: Whom have you relegated to insignificance because he or she comes from "Nazareth"?

SATURDAY, JANUARY 15 • Read 1 Corinthians 6:19-20

A temple or refuse site?

The Corinthian Christians are beginning to be morally extravagant in their freedom. They deem anything that the body engages in, from food to sex, as acceptable. After all, if the spirit belongs to God, then the body is free to do as it chooses. This widespread thinking has led to behavior that makes these Corinthian Christians resemble those who do not follow Christ. Yet Paul reminds them that the body is a "temple of the Holy Spirit."

We cannot imagine entering a sanctuary and discarding our daily trash and garbage upon the altar. Even to think of scrawling graffiti on the walls and pews would appall us. To litter the floors voluminously with debris is not a thought that we entertain.

Paul, in writing to the Corinthians, reminds them that for Christians all things may be lawful but not all things are beneficial. Why then do we subject our bodies, in which the Holy Spirit resides, to excesses in eating, work, and illicit pleasures? What we would find unthinkable in the physical sanctuary is commonplace in the temple of our bodies.

Pause a moment and consider—to what are you subjecting your body that may offend the Holy Spirit who dwells within you? God will glorify your divinely precious body even as God glorified the body of Jesus.

Do you treat your body as a dump heap for indiscriminate yielding to passions or as a field sown continuously by divine power, gifts, and grace?

PRAYER: God of Resurrection power, help me treat my body as your Temple. Make me aware of ways I offend your Holy Spirit who dwells in me. Amen.

SUNDAY, JANUARY 16 • Read 1 Corinthians 6:12-20

Can you prove your worth?

Often through our employment, professions, affiliations, possessions, or physical prowess we try to prove how worthy we are. Our world's goal orientation pushes us to accomplish and achieve. However, once we join the group, achieve to the nth degree, become the most captivating of persons, we find that something is still missing. The void that existed still exists. The external simply camouflages the internal.

For the Corinthians, the external has no tie to the internal. They place no constraints on external behavior, because the internal and external have no link. Yet Paul reminds them of their link to Christ through the Spirit, so that their external behaviors and sins become sins against Christ. Finally Paul states that the Corinthians—despite affirmations otherwise—do not belong to themselves. Even their bodies belong to God. Those redeemed through the death of Christ must honor God with their spirits and their bodies.

Perhaps our society's emphasis on externals helps us separate body and spirit. Perhaps we need to consider letting go of accomplishment and achievement in order to spend more time *being*—being who we are and appreciating our uniqueness.

We recall the psalmist's words: "Wonderful are your works!" The world needs folk who like themselves inside and out! Without all the trappings of so-called success and popularity, each is exquisitely beautiful. Our bodies and our spirits contribute to God's creation. When we gratefully acknowledge what God has made in us, then we are less likely to violate ourselves or others. "For you were bought with a price: therefore glorify God in your body."

PRAYER: O God, I come to you with praise for that which is within and without. "Wonderful are your works!" Amen.

Obedience Is the Key

January 17–23, 2000 • Sheron C. Patterson*

MONDAY, JANUARY 17 • Read Jonah 3:1-5, 10

My vehicle and I came to a standstill at a red traffic light, a clear indication that I must stop. Traffic lights tell us when to start, when to slow, and when to stop, giving direction to our comings and goings.

In a sense, God serves that same function in our lives. Even though God's signals don't always come in vivid greens, yellows, or reds, God's love is the basis of the directing. God desires the best for us and God continually communicates directions for our lives. It's up to us to watch and obey. Obedience is the key. Looking, listening, and watching for God are keys to obedience.

Refusal to obey often occurs. Either we do not understand the work God is doing in our lives, or we do not understand why God is directing us down unknown paths. Sometimes we simply don't like the direction that God is steering us in.

The people of Nineveh hear the words of the prophet Jonah and obey because they believe the God whose message Jonah proclaims. They may not like the message; they may not understand it. It may wreak havoc with their schedules, but they obey. Imagine the bustling city of Nineveh coming to a complete standstill as the people fast and don sackcloth.

The obedience of the Ninevites results in God's favor: God relents of the promised calamity. What will it take for you to do God's bidding—not later, not next week, but now?

PRAYER: Lord, I want to start, slow, and stop today according to your directions. Amen.

---

*Senior pastor, Jubilee United Methodist Church, Duncanville, Texas; author of three books and countless articles.

TUESDAY, JANUARY 18 • Read Psalm 62:5-6

Our souls need an oasis from the relentless sense of frenzy, rush, and hurry up. Deadlines, meetings and schedules squeeze serenity out of us. We knowingly throw ourselves into this whirlwind of commitment, responsibilities, and calendars—often for good causes. Yet in the end, we find that we are irritable, exhausted, and overwhelmed. In the face of our misery, the psalmist suggests that we find rest in God alone.

One day I wearied of the gasping, heart-racing episodes of stressed-out fear. My soul sought the Lord alone through a process of trial and failure. My flesh wanted a remedy that I could control, manipulate, and deal with tangibly. God remains out of our grasp yet within our reach. The psalmist seems to know that the practice of seeking for God helps us develop a deeper appreciation for God. The seeking enables us to rest.

It takes guts to shout No! to all the demands of life, to focus on God and plunge into God's rest. Seeking rest in God alone is an assertive act on the part of the soul. The soul must find rest; therefore, it seeks rest. Our souls must realize when they need rest, or we burn out. Fast-paced living is addictive. It gives us the illusion of power and control.

We can rest in God who offers divine relaxation and an invitation to slow down, pause and meditate on the One who made all things possible. We can release our need for control over things for a while and let God restore and revive us. Only in God's care will we find a sweet peace.

PRAYER: Lord, I want to accept your care for me; relax my need to control. Amen.

WEDNESDAY, JANUARY 19 • Read Psalm 62:7

How different would our lives be if we lived out this verse: "My salvation and my honor depend on God"?(NIV) Would it mean that we invest less money in designer clothes, luxury cars, or prestigious addresses? Would it mean we might experience less pressure to be the best, to know the most, and to climb the highest?

A spirit of competition envelops us and the fracas of self-serving drives us to concern ourselves with what we have and what others don't have. Such identifications tear us apart rather than bringing us together. Most importantly, our frenzied way of life—that of acquisition and self-serving—removes God from the equation of honor and salvation. We rely on "things" or people or prestige to give us honor and salvation. We have forsaken God's original design; we have forgotten that we are "fearfully and wonderfully made" (Ps. 139:14) by the Lord—the Lord alone.

The psalmist speaks with confidence about an inner source of strength, a "mighty rock." The world cannot give or take away this strength. God offers it to us constantly. Sometimes we lose sight of God, but God continually offers us honor and salvation. Honor and salvation from God come to us with no need to purchase anything, to live anywhere, or to clothe ourselves with designers' plans. They spring from an inner source.

The honor and salvation of God come to us when we identify joyfully with God. We can live in God, base our whole life in God. This freedom comes when we acknowledge that God's resources are greater than our own. This is a difficult admission because our flesh tries to wrestle with God for top billing—every day of our lives!

PRAYER: Lord, remind me daily that I have it all through you and you alone. Amen.

THURSDAY, JANUARY 20 • Read Psalm 62:8-12

During rush hour, I found myself stuck in fierce traffic: numerous stalled cars and collisions. I crawled along at a snail's pace. The slow traffic aggravated a greater concern—I needed to talk to someone soon about an issue simmering in my heart. *Whom should I call?* I wondered as I reached for my mobile phone. One friend was out of town on business; another friend was hard to reach. I could not remember the phone number of a third friend.

Suddenly the answer to my question came to me: *I will talk to God.* Why had I not thought of that earlier? God is such a convenient friend. Talking with God means I have no need to remove the mobile phone from the purse and make a call that will be billed by the minute. With God I have no need to remember a phone number. At that point, I just let loose all that I held tightly within. I let it flow. Even with good friends, the issues are sometimes too deep and painful to speak aloud. With God, I have no need for words; God already knows the needs I am unable to voice.

To whom do you talk? All of us need someone to hear our pain, our dreams. Most of us have a confidant, but is that person the best choice? Can that person listen without judgment or condemnation? Can that person pour balm on the wounds inflicted by life and heal them? Can that person put joy back in your spirit? Probably not. Only the Lord can do all that.

The psalmist instructs us to pour out our hearts to the God who offers refuge. God knows the hurt we experience as a result of the issues, concerns, and worries that fill up our hearts. God also knows that we need to empty our hearts, to release the pain and acknowledge God's availability. Let it out.

PRAYER: God, I want to pour out my concerns to you instead of holding on and cluttering my heart. Amen.

FRIDAY, JANUARY 21 • Read 1 Corinthians 7:29-31

I am mulling over Paul's words as I drive a carload of children to school. He calls for a radical reordering of life in light of the return of Christ. How should we respond in this new age? Is Paul speaking literally or figuratively? Should I pull over to the shoulder of the freeway, park the car, and walk away from my family in order to focus solely on Christ? Should I renounce all the other joys of life—friends, career, and possessions—to prepare properly for Christ's return?

Paul's words offer as much a challenge to us in the year 2000 as they did around 54 C.E. when he wrote them. Paul probably knew and acknowledged that many of Christ's followers had families and friends, as well as other commitments to their present world. But sometimes our commitments resemble cement bricks that pull us down and away from our desired relationship with Christ.

Paul knows that Christ must occupy a primary place in our lives. We must reorder priorities: Important people become less important. Possessions lose their power in our lives. Our adjusted attitudes reflect the love of Christ, and we constantly seek the face of God.

Is this a realistic course of action for today? Can we make this commitment without seeming fanatical? Yes. Evaluate your life and honestly appraise where the Lord reigns and where the Lord's presence is nonexistent. We know from Hebrew Scriptures that our God is a jealous God. Paul calls us to release any idols: money, cars, family, careers. Oddly enough, the very things we ask God to give us ultimately may become our spiritual undoing. We must keep in mind the gift and our relationship to the Giver.

PRAYER: Lord, keep me ever mindful of you and my responsibility to our relationship. Amen.

SATURDAY, JANUARY 22 • Read Mark 1:14-15

The car radio blares out report after report of violence, crime, and mayhem across the world. Parents kill their children, and children kill their parents. Suicide bombings destroy entire villages, and drug-motivated robberies sour the lives of families. This sense of lives in continual turmoil, with no break in the action, saddens me. I respond by forming a callus around my soul to avoid susceptibility to hurt. We can easily allow bad news to escort us to despair. Good news seemingly is hard to find; the chaos and violence seem to drown it out.

Perhaps the people to whom Jesus comes proclaiming good news feel the same way—overwhelmed by bad news. After John's imprisonment, Jesus begins preaching the good news in the Galilee area. His words bring excitement and interest; perhaps they break through the sadness of people's experience. The audacity of the good news in the face of tribulation is just like Jesus—fearless. Jesus stands on the word of God. He does not allow bad news and downcast situations to control him or dictate to him. The good news of the gospel brings light to any darkness.

How dare we get excited when suffering a setback or a downfall? How can we celebrate when a deluge of moral depravity overpowers our existence?

Jesus preaches the good news, and he also tells the people: "The time is fulfilled, and the kingdom of God has come near; repent, and believe in the good news." Jesus invites his hearers to take a role in this good news. Goodness draws its potency from believers who participate in its existence. We have a responsibility to turn the tide on bad news by living our lives as believers in the good news.

PRAYER: Lord, help me participate in the good news you have today. Amen.

SUNDAY, JANUARY 23 • Read Mark 1:16-20

Can you imagine Jesus walking along the seashore selecting his disciples? Some may assume that he is making random selections. Actually Jesus invites those who will obey. Obedience is the key to following Jesus. Jesus tells the men that they will become fishers of people. They believe him, put down their nets, and follow him. Do any of them think Jesus has made a mistake? Do they ever feel unworthy? What causes them to obey?

Simon and Andrew, James and John make quite a transition from being catchers of fish to becoming fishers of people. Jesus asks them to move from sight walking to faith walking. What are the job requirements? Jesus doesn't ask for college degrees, internships at Fortune 500 companies, or the completion of impressive reading lists. Jesus does not send them through a gauntlet of interviews. These unlettered men with limited skills and exposure have one necessary quality: They willingly allow Jesus to teach them; they exhibit openness to Jesus' leadership.

Many people balk at following Jesus and accepting assignments for Christian service because they don't feel qualified. Perhaps they feel the requests are a mistake—surely they have nothing to offer. They forget that those whom God calls, God also equips. They forfeit the opportunity for endowment, enlightenment, and empowerment by the Lord.

These disciples—Simon, Andrew, James, and John—demonstrate that the second we turn away from our own agendas and accept what the Lord has in store for us, we will receive all the training we need. We must strive to follow the disciples' example of pure obedience, lack of questions, and complete trust.

PRAYER: Lord, I will open myself to you today and follow wherever you lead. Amen.

Power and Authority

January 24–30, 2000 • Jerry Owyang*

MONDAY, JANUARY 24 • Read Deuteronomy 18:15-17

Challenges

It's a little over three weeks into the new year, and hopefully all the challenges of the much-ballyhooed Y2K computer bug have been solved. If only Moses had it that easy! As Moses begins to recognize the challenges of life on the desert plains of Canaan, he attempts to prepare the Israelites for Yahweh's future revelations.

Moses' preparation includes establishing the institution of prophecy. He requires that the people wait for God's words through a prophet just like Moses—to counter the temptation of following the pagan Canaanite religious practices of magic, sorcery, occultism, and divination.

The establishment of prophetic ministry is a shift from the traditional priestly conservation of known truths; the prophet, as the ordained spokesperson of this faith community, breaks new ground by declaring God's revelation for growth. Prophecy goes beyond prediction to interpretation—enabling people to know the contemporaneous mind of God.

The true prophet of today is impassioned with God's righteousness, sovereignty, and love so as to call people to remember and live the covenant relationship they have with God in a compassionate way.

PRAYER: Knowing God, help me listen to your words spoken by the prophets of my time that call me back into a God-centered relationship with you. Amen.

---

*Ordained deacon; Minister of Christian Education at Garden Grove United Methodist Church, Garden Grove, California.

TUESDAY, JANUARY 25 • **Read Deuteronomy 18:18-20**

Accountability

What important qualities must a prophet possess? What benefits accrue to one serving as a prophet? Why would anyone want to be a prophet? How would you respond if God called you to be a prophet?

When the need arises, God will raise up a prophet from among the community of faith to speak divine truth and righteousness. The prophet, then, has authority to speak, since such words come directly from God. To see and hear God's prophet is to see and hear God. The prophet, while vested with sacred authority, is accountable to God for speaking only those theocratic words given to communicate God's will directly. As recipients of true prophetic words, we too have a responsibility: to "heed" (NRSV) or "hearken" (KJV) to the words of God spoken through the prophet. We are to give more than passive listening; we are to give undivided attention and to embrace God's truth and knowledge, not that of society.

Accountability is not everyone's favorite word. While we all desire independence, the word *accountable* implies that we have a responsibility to someone other than ourselves—even to someone who may have authority over us. The revelation of God's word to us (intellectually or spiritually) makes us accountable to act on the new knowledge or the remembrance of the covenant that is now in our possession. It does not serve us well to listen and then ignore that which is authoritative and designed for our benefit. The prophetic word makes known to us the mind and will of God, upon which our hearts and destiny depend.

PRAYER: God of prophecy, reveal to me your will for my life; cause me to hear, embrace, and act on your truth spoken by prophets of yesterday, today, and tomorrow. Amen.

WEDNESDAY, JANUARY 26 • Read Psalm 111

Praise and wisdom

Every once in a while we come across the words of a poet or lyricist who captures something of the feeling we may have about God. Even a composer's haunting refrain may mirror a special longing of ours. In today's reading, the psalmist successfully frames praise of God that celebrates the Lord's goodness to Israel within a hallelujah chorus for use in a worship setting. Through both "lyrics" and "melody," the psalmist seeks to evoke gratitude in us for both the creative and formative attributes of God: compassionate, faithful, generous, steadfast, and redemptive.

Poetry, which has a quality of spontaneity and grace that evokes imagination, is a special art form, crafted and influenced by culture. For instance, *haiku* is an unrhymed Japanese verse form of three lines containing five, seven, and five syllables respectively. Another unrhymed Japanese verse form is *tanka*, which consists of five lines of five, seven, five, seven, and seven syllables respectively. Creating poetry within these structures is a work of beauty.

The psalmist composes this psalm as an acrostic within a unique Hebraic cultural context of being framed by the first and last verses of praise and wisdom. The poem offers richness of imagery, passion, and metaphor; its words are as vivid as they are concrete. The psalm, in its distinctive parallelism and repetition, focuses our attention on God's works in nature, history, and covenant relationship with God's people. How could we withstand this evidence and not be at the starting point of wisdom in our efforts to know God?

SUGGESTION FOR MEDITATION: **Write a personal prayer or psalm in *haiku* or *tanka* verse style.**

THURSDAY, JANUARY 27 • Read 1 Corinthians 8:1-6

Freedom in Christ

How do knowledge and wisdom differ? Try this: Wisdom is knowing when to use knowledge. Everyone knows something, but it matters how you communicate that something. Paul correctly reminds us that while knowledge puffs up, love builds up. I once attended a gathering and found myself in the midst of an exchange of insensitive jokes. I stood silently by until an opportune time arose and then responded in an appropriate manner; the ribald humor ceased and apologies were made.

How easily I could have alienated people by speaking the correct word at the wrong time! Are we totally free to be who we are in Christ Jesus? Well, yes...and no. The issue at hand in Corinth was the eating of food offered in pagan rituals: May a Christian eat such fare? Paul gives a qualified positive nod to Christians who know that an idol has no substance and that there is only one God; but these knowledgeable persons are to display sensitivity to Christians who struggle with this issue.

Wisdom allows us to use love rather than knowledge as the better guide, for love takes the more mature Christian into a warmer fellowship with others. While knowing the truth is important, it is equally important to speak the truth of the gospel of Jesus Christ in love. Having a certain knowledge of faith does not give license to assert freely such enlightenment in a manner that results in manipulation, exploitation, or inducement of guilt in a person less advantageously positioned in the faith. Paul quickly reminds us that such knowledge can be self-serving and can lead Christians into sin: It is better to love and to be known by God.

PRAYER: Omniscient God, may the knowledge I have *of* Christ be perfected in my love *for* Christ. Amen.

FRIDAY, JANUARY 28 • Read 1 Corinthians 8:7-13

Conscience

Our culture teaches us that the corporate ladder goes in one direction: up. Once on it, we must climb as hard as we can for as long as we can toward more recognition and reward, bigger titles, more people working for us, and longer hours on the job to achieve worldly success. I have met Christians who seem to be on a similar path on their journey of faith.

Paul continues his admonition to fast-track Christians: He encourages sensitivity on the part of those who are confident in their knowledge of God to those whose faith has not yet matured. The example of Christians secure in their knowledge of God may unduly influence those who still struggle in certain areas of the faith. Paul wrote that those strong in their understanding of God may, by knowingly eating the meat dedicated to idols, encourage those Christians who want to be Christian yet still have idolatrous leanings to act against their conscience. Then doing wrong becomes easier. The result is that knowledgeable Christians sin against Christ because Christ died for all believers—even those without knowledge and awareness.

We subject our freedom in Christ only to the self-imposed constraint of Christian love. If the exercise of a certain liberty harms the spiritual life of another, we should voluntarily refrain from exercising that freedom. The exercise of spiritual freedom will not lead Christians into activities that controvert the conscience; true freedom results in a commitment to the healthy upbuilding of the whole believing community, the body of Christ.

PRAYER: God of conscience, grant that I may, in love, limit my freedom in Christ out of sensitivity to those whose awareness has not yet matured. Amen.

Authority

It is one thing to have power; it is another matter to have authority. While a traffic officer may have authority to blow a whistle and hold up a gloved hand to halt traffic, that same officer does not have the literal power to stop a vehicle from traversing the intersection at a high rate of speed.

Power and authority: They must be used in tandem to be effective. Jesus had both. In the synagogue, Jesus the teacher expounds on the kingdom of God with authority, seemingly in marked contrast to the scribes who only quote the words of others. The passage does not state Jesus' teachings. However, we can surmise that his words and mannerisms rang true with those in the synagogue, resulting in their utter amazement.

Jesus Christ discloses to the world a new understanding of the meaning of omnipotence. As the son of God born to earth, Jesus teaches with an inherent authority that comes directly from God, not humans. That authority supersedes all other claims: Jesus has authority to reconcile relationships, forgive sins, heal the infirm in body and spirit, and transform lives. With that same authority, Jesus also has power over the evil one, Satan; Jesus demonstrated both divine power and divine authority in the wilderness.

How can we allow Jesus' power and authority to work in our lives? in the lives of others? in the lives of our churches? In what ways will you submit to Jesus' authority in your life throughout this week?

PRAYER: Divine Authority, revive in me the willingness and desire to be amazed once more at your teachings about the kingdom of God, to which I belong. Amen.

SUNDAY, JANUARY 30 • **Read Mark 1:23-28**

Power from above

The Gospel of Mark has barely begun and Jesus now faces his second challenge with evil (the first being Satan's temptation in the wilderness, Mark 1:12-13). The gauntlet has been thrown. With the exorcism that takes place in the synagogue, the battle begins between the Son of God and Satan.

Doesn't it seem strange that the man with the unclean spirit worships in the synagogue? Perhaps it really isn't all that uncommon to find in worship people possessed of all sorts of excess baggage. This baggage might include addiction, denial, bitterness—in a word, *sin* and unclean spirits. The new and fresh teaching of Jesus touches the depth of the man's soul and triggers the spirit's confrontational cry. Divine deliverance takes place but not before the evil spirit acknowledges who Jesus is and, in a fashion, sounds the alarm that the kingdom of evil is now under attack by the kingdom of God. That Jesus would silence the evil spirit always intrigues me; what better testimonial of God's power than from the vanquished!

But Jesus always has a sense of timing that escapes most everyone, myself included. Perhaps Jesus' power binds the spirit from espousing fear and confusion or from acting in any form, except to leave the man. The man's restoration amazes the crowd, for they recognize that Jesus offers more than deliverance: His new and fresh teaching challenges not only evil but the all too familiar, stale pharisaic party line of staid religiosity. May Jesus do so for us and our churches!

PRAYER: Deliver me, O Lord, from familiarity that blocks and blots out your freshness for my life. Amen.

The Breadth of God

January 31–February 6, 2000 • Valerie M. Griggs*

MONDAY, JANUARY 31 • Read Isaiah 40:21-31

Lift up your eyes on high, and behold who hath created these"
(v. 26, KJV). Isaiah reminds us to gaze at creation to learn
God's purposes. Is that God's laughter we hear? "Have ye not
known? have ye not heard?…have ye not understood?" (v. 21,
KJV). What is it we're supposed to understand? That God
intends good to us.

"Behold, the Lord God will come.…he shall gather the
lambs with his arm, and carry them in his bosom" (vv. 10-11,
KJV). Christmas celebrates the fulfillment of Isaiah's prophecy:
God has come to us. The radical message of the gospel is Yahweh's continual coming. Christ's birth comes to each of us in
loss, in dreams, in our need to grow into his likeness. We have
the historical fulfillment of God's promise in Jesus of Nazareth and the good news of the Christ in our personal history.

This chapter is a trumpet blast. The Creator who sits above
the circle of the earth is the Understanding One who empowers the weak. The Holy One who determines who shall rule
and when, renews those who wait on the Lord. In today's reading, Isaiah helps us glimpse the breadth of God.

What other all-powerful, creator god in any religious system promises to come to us? What other god desires to gather
us, teach us, and reward us? "To whom then will ye liken me,
or shall I be equal? saith the Holy One" (v. 25, KJV).

**PRAYER: O Lord, I am slow to hope in your promises because
they are too wonderful. I can scarcely take in your power and
compassion. Your heart and mind are unfathomable. Still you
keep coming to me. Thank you. Amen.**

---

*Spiritual director and Spiritual Growth Associate at Old First Re-
formed Church, Brooklyn, New York.

TUESDAY, FEBRUARY 1 • Read Psalm 147:1-11, 20*c*

Today's psalm praises God as creator (v. 8), God as sustainer (v. 9), and God as redeemer (vv. 2-3). Other verses describe the divine character: healer (v. 3), lifter of the meek (v. 6), keeper of the seasons (v. 8) who cares for all, gatherer of outcasts (v. 2). God does not dwell in some obscure place, remaining aloof and skeptically believing that none can reach the divine. God takes pleasure in those who hope in God's steadfast love (v. 11). God binds up wounds (v. 3).

What a busy God. What a different kind of busyness from ours. We hope to gain and get from our busyness. But the Lord's activity is meant to assure us of God's presence and love for us. No wonder this transcendent and immediate God has no interest in strength as displayed and prized in human terms.

I wonder if we, in our flesh and blood, believe God—believe what God has said, done, and is still doing? Perhaps we mechanically praise God for the attributes listed in this psalm. Occasionally we may muster what Jonathan Edwards called "holy fear." Do our work, play, hopes, and dreams clearly reflect our belief in God?

SUGGESTION FOR MEDITATION: Too often we focus on what we think we have done for ourselves. Ask the Holy Spirit to remind you of the times you experienced God's healing and protection. Recall times when you recognized God at work in your life. Think about where and when you have sensed God's presence most strongly. Let the recollections turn to praise for who God is in your life.

Praise psalms do more than remind us of God's all-powerful goodness. They correct erroneous ideas we have about our relationship with God.

Israel vacillated between worshiping Yahweh alone and worshiping Yahweh alongside other gods. If religion is only ritual, Yahweh can look like any other god. Even we moderns fall into the ritual rut. We narrowly focus on form. We offer rites, programs, or atmosphere to God, rather than our hearts. Soon we confuse God with mysterious forces and a natural religiosity. One god is as good as another, as long as we are sincere and consistent in ceremonies and practices.

Or we fall into the mystical labyrinth. Here we twist the truth that God is in hearts, not altars, to the other extreme. Through somatic exercises, fantasizing or self-actualization methods, we strive to break into sacred dimensions. Using prayer formulas or mantras, we seek to unleash sacred powers. Yahweh is a symbol like any other concept and philosophy of god. We give God any face or name we desire. Emotional states and ecstasies convince us we are holy. In time, we become equal to God.

How do we approach the glory, majesty, and holiness of God? Through praise. The Holy Spirit brings God's reign to our hearts. Jesus has revealed God's character and intention toward us. Jesus has opened the gates of relationship through his death and resurrection. Our hope is in praise for what God has done to restore the divine image in us.

PRAYER: Lord, there is none like you. Forgive me for diluting you and trying to manage you. Forgive me for wanting a relationship with you on my own terms. Make me one of your people. Make my freedom in Christ real until my heart, mouth, and deeds overflow with praise for you. Amen.

THURSDAY, FEBRUARY 3 • Read 1 Corinthians 9:16-23

Paul's self-disclosure often astonishes me. Today's professional religious leaders rarely evidence such transparency. What quality allows Paul to be so honest about himself? "For though I am free with respect to all, I have made myself a slave to all" (v. 19). Paul, Gamaliel's pupil, the chief priests' hired gun, now insists that he does not abuse his power in the gospel (v. 18) A man who once traveled freely to do violence for the powerful endured shipwrecks, stonings, whippings. "I take pleasure in infirmities, in reproaches, in persecutions …for Christ's sake " (2 Cor. 12:10, KJV).

Consider Paul's breadth: "Unto the Jews I became as a Jew.…To them that are without law, as without law.…To the weak became I as weak" (vv. 20-22, KJV). At one time, Paul lived his faith expertly and narrowly as a "Hebrew among Hebrews" in observing the rigorous piety of the Pharisees. But after meeting the resurrected Christ on the road to Damascus, he became *the* apostle to the Gentiles, recognized as such by the pillars of the Jerusalem church, Peter, James, and John.

What accounts for the radical expansion of his heart? The life of Christ—the height, depth, and width of divine love broke Paul's heart wide open. Humility and redemption transformed the heart of one who held coats while Stephen was martyred into the heart of one who sang while chained to a prison wall.

SUGGESTION FOR MEDITATION: Find your heart today. Sit quietly with your heart. No matter what its shape, welcome your heart. Remember the Lord wants to give you a heart of flesh to give power to the faint. The Lord desires to heal the brokenhearted, and to give us holy boldness in times of distress. Offer your heart to God—ask the Holy Spirit to breathe into your heart today.

FRIDAY, FEBRUARY 4 • **Read 1 Corinthians 9:20-22;**
2 Corinthians 11:22-23; 12:10

Lips that once breathed threats and death now speak of becoming all things to all people. Paul's empathic connection with those who need to hear the gospel reflects God's character. Paul has let go of narrow theology and imitates God's determination to reach everywhere.

Scripture proclaims God's thorough entanglement in history. Through unlikely heroes in lost cities and despised prophets; in foreign kings and inexplicable battles; in dreams, sibling rivalry, and reluctant messengers; finally, in the flesh, the Eternal has taught, promised, and revealed Godself.

Paul has learned God's way of engaging the universe. Paul freely serves all—non-Jews and Jews alike. He serves while imprisoned and while facing deprivation, knowing that physical death is his sure reward for such service. Christ's narrow way leads to a breadth in serving others that earthly standards can never match.

Can we say with Paul, "Woe to me if I do not proclaim the gospel!" (1 Cor. 9:16)? Paul's reliance on God expands his vision. In what areas does our vision need expanding? Does our worship life need a breath of fresh air? Do we rely on old forms to affirm our faith? Do familiar patterns assure us the church is alive? Where are the new faces that don't look like our own? Do we pray with people who differ in vocational or educational background? Are we ready to commune with the isolated and the despised in our society to win some to Christ?

SUGGESTION FOR PRAYER: Consider the people in your church to whom you never speak. Begin praying for them. Make it a point to sit with them during worship or to visit during fellowship time. Who are the people whom you consider so different from yourself? At work, around town, in your family, begin praying for them. Begin asking the Lord to help you see people the way God does.

SATURDAY, FEBRUARY 5 • Read Mark 1:29-39

In Mark's Gospel we meet the promise we've been coming to understand all week. We see Jesus in an ordinary home with ordinary people. In specific space and time, a carpenter from Nazareth speaks God to the world.

After a grueling day of teaching in the synagogue, Jesus goes with his friends to the home of Simon and Andrew. Perhaps they hope to have a good meal and unwind. Jesus heals Simon's mother-in-law, but that doesn't end the day. Evening falls, and people come with their sick and with the demon-possessed. The whole town comes to that door, a door they probably have walked by day after day before without a thought.

The next day, before daybreak, Jesus goes to a solitary place to pray. When his friends find him, they pass on the message that "everyone is searching for you." Jesus insists they move on to other towns. He cannot contain God's purposes to one place. Jesus embodies the Father's untiring compassion. Every breath of Jesus brought teaching, healing, and prayer.

How often do we call it a day only to be met with some friend's need or a small family crisis? What is our initial response to these demands? After a long, productive day, don't we put out the "Do Not Disturb" sign? We are weak and limited, but God is not. The God who promises to come to us does so wholeheartedly, holding nothing back.

SUGGESTION FOR MEDITATION: One reason we run out of steam is that we don't know how to rest. We feel that our value comes from performance and production. Remember Jesus' invitation to come to him for rest. Prepare to celebrate this Sabbath by putting away your own busyness and praising God for the gift of God's presence in the details of your life.

SUNDAY, FEBRUARY 6 • **Read Mark 1:29-39**

Thinking of that home that evening stirs my heart. I picture family, a meal, healing—the precious delights in life—and Jesus is the center of it all. Tired friends, a healed mother-in-law, an overflow of neighbors—Jesus is living out his mustard seed parables.

The kingdom of God starts as something small and intimate, something between friends. Then steadily God increases the sphere of influence. An ordinary home becomes a sacred place where God's presence in flesh and blood changes lives. The first-century church shares in this legacy: "They, continuing daily with one accord in the temple, and breaking bread from house to house, did eat…with gladness.…Praising God, and having favour with all the people" (Acts 2:46-47a, KJV).

Many analyze the condition of the North American home at the end of the twentieth century. Few would describe our homes as sacred places. More often homes spawn substance abuse, violence, sexual abuse. They are filled with the silence of alienation, the anguish of illness, and the fear of neighbors.

With so many conditions working against our homes as sacred places, let's remember God's busyness. Let's remember God's understanding of and care for us. Can we praise God even in the debris of our broken homes? Are we willing to companion those who find suffering instead of sanctuary at home? Are we ready to be Christ-bearers at kitchen tables, on front steps, and in living rooms?

SUGGESTION FOR MEDITATION: **Read this story and put yourself in the scene. Imagine the scent of supper being cooked, the voices of Jesus and his friends. Maybe you are with them. What would you say to Jesus? Or maybe you are a neighbor who needs healing for yourself or someone you love. See Jesus reaching out to you. What does Jesus say to you?**

Healing People, Healing Places

February 7–13, 2000 • Thomas F. Tumblin*

MONDAY, FEBRUARY 7 • Read 2 Kings 5:1-14

Naaman knows success. He has conquered armies and serves as the king's chosen military leader. Thousands follow his every command, laying their lives on the line to win battles. His strategies route the enemies of Aram. As a warrior, he knows how to stand face-to-face with violence and death. He influences the destiny of the nation. He has arrived at his vocational pinnacle.

However, one of the liabilities of reaching the top is that we bring our weaknesses with us. Naaman's liability is leprosy. The spotlight of leadership brings both fame and shame. His resulting anger from such a disease might have stoked his passion to succeed. Ultimately Naaman has to face his weakness.

All of us carry dis-ease, whether externally or internally. Regardless of our status, the frailties of being human temper our strength. God uses a Jewish servant girl to initiate Naaman's healing. The vanquished slave becomes the guide to wholeness. While everyone sees Naaman's dilemma, only one of God's chosen seems able to offer the solution.

Often we are so intent on reaching the summit that we miss the healing God has placed right in our path. We covet the destination and miss the journey's transformations. What does it take for God to capture our attention en route?

PRAYER: God, help me see and hear your healing grace in the unexpected places and people. Lead me into the best success— wholeness as I follow Christ day by day. Amen.

---

*Associate Professor of Leadership and Associate Director of the Doctor of Ministry program, Asbury Seminary, Wilmore, Kentucky.

TUESDAY, FEBRUARY 8 • Read 2 Kings 5:1-14

Imagine the king of a small country getting unexpected company: a huge military entourage sent by a world leader. Ready to pay 750 pounds of silver, 150 pounds of gold, and 10 sets of clothes, the guest, who happens to be an infamous general, expects the impossible—healing from an incurable disease. An impending sense of "do or die" looms large!

Enter Elisha, the former apprentice of the century's greatest prophet Elijah. Unable to meet the general's need, the king gladly diverts the general and his chariots to Elisha's house. When kings fail the challenge, try God's messengers.

Elisha's servant greets the arrival of the all-important Naaman. The servant offers Naaman a demeaning prescription for his leprosy: Take seven baths in the Jordan River to be cleansed of the skin disease. "I thought that for me he would surely come out, and stand and call on the name of the Lord his God, and would wave his hand over the spot, and cure the leprosy!" Naaman wants magic; Elisha intends a miracle.

The quiet dramas of God's simple solutions may seem anticlimactic. In an era of multichoice spirituality, the dramatic draws crowds. For Elisha the crowd has already been provided, complete with servants, chariots, horses, royal commendation, and elevated expectations. Yet the prophet is unwilling to outact God. Divine answers provide their own drama without the hype.

How do we attempt to stage our own healings? With great entourages and high stakes? Some of the best miracles are the quiet ones. Simple follow-through on God's instructions suffices. Seven baths in the Jordan, living healthy lifestyles, listening to medical professionals, believing God in prayer— none of these options necessarily makes the headlines. Preludes to miracles seldom do.

PRAYER: Forgive me, Lord, for preferring magicians over prophets and drama over the divine. Teach me to trust your path to healing. Through Jesus Christ. Amen.

WEDNESDAY, FEBRUARY 9 • Read Psalm 30

Although the superscript mentions David's name, we don't know that David actually wrote this psalm. However, this song, written for the dedication of the Temple, pulses with David's emotional cycles of deliverance and despair. When healthy, David asserts that God "had established me as a strong mountain." When overwhelmed with illness, David shifts to the power negotiator mode: "What profit is there in my death?...Will the dust praise you?" These words convey the sense that we must fight God for our lives.

Dependence on God does not come with a Kevlar vest to stop the bullets of disease and disappointment. Of all people, David experienced the shifting of life beneath his feet. In the sheep fields he learned how literally to lay down his life for his animals. In the Valley of Elah (1 Sam. 17), he learned how to face down giants in God's name. He stood steady and submitted to King Saul when Saul became schizophrenic and jealous of God's anointing of David.

At the time of the Temple's dedication, the psalmist's witness resonates with the covenant God makes with David in 1 Samuel 7. David wants to build a house for the Ark—the symbol of God's presence with Israel. God declines the offer and instead promises to build David's house through future generations. In fact, David does not construct the Temple, but this psalm sings his testimony in absentia.

What is our witness to God's sustaining care through all of life's highs and lows? Life is deadly without God; it is witness with God. We point to the markers of Divine Presence along the path, staking our future on God's faithfulness in the past.

PRAYER: **God of all seasons and experiences, make new your covenant in my life. Make me a testimony to your unfailing care in every moment of life. Amen.**

THURSDAY, FEBRUARY 10 • Read 1 Corinthians 9:24-27

Millions of dollars and hundred of hours go into making athletic heroes. Olympians sequester themselves and focus their lifestyles to attain the one goal: winning the race. For the athletes and their sponsors, the cost is worth the prize. Early morning practices, pulled muscles, relocation of the family—"no pain, no gain." Outlasting the competition requires strategic resources for the athlete. The young champion then must push beyond exhaustion daily in his or her physical regimen. Distractions must be limited. Settings conducive to excellence must be maintained.

Elsewhere, Paul prays that we will prosper as well spiritually as we have physically. For some of us, that might be a dangerous exchange. We forget that God created us holistically. Our physical well-being impacts our spiritual and mental well-being. Exceptional mental focus takes the body to greater heights in the competition. Testimonies of those who have suffered physically for their faith tell of the magnified grace God gives during the torture, which offsets the pain.

Current research has linked the release of endorphins of a runner's "high" to what occurs when individuals practice generosity. We no longer give until it hurts; we now give until it feels good.

Take a few moments to perform a check-up. How are your physical, mental, and spiritual vital signs? What health plan would a personal trainer in each of these areas prescribe for you? With the help of a wise spiritual friend and possibly your physician, design the new habits that optimum health in every area of your life requires. People seek models of the integrity of God's creation—a sense of congruence in all aspects of life. With God's help, we all can live as God's holistic champions.

PRAYER: Make us, O God, champions of your best design, spiritually, mentally, and physically. Help us run the whole race well. Amen.

FRIDAY, FEBRUARY 11 • Read 1 Corinthians 9:24-27

In my naïve college days, the prevailing formula taken from James 1 implied that trials produced spiritual maturity. In the cloistered setting of the academy where most challenges were more in our heads, we faced some fairly mundane trials. Yet we wanted to be spiritual heroes, model Christians. So, in a sort of holy masochism, I began to pray for trials, a little suffering for Jesus so I would mature. (Thankfully I stopped short of actual flagellation as a self-imposed trial.)

Spiritual maturity takes practice. We cannot treat our Christian walk like the foreign language we learned in high school and have long since forgotten. The Wesleyan mix of vital piety and social outreach demands the authenticity of a crisp devotional life and an evidence trail of faithful acts of kindness and justice done in Christ's name. We mature in our vulnerability and accountability, the fruit of building trust with God and one another. We create maps of faith oases, the people and resources God has provided through the ages, and then help others find the same oases.

My passion is tempered now. Instead of praying for additional trials, I seek to live into the trials and joys that come in God's providence. I am learning a "pace of grace," as Susan Muto calls it, a pace that keeps all of my senses sharp and attentive to God. I continue to discover new ways to grow a healthy spiritual center out of which God's spirit can flow. Healthy maturity results from centering on the Eternal Hope.

PRAYER: Focus me, O Lord, on nurturing the spiritual center that provides the calm when surrounded by chaos. Discipline me to mature me in your joyful presence. Amen.

SATURDAY, FEBRUARY 12 • Read Mark 1:40-45

What does it feel like to be an outcast? I don't mean the occasional snubbings we remember from high school; I mean real ostracism. For the lepers, once society discovered their disease, the break came swiftly and totally. No more going to the Temple or synagogue. No more living in town with the family. People stopped greeting you with the traditional kiss. Everywhere, instead of "Shalom," the cry became "Unclean!" As if the malady was not pain enough, the status as social pariah compounded the shame. The leper's livelihood came from begging for mercy and sustenance on the outer edges of the city.

God's first choice for all humanity is healing. On this side of eternity, diseases and tragedies—both natural and human—happen. Yet in God's divine balance of power in a fallen world, God's first choice is to be clean. We have trouble believing that truth when we are hurting, when God seems to be making us the example of fallenness. The leper in Mark 1 does not know how the Teacher will respond to his pleading request as he kneels before the One whose reputation for healing has started to spread through the region. "[Jesus,] if you choose, you can make me clean." Jesus appears annoyed at the interruption—or does it disturb him that the leper doubts his good intentions?

Before he utters a word, Jesus reaches out and does the unthinkable—he touches the unclean leper and technically becomes unclean himself. Then the leper hears those words that he has imagined impossible: "I do choose. Be made clean!" Authority and compassion combine to change the leper's life again, this time for the good and forever.

What diseased places in your life need God's touch?

PRAYER: **Loving God, you do not allow anything or anyone to put you off. Choose to touch me in my ugliest places and make me whole. Amen.**

SUNDAY, FEBRUARY 13 • Read Mark 1:40-45

Unbridled joy! Reckless excitement! Got to tell somebody! Jesus tries to channel the former leper's enthusiasm when he says in effect, "Let's play this by the book. Go straight to the priest who declared you unclean and let him declare you clean. Take the required sacrifice for cleansing with you as a testimony to God's miraculous touch. Do not tell anyone else—just the priest."

Simple, clear instructions. It seems the former leper lacks discretion, at least at the outset. He cannot contain restoration to a life of promise and social acceptance, a life with family and touchable friends, in legalities. The former leper blows Jesus' cover. His publicity campaign does not permit Jesus to be in town without being mobbed. The former leper simply does not think through the implications of his spreading the good news.

What will you do with God's healing in your life? You may have a soulmate with whom you need to share the miracle as an act of accountability and testimony. You may be given the opportunity to spread the word throughout the region.

Be ready for the change. Miracles can draw crowds, especially when they restore a person from being a despised beggar to being certifiably clean. Every human being yearns for bona fide transformation.

Our challenge is to walk in wholeness once the miracle has taken place. The former leper no longer lives as an outcast at the edge of town. His cry no longer resounds, "Unclean!" Relationships are restored, family regained. The world opens up again. Walk boldly in the whole life God has given.

Prayer: Protect me, O Healer, from acting sick when you have made me well. Extend your shalom to others through me. Amen.

A New Thing

February 14–20, 2000 • L. Cecile Adams*

MONDAY, FEBRUARY 14 • Read Mark 2:1-4

You hear that Jesus is at home, so you rush to see him and find you cannot get in because of the crowd. You stand at the front door, feeling the press of later arrivals.

You hear the sound of Jesus' voice and the whispers of those around him who comment on his words. You hear flies buzzing, women chattering at the village well, the clip-clop of donkeys, children's laughter, and people passing.

Slowly you become aware of shuffling feet and rustling fabric as people move. You hear quickened breathing and not-so-hushed directives: Make way; make way. You hear footsteps on the outside stairs, and scratchings and scrapings tell you something is happening on the roof.

Suddenly the silence inside the house becomes obvious. You slip just inside the door and see a bed being lowered through the ceiling. You hear the ropes scraping the roof. Then you see a person lying on the bed that now rests on the floor. Neither that person nor the people on the roof speak a word, but you hear their pleas for healing in the look on their faces. Jesus bends over, and you lean forward to hear what he says.

Stop the story here and reflect on your experience. What keeps you from drawing closer to Jesus to hear his words? Whom are you bringing to Jesus for healing? If you were the person in the bed, what healing would you hope for? What words would you want to hear Jesus saying?

SUGGESTION FOR PRAYER: Use the answer or question that most disturbs you as a guide for your prayer. If you have difficulty forming the prayer, ask God to pray the prayer in you. Trust that the words will come.

---

*Pastor to Families with Children, Rome First United Methodist Church, Rome, Georgia.

TUESDAY, FEBRUARY 15 • Read Psalm 41

Considering the poor brings happiness. Regarding the poor brings blessing, reward, protection, deliverance, and healing. However, considering the poor is not a good luck charm or an insurance policy. Rabbi Kushner has named our fear and our reality: Bad things do happen to good people. The psalmist reels off a litany of calamities: isolation, the appearance of and harassment by enemies, empty words offered as solace, gossip, illness, and betrayal.

So how can you be happy in the midst of life's more painful side? The psalmist's response: Consider the poor, and trust God. Maintain your integrity by living as compassionately, graciously, and steadfastly as you have experienced God to be. God's public vindication of your faithfulness will be your reward, and your happiness will abound.

Sister Helen Prejean grew up in a middle-class family. For a long time, she believed that she could interpret the word *poor* liberally rather than literally whenever it appeared in the Bible. She thought she would be content to minister to the poor in spirit or the poor in attitude. One day, however, she realized suddenly that *poor* meant poor; and she immediately set to work with people who were economically and socially poor. Her work led her to respond to a letter written by a man on death row. Eventually she visited him and began providing him with pastoral care. You can read the rest of the story in her book *Dead Man Walking* or see the movie with the same title.

Sister Helen's grace, sense of humor, centeredness, and hopeful loving resonate in a hymn of blessing to the God of Israel, the one who creates, redeems and sustains—not only her and us but the whole universe. God calls us to do no less where we are and in our own way.

SUGGESTION FOR PRAYER: Ask God to guide you in considering the poor. Listen for God's response that will indicate what God wants you to give up, put down, take on, move toward. Pray for courage and wisdom in doing what God has asked of you.

WEDNESDAY, FEBRUARY 16 • Read Psalm 41

What a beautiful psalm of trust in God's healing mercies! The psalmist's trust comes from the same root as the trust of those who let their friend down through the roof to Jesus. Both situations operate on the societal belief that illness and deformity result from sin. Yet that belief deters neither the psalmist nor the men in Mark 2. Instead they believe that healing is possible and will happen.

"O Lord, be gracious to me" appears in verses 4 and 10. The repeated phrase serves as a prayer of repentance and petition. You may use this breath prayer (one you can pray silently or aloud in one breath) at any time. Try it now. Take in a breath, say the phrase, let your breath out. Repeat the cycle several times. Perhaps the man on his bed and his friends were praying the same prayer as they moved toward Jesus.

This psalm projects a communal aura. Those who speak empty words, gather mischief, hate others, and imagine the worst contribute in a major way to the illness of the society. Yet they focus on the illness of an individual. (Didn't Jesus say something about removing the log from our own eyes before trying to remove the specks from the eyes of anyone else?)

Likewise, we cannot pray for God's gracious healing for us without affecting not only ourselves but the whole fabric of society as well. With the psalmist, we move from a desire for retribution to trust in God's justice, realizing the benefits of integrity and praising God for being set in God's presence forever. God's grace heals us; we offer the same healing to our friends and enemies.

SUGGESTION FOR PRAYER: **Pray the breath prayer above or use a more appropriate breath prayer. Spend five minutes (or more) with this prayer. At the end of the time, rise slowly with awareness of and thanksgiving for how God's graciousness is already at work in you, healing you and the world.**

THURSDAY, FEBRUARY 17 • Read Isaiah 43:18-21

This passage follows a lengthy recital of the ways in which God loves God's people. Whatever needs to be done for redemption, restoration, and protection, God will do. Something new will be brought forth by God. In fact, even as God speaks, the new is appearing. *Shalom*, that wonderful Hebrew word that has no exact translation in English, comes to mind. Healing, wholeness, joy, right relationship will characterize the "new thing" that God brings into being. The desert will have water; the wilderness will have a way.

Often we can see what God is doing only if we face a certain direction; we must turn toward God rather than away from God. If we want to see the sun rise, we must look east. Yet how often we get confused and look the wrong way.

Even when we get the direction right, we find it difficult to see the new thing God is doing. Delays become major impediments to our future. Detours become catastrophic events. Dismantling of the way things have always been done leads to panic in the face of change. Despair and depression blot out the sun and the Son.

With God, unimaginable new things are possible: bread in the wilderness, light in the darkness, calm in the storm, life in death. Envisioning these new possibilities is as simple and as profound as viewing the jar of water that holds angel-wing begonia cuttings on my kitchen windowsill. The top of the stems are black, dying, dead. Yet, at a joint further down on each stem, new leaves emerge and roots form. Soon I will be able to pot them and enjoy the growth of a new plant. So it is with our lives and our world. Thanks be to God!

PRAYER: God, shine your light upon my life that I may see the new thing you are doing. Unstop my ears so that I may hear the new thing you are doing. Wash me with your love so that I may be the new thing you are doing. This is my prayer in the name of the Christ. Amen.

FRIDAY, FEBRUARY 18 • Read Isaiah 43:22-25

Being reminded by God of what one has *not* done to honor God is terrible indeed. The writer records the sins of omission of God's people, and we see them right before our eyes.

Being Christians rather than members of the tribes of Israel, let's give attention to some contemporary equivalents of the list in verses 22-24. These charges are communal in nature, rather than individual, although they may represent a collection of private negligences.

We have put our trust in technology or education or wealth or (*fill in the blank*) instead of trusting God's promises. We have neglected to pray the psalmist's prayer: "O Lord, be gracious to me; heal me, for I have sinned against you" (Ps. 41:4).

We have placed a premium on having fun and have missed the joy of delighting in God and one another. We have related to our time, our money, our work, our creativity, our skills, our homes, or our children as if God has no relationship to us.

We have stuffed our bodies and neglected to taste God's goodness. We have filled our lives with busyness instead of becoming partners in God's business. We have wearied God with our sins and worn ourselves out in the process.

Even if this is only the beginning of the list (and who is to say that it isn't?), the news is good: Everything in the debit column has been erased! God will not remember our sins! This begins the new thing God is doing. We have a second chance, another opportunity, a clean page, a new day. Let's trust that God's promise is being fulfilled in our lives today.

PRAYER: Dear Holy One, you reduce my sins to ashes. Raise me up from the charred ruins of my life to complete the work that you have begun in me. Amen.

SATURDAY, FEBRUARY 19 • Read 2 Corinthians 1:18-22

Being resurrected is not easy, at least not for the one being resurrected. How Lazarus walked out of his tomb is still something of a mystery, not to mention what happened on that first Easter morning. Being resurrected means that we have to get on with our lives, but we cannot pick up exactly where we left off. Somehow our thinking and doing differ.

This letter to the church in Corinth reminds the Corinthian Christians and us of the difference: Christ fulfills all of God's promises. Jesus is the Yes, the exclamation mark, to the life God intends for all of us.

The writer does not always employ tact to persuade people to believe in Jesus Christ. Sometimes the zeal becomes more offensive than persuasive. Nonetheless, the writer sees himself as marked with God's imprint, anointed, filled with the Spirit.

For the early Christian, this writer conveys the faith in obvious, even contagious, ways. Consider what Paul endured: shipwrecks, beatings, jailings, murder threats, congregational conflicts, and yet Paul perceived that God was keeping God's promises. In all things, Paul said Amen to the glory of God.

So where is our zeal? How do we take what life brings us and, in partnership with God, create a garden that blesses and restores us and others? How do we stand so firm in the faith that all we do becomes a yes!, an alleluia, and an amen?

What promises of God are finding fulfillment in your life? in your congregation? How do you tell others about that fulfillment, giving specific examples? What is your resurrection story for today?

SUGGESTION FOR PRAYER: In your conversation with God, include thanksgiving and petition for those matters that are most obvious to you. Remember to include times of silence and to listen carefully for God's word(s) for today.

SUNDAY, FEBRUARY 20 • Read Mark 2:5-12

We have come full circle, back to where we began. Now we are ready for the rest of the story. Or are we? Something about what happens next feels too familiar and uncomfortable. Whether we identify with Jesus' critics or with the man on the mat, we find ourselves face-to-face with the truth of God's healing power. To what extent will we trust ourselves with God and be healed? And to what extent will we trust others to bring us into the presence of the Christ so that we may receive healing?

Who would not desire healing for someone? In this story, obviously, the scribes do not. They have no concept of God made flesh. They imagine the worst for the man on the mat (Ps. 41:7b). They have no expectation for miracles, much less the miracle of forgiveness. Their whisperings draw Jesus' attention. Suddenly the man on the mat becomes the center of attention; and that is not good.

How do you suppose Jesus looked, and how did he sound as he addressed the scribes? Do you imagine anger or tenderness in his face and voice? weariness or resoluteness? compassion or sharpness? Can you hear the questions piercing the layers of legalism and skepticism in your life?

Suddenly the focus shifts again; Jesus speaks to the paralytic in direct and emphatic words. Can you allow his statement to lift you from immobilizing forces?

Like the man who has been paralyzed, we are forgiven. That burden no longer weighs us down. We stand up, take our mats of affliction, and go to our homes in the presence of God forever. *We* are the miracle God is working in our midst. We have never seen anything like this. Thanks be to God!

SUGGESTION FOR PRAYER: **Identify the healing you desire. Ask several friends to pray with you, either together or individually, for that healing.**

The Divine / Human Relationship

February 21–27, 2000 • A. Heath Jones III*

MONDAY, FEBRUARY 21 • Read Hosea 2:14-20

We finite, mortal humans by definition have difficulty conceptualizing the infinite God; and when we do, we frame our attempts in human terms. That may account for the power of Hosea's graphic descriptions of the divine/human relationship. He understood the relationship between the Lord and Israel as tumultuous and intense, much like the roller-coaster ride of a passionate but at times troubled marriage.

In this passage Hosea presents a picture of a wife who has strayed, who in the most intimate of times still calls out the name of her lover rather than her husband. He recalls for the reader the Valley of Achor, a reference to the terribly disturbing story in Joshua 7 in which Achan and his family are stoned to death in the Valley of Achor ("trouble") for the trouble Achan has brought on Israel.

In spite of the wife's (Israel's) infidelity, Hosea sees compelling hope for the recovery of the relationship, a return to the time of wooing, of first kisses. He confidently believes in a complete turning around from the low point of the Valley of Achor to hope, and he reminisces about the excitement of eager young lovers as a canvas for the emotions and hope that must have accompanied the people's escape from Egypt. Finally, Hosea envisions a covenant of nature at peace, of love and fidelity forever.

PRAYER: Faithful God, rescue me when I stray. Amen.

---

*Adult church school teacher, active grandfather, member of West End United Methodist Church, Nashville, Tennessee.

TUESDAY, FEBRUARY 22 • **Read Psalm 103:1-5**

In a relationship, parties both give and receive. Sometimes it is hard to tell if the parties give because they receive or receive because they give. Which came first, the chicken or the egg? An altruistic spirit among us might say that loving God is the only proper response for all that God has given us. But do the potential benefits of loving God motivate us in part? This passage urges us not to forget all the benefits of blessing God, and then the psalmist boldly lists some of those benefits, seemingly encouraging us to bless God in order to reap the benefits package.

The psalmist writes in extreme terms, blessing God not simply with words but with every ounce of his being. The psalmist is given to extremes on the benefits side too. Surely God doesn't guarantee the healing of all diseases as the psalmist claims, even in our time of miraculous strides in medicine. And does God promise to renew youth as long as a person lives? Of course not.

But these are not entirely false promises on the part of the psalmist. What we glimpse in reading this passage is the truth of the relationship, the extreme abandonment of the self in someone else, crying out love with every ounce of one's being, achieving the extreme fulfillment of one's wholeness in this relationship. Even in illness or the frailties of age, the relationship invigorates. And whether one loves first, then receives the benefits or loves as a result of vested interest in the benefits is indistinguishable and irrelevant.

PRAYER: God, teach me to love as the ancient psalmist loved— with extreme abandonment. Amen.

WEDNESDAY, FEBRUARY 23 • Read Psalm 103:6-13, 22

Surely 1 Corinthians 13—Paul's familiar description of the character of love—is the most commonly used biblical text in marriage ceremonies. But this section of Psalm 103 also depicts in a significant way God's love for Israel and for us. We get a powerful glimpse into the psalmist's theology, almost a creedal statement of how God relates to the people.

In some ways this description of God's character in relationship subtly indicts human behavior in relationship to other humans and to God. God works vindication for the oppressed, but it is humans who oppress. God doesn't continually accuse and remain angry, and the implication is that humans do. God doesn't deal with people in accordance with their sins, even though humans enumerate eyes for eyes and teeth for teeth. And in two places in these few verses the psalmist refers to the almost unimaginable bounty of God's steadfast love, again implying that humans find themselves quite limited in that area.

Just as Paul does in 1 Corinthians 13, the psalmist lists here the attributes of a loving relationship: justice, mercy, self-revelation, graciousness, slowness to anger, the forgiving of transgressions.

A summary statement compares the love of God for the children of God to the love a human father has for his children. That comparison serves two purposes. First, it helps us once again as we try to grasp the infinite with our finite minds: We do that through human terms and our experience of parental love. Second, it challenges us to reflect the character of God's love in our own loving.

PRAYER: God, teach me to love in the reflection of your infinite love. Amen.

THURSDAY, FEBRUARY 24 • Read 2 Corinthians 3:1-6

Several things are going on in this passage, not the least of which is the argument against the letter of the law, the Mosaic tablets of stone, which the Spirit replaces with a life-giving new covenant written on the tablets of the heart.

Beyond this polemic, the text addresses issues of competence, confidence, and authority. The Christian church often faces questions of credentials and credence: Who is authorized to speak for the church or for the faith? When differences in perspective and interpretation of God's word arise, whom should we believe?

Buried beneath and around these issues, though, is how Paul frames the questions: The church at Corinth itself becomes a letter written on the heart and read by all. Relationships, as with Paul and the church at Corinth, inevitably become influential. Each party influences the other to such an extent that others can readily identify the influences.

In child rearing the recent question has been genes versus environment: What influences the child? Clearly both do. Adults often find that their attitudes or behaviors mirror those of their own parent, grandparent, or teacher. Paul sees his own stamp on the church at Corinth, and conversely he sees the influence of the Corinthian Christians on himself. Ultimately, Paul sees them all bearing the influences of Christ and thus of God. If I have a relationship with God, I will inevitably exhibit some of the character of God. Therein lies my commendation and authority.

PRAYER: God, grant that I may be worthy of reflecting your own character in my life. Amen.

FRIDAY, FEBRUARY 25 • Read Mark 2:13-14

The first verse of this passage reports only three items: Jesus went out beside the sea, a crowd gathered around, and he taught. Yet in the reader's mind, this simple report conjures up a magnificent scene that is common in the Gospels: the teacher with a crowd of eager listeners gathered around.

Most everyone can point to at least one influential teacher in her or his life, someone whose words, character, or actions made a lasting impression, often changing the course of the student's life. How much more influential is this teacher Jesus whose words and teachings are preserved for us and whose influence is far more widespread geographically and through the centuries than we can enumerate!

Juxtaposed with this picture of Jesus teaching beside the sea is a verse that abruptly interrupts the scene. It's almost as if we are in an art gallery looking at paintings by the same artist but hung with no theme in mind, and we move from one scene to the next. Suddenly Jesus is no longer beside the sea. Instead, he is walking along, perhaps in the business district of a town. Either we don't receive the full story, or the incident is far more radical than we might like to imagine, but Jesus says simply, "Follow me"—and Levi does.

Ostensibly the two scenes have no relation, but perhaps in the Gospel writer's mind they connect in the way that Jesus, this ultimate teacher, relates to those who listen. Persons experience an undeniable compulsion to listen to this God/man, to allow his words, his manner, his character to draw them in, resulting in radical change.

PRAYER: God, grant me courage to listen because of and in spite of the possibility that I'll be radically changed. Amen.

SATURDAY, FEBRUARY 26 • Read Mark 2:15-20

Here we read two of a number of similar stories in the Gospels that pose a rather unusual or puzzling situation involving Jesus. The scribes question Jesus' disciples about his behavior. The meaning of Jesus' parabolic answer is not entirely clear. Because of Jesus' elusive responses, we frequently focus on the behaviors rather than the answers as models. In doing so, we come to understand clearly that social norms and rules of etiquette do not bind Jesus—not even those rules bound up in the faith.

So is Jesus a rebel, a loner, someone who simply cannot tolerate society's rules? Perhaps. But we may learn more by looking at Jesus' relationships: With whom does Jesus associate, and what does Jesus invest in the association? From this vantage point, at least in these two stories, clearly Jesus seeks relationships and values them. He doesn't invite a few poor people to dinner as a charitable contribution; he lives with the sinners, normal people like you and me. According to the second story, Jesus relishes his association with the disciples, living the friendships to the fullest in a *carpe diem* sort of way. Rather than separating himself, Jesus appears to drink up relationships, thriving on them and valuing them for the hope they offer.

Jesus thrived on relationships with people who had not done anything in particular to earn that relationship, other than to commit to the relationship themselves—a tremendous demonstration of God's grace.

PRAYER: God, help me accept your grace, to invite and accept relationship with you and drink it up. Amen.

SUNDAY, FEBRUARY 27 • Read Mark 2:21-22

This passage occurs in Matthew (9:16-17) and in Luke (5:37-38) as well, and in all three Gospels it follows the issue of John's disciples fasting while Jesus' disciples do not. So the context for this saying about wineskins is always one of some discomfort with Jesus' apparent disregard for the rules, where he seems to promote throwing out the old in favor of the new.

In some sense, the wineskins' saying seems to ratify our current insatiable appetites in a throw-away world where it is cheaper and easier to get a new appliance than to fix an old one, where one can do nothing with an old computer other than throw it into a landfill. But in all three of these Gospels, Jesus has just said that the wedding guests cannot fast while the bridegroom remains with them, pointing up his urgent appetite for relationship with the disciples.

Wine connoisseurs know the value of an old wine, so perhaps the issue here is not one of tossing out the old in favor of the new but one of appropriateness: Fasting has its place but not while the bridegroom is still around; old wineskins have their place but not to hold new wine; rules about rejecting sin have their place but not when they prevent someone from relating to a person—even to a sinner. In fact, each vignette in this week's readings from Mark focuses on the relationship of Jesus to people, and it is clear in each instance that Jesus will not let anything interfere with that relationship. How uplifting to think that God is so eager to relate to people that nothing can interfere!

PRAYER: God, thank you for your willingness to relate to me, sinner though I am. Amen.

God's Glory Revealed

February 28–March 5, 2000 • Lynne M. Lepley*

MONDAY, FEBRUARY 28 • Read 2 Kings 2:1-6

As I write this meditation, a replica of the Vietnam War Memorial is on display in my city. I was not prepared for the power of this symbol to evoke vivid memories of an emotional time in our national history. As people make their pilgrimage to the Wall, they touch, see, and remember again those things that had almost been forgotten.

God leads Elijah and Elisha on their journey to the Jordan River in a deliberate manner. Each place along the way takes on symbolic significance, evoking memories of God's presence with Israel: At Gilgal, the Hebrew people made their first encampment after God brought them across the Jordan. Bethel served as the chief sanctuary of the Northern Kingdom. At Jericho God gave the Hebrew people their first victory after crossing into the Promised Land.

As Elijah and Elisha pass through each place, no doubt they remember all these events. The history of God's covenantal revelation lives in their memories. Their pilgrimage to those historic places calls to mind and reveals God's glory once again in all its living power.

SUGGESTION FOR MEDITATION: Think back to an important time in your past. Close your eyes. Envision yourself in that environment. What do you see? hear? smell? What can you touch? As you immerse yourself in this past experience, are you aware of God's presence? Where is God's glory being revealed to you?

---

*Director of Leadership Development for the Statesville District, Western North Carolina Conference of The United Methodist Church.

TUESDAY, FEBRUARY 29 • Read 2 Kings 2:7-12

My first pastoral appointment presented me with many challenges. I recall with fondness the ministry of nurture and support from my friend Vernie. My strongest memories of Vernie are the last: how she continued to minister even after a spreading lung cancer and months of treatment began to sap her energy. Eventually she could no longer leave her bed and, at the end, even speaking became a struggle. During our last visits together, I remember that her positive and loving spirit remained unchanged. Whenever I prayed for her, she always responded with prayers of thanksgiving. Over the years, Vernie's prayers have reminded me to look heavenward when temporary circumstances would have distracted me from God's glorious presence and power.

In today's reading, the time has come for Elijah to return to heaven. Elisha, his servant, grieves at the thought of separation from his beloved friend. Sensing his grief, Elijah says to Elisha, "Tell me what I may do for you, before I am taken from you." Elisha asks for a double portion of the spirit his mentor possesses.

How can Elijah grant such a request? Elijah explains that Elisha will receive the spiritual blessing he seeks in only one way: Elisha must witness Elijah's return to heaven. When the moment arrives, Elisha turns his eyes heavenward to see the glory and power of God catching up Elijah in a mighty whirlwind and a chariot and horses of fire. Elijah knew that only the glory of God revealed to Elisha can grant him the spiritual strength he seeks. Only the vision of God's glory can move him beyond the temporary to the eternal.

How might God use you and your life's circumstances to help others experience God's glory?

PRAYER: God, help me point the way to you. Amen.

WEDNESDAY, MARCH 1 • Read Psalm 50:1-6

These verses were written as a call to worship for God's people. This call to holy assembly recognizes the nature of God as judge and affirms that all who worship God must submit to God's judgment. Consuming fire and mighty tempest reveal God's glory; and all who come to worship come in submission to God's divine judgment.

The psalmist, however, sees God's judgment as a freeing experience in which to rejoice rather than a repressive experience to be feared. How can this be?

Centuries after this psalm was written, John Wesley understood "Christian conferencing" to be an important means by which Christians could experience God's grace. Wesley encouraged the Methodists to meet in small groups. In these "classes," participants earnestly and honestly shared the joys and struggles of living the Christian life in the world. Within this community of love, believers both encouraged one another and called one another to account when necessary. Class members understood this mutual accountability as an act of love to keep one another close to God.

This same understanding allows the psalmist and the members of the faith community to rejoice in God as judge. They delight in knowing that God will judge them in order to guide them in the divine way. In the awesome power of the consuming fire and tempest blast, they witness God's glory and experience God's love.

SUGGESTION FOR MEDITATION: **In a time of silent contemplation, allow God to reveal to you those things that have become barriers and burdens in your life. Imagine God's glory cleansing and burning away all those things, destroying them forever. Offer up worship and praise!**

THURSDAY, MARCH 2 • Read Psalm 50:1-6

With the help of the media, we have now elevated courtroom drama to the level of personal entertainment. We have become spectators of the real-life judgment of others as it unfolds from the safe distance of our living rooms. We casually take sides, debating at trial's end as to whether justice really was carried out.

In Psalm 50, a psalm of justice and judgment, God serves as judge in a trial that does not lend itself to a debatable human interpretation of justice. God has declared the need for the trial, a trial of cosmic proportions from which no one is exempt. What is the charge? God's people offer God worship that is empty and void of genuine feeling. In their indifference, they violate their part of the covenant.

These opening verses graphically depict a God who is anything but insincere, hollow, and lax. God can no longer ignore the offense of God's people. This glimpse of the authentic and unabashed glory of God's righteous anger almost overwhelms us. God's passion for the covenant people shines forth, and God expects nothing less than an authentic, passionate response from all that God has created and loves.

Lest those on trial dare to protest, God has summoned witnesses: all who have kept the covenant and who worship God in all sincerity. God calls the natural world as witness to the covenant. And God also gathers faithful human creations to speak as defendants.

These verses set the stage for a real-life judgment drama that involves all of creation. Where are we in this scene? Does our lax fulfillment of the covenant indict us? Or do we find ourselves among the defendants, those faithful ones who genuinely reflect God's glory?

PRAYER: God, I stand in awe of your glory. May I keep covenant with you in a way that reflects your passionate love for humankind. Amen.

FRIDAY, MARCH 3 • **Read 2 Corinthians 4:3-6**

Paul observes that the revelation of God's glory to God's people "has shone in our hearts." As he speaks of the "glory of God in the face of Jesus Christ," the phrase reminds us of the undeniable connection between the content of the heart and its outward expression.

As Moses returns to the people after talking with God on Mount Sinai, his heart and mind have been filled with God's glorious power; yet Moses remains unaware that his own face is now aglow with the glory of God until the people tell him.

If Moses is unaware that being in God's presence has affected more than his heart, how often are we unaware that our outer expression reflects our inner spiritual condition? At times worry, anger, or fear overcomes my heart. I usually think I'm concealing my anxieties, but then someone looks into my face and asks, "What's wrong?" I've come to learn that I "wear" my heart's spiritual condition on my face—no matter how hard I try to conceal it.

We need to ask ourselves: With what am I filling my heart and mind? How do these things negatively affect my overall spiritual health? How does neglect of my spiritual life affect my Christian witness?

Paul writes these words in light of his own life experience. Paul never forgot the vision of the glory of God revealed in the face of Christ. This revelation had the power to change his heart and life forever.

What can the glory of God in my heart, shining through me, do in the lives of others?

SUGGESTION FOR MEDITATION: **Imagine the glory of God filling your heart—dispelling negative or hurtful thoughts and influences. Notice how it makes you feel inside. How does your face reflect what you are feeling? Go out into the world, conscious of God's glory shining from your countenance as you encounter others. Look for its reflection in their faces.**

SATURDAY, MARCH 4 • Read Mark 9:2-9

Jesus takes Peter, James, and John and goes to the seclusion of a high mountain. In that quiet place, away from the usual din of the pressing multitudes, the disciples witness Jesus' becoming transfigured—aglow with the light of God's glory—right before their eyes. Can it be that Jesus knows his disciples need a quiet place, free from distractions in order to see God's glory revealed in him? The fullness of God has always been present in Jesus. Can it be that Peter, James, and John are able to see it clearly for the first time in the solitude of this remote place?

Perhaps Peter personifies our reaction to the silence and sense of isolation that accompanies a time apart. In the powerful stillness of that moment as Jesus is transformed before them, Peter breaks the silence, perhaps because he is afraid. Peter doesn't know what to say—but that doesn't stop him from speaking! Peter's awkward situation becomes the very environment for the revelation of God's glory.

Do I, in my discomfort with silence, avoid "awkward" situations where I simply don't know what to say? Could it be that in my avoidance, I am missing some opportunity to witness God's glory revealed?

As a pastor, I find it freeing to realize that I don't have to possess the "right" words for every occasion. Sometimes the most powerful statement we can make is to say nothing—and in the silence of those moments to allow the power and glory of God to shine forth.

PRAYER: O God, help me not to fear the times of silence but to seek your glory in the stillness of the moment. Amen.

SUNDAY, MARCH 5 • Read Mark 9:2-9

TRANSFIGURATION SUNDAY

When Peter, James and John accompany their Lord up the mountain, the sight of Jesus transformed before them fills their eyes. They hear the voice of God speaking from the cloud, declaring, "This is my Son, the Beloved; listen to him!" The Transfiguration comes just after Peter's declaration of faith, "You are the Messiah" (8:29).

On the night of his arrest, Jesus again calls Peter, James, and John to accompany him. Do these three men recall that transfiguration moment of Christ's glory as Jesus again calls them apart to be with him? Events take a very different turn in this time apart: Jesus is arrested, and the disciples flee. How can they turn from Jesus after witnessing his transfiguration? Yet how many times do we experience the reality of God's glory in our lives, only to struggle with our faith when confronted with real-life fears and temptations.

Some of my friends have just returned from a Walk to Emmaus. Their "Fourth Day"—the rest of their lives after this spiritual retreat—have begun. In the years since the "mountaintop" spiritual experience of my Walk, many times I have forgotten—even denied—Christ by failing to follow him.

Despite the failure of Peter, James, John, and the other disciples to follow Jesus to the cross, the greatest news is that God responds to their failures with nothing less than another display of God's glory: the appearance of the white-robed "young man" who bears the amazing message that Jesus is alive and goes ahead of them to Galilee. In the midst of the most dismal human shortcomings, God's glory and grace shine forth to heal, reconcile, and restore.

PRAYER: Gracious God, I ask your forgiveness for those times when I fail to live as one who has witnessed your glory. Do not allow my shortcomings to overwhelm me, but help me see the glorious gift of your love and grace. Amen.

Remember Your Baptism!

March 6–12, 2000 • Rebecca Irene Foote

MONDAY, MARCH 6 • Read Genesis 9:8-17

As rain poured down on seminary students running in the quad to reach protection from the deluge, my professor would amble along holding out his upturned hands and shout, "Remember your baptism! Remember your baptism!" In other words, let this rain be a symbol to remind you that with water you were initiated into the Christian community of faith. You are a loved person—a new creation!

We have many signs and rituals in the church to remind us of God's love in our lives through Jesus Christ. Water is one of the most powerful symbols that was used in both the Old and New Testaments, and it continues to be a part of our tradition today. On Wednesday of this week we begin the season of Lent—a time when we purposefully recall the covenant that we made in our baptismal vows, our water vows, in response to the everflowing river of God's grace that runs through us all. It is, therefore, important that the onset of Lent be a time when we look at our vows and commit again to the covenant we made at baptism and affirmed at the time of confirmation. This covenant goes far beyond a legal agreement—it calls us to take a risk and to believe that God loves us. Then it calls for our faithful response as we live out the joy we know as new creations, beloved creations of God.

PRAYER: Most loving and gracious God, like Noah, lead me to step out in faith as I renew my covenant with you this coming season of Lent. Help me remember my baptismal vows each day this week and respond in active service, knowing you love me dearly and will always be with me. Amen.

---

*Elder in the Detroit Conference of The United Methodist Church, currently living in Chattanooga, Tennessee.

TUESDAY, MARCH 7 • Read Mark 1:12-15; Psalm 51:1-17

The first vow in the baptismal covenant of my faith tradition asks us to renounce the spiritual forces of wickedness, reject the evil powers of this world, and repent of our sin.

The prefix *re-* begins every verb. *Re-* simply denotes an action in the reverse direction. We *re*-nounce the spiritual forces of wickedness. We *re*-ject the evil powers of this world. We *re*-pent of our sin. We covenant with God, through the outward sign of baptism, to turn our back on wickedness, evil powers, and sin. We promise to turn completely away, moving in the opposite direction from injustice and oppression in whatever forms these evils present themselves.

We answer this first vow with Yes! Yes! If I walk into an unhealthy situation that causes pain to others and is destructive, I am going to renounce it, reject it, turn from it, and walk with God. I will refuse to support anything that does not build up the kingdom of God, God's children, and myself. Turning once and forever?…probably not. Every day?…more like it. For some of us, turning from the unhealthy and the life-destroying is an hourly or minute-by-minute endeavor. We must say repeatedly, "Yes, I will repent and turn toward God, with God!"

One Sunday a man who had lived all his life causing pain and destruction to others came forward in the small church of the village to repent and start anew with God. The minister started to dip his hand into the baptismal water when from the back of the church a woman stood up and cried out, "Stop! Wait! That little dab of water will never do. You'll have to anchor him in deep water overnight at least!" Lives change, not through the amount of baptismal water but the amount of grace God gives us to live out our desire to change.

PRAYER: O Lord, help me turn from all the destructive forces in my life and walk with you. I do this only with your love and grace, symbolized with the water of baptism. Amen.

WEDNESDAY, MARCH 8 • Read 1 Peter 3:18-22

ASH WEDNESDAY

The second vow of The United Methodist baptismal covenant involves our acceptance of the freedom and power God gives to resist evil, injustice, and oppression in whatever forms they present themselves. The world must think us peculiar that we use the word *freedom* to express giving up the way we have been conducting ourselves.

A simple analogy may help us understand this concept. Think of the most exotic car that one could ever purchase. Owning the car, one would want to know about it, get the most out of it, and certainly understand what could damage it and cause it harm. If the car needed repair, one would go to the mechanic who knew the car inside and out, otherwise the car's maintenance would be limited by one's ability to understand everything about the car.

Christ came to show us our Creator's direction for the healthiest, most abundant life we can have—a life that gives us the freedom to be all we can possibly be. Not a life without difficulties, not a life without pain, not a life without struggle but a life in which we turn daily to walk with our Maker who knows us best.

The baptismal imagery implies that we are buried to the old direction and rise again to walk in the new life imbued with the freedom and strength to do it. We face deaths all the time in our lives—events and relationships that cause us to wonder if we can go on, get beyond them, cope, live. So on this holy day of Ash Wednesday, we remember our baptism and all the deaths we experience, and we know, though deaths come and ultimately even our mortal life ends, we have the freedom and the power of our Creator to rise again in newness of life.

PRAYER: Loving God, may the ashes of this day be a sign of the deaths I often face in my life, but may the remembrance of my baptism be the sign of hope and freedom through Christ. Amen.

THURSDAY, MARCH 9 • Read Mark 1:9-11;
2 Corinthians 6:1-2

The third baptismal vow of my denomination asks the question: "Do you confess Jesus Christ as your Savior, put your whole trust in his grace, and promise to serve him as your Lord, in union with the church which Christ has opened to people of all ages, nations, and races?"

We, the baptized, answer, Yes! To put Christ above all in our lives and to make service to Christ the highest priority in our lives is quite a declaration.

I am reminded of a story of a missionary to Vietnam in the late seventies. Sam was trying to help with the rebuilding of that country after the ravages of war, but he received little cooperation. One particularly exasperating day, he left his work and started home in his jeep through the jungle. His vehicle broke down; and when he finally arrived, exhausted, at his cottage, Sam found that all of his possessions had been stolen. He fell on the floor and cried. He started to call out to God in his anger saying, "You led me here. I am following you. I confessed you as Lord of my life. And look at all that has happened. I don't love these Vietnamese anymore!" The Lord spoke to his heart, and he heard so clearly God's answer: "Sam, you are not here because you love these people; you are here because I love them!"

Often we confess Jesus Christ as Savior, but we forget what that affirmation has to do with our lives—every day. It is a difficult challenge to trust that God is with us, gracing our lives, and that we are, in response to the Lord's love, to share God's grace with others. In this season of Lent, we remember that whatever befalls, God's grace is sufficient to see us through—we have been baptized!

PRAYER: Gracious God, help me remember just that—you are gracious. Help me trust and obey, for I have vowed to do so knowing that it guides me to abundant life. Amen.

FRIDAY, MARCH 10 • Read 2 Corinthians 5:20-21;
Isaiah 58:1-12

The fourth baptismal vow asks, "Will you remain faithful members of Christ's holy church and serve as Christ's representatives in the world?" Martin Luther called Christians "little Christs." This is our mission. I belonged to a church called The Church of the Incarnation. Is that not a wonderful appellation for us: to be incarnate, in the flesh, those whose mission it is to represent the holy—to exit the church on Sunday understanding our life to be one of loving and serving those around us. Each church building needs a sign over the door inside that reads as congregants exit, "You are now entering the sacred." We need reminders of our vow that calls us to be Christ's representatives in our home, in our relationships, in our workplace, in the midst of issues that impact any of God's creatures and creation.

The movie *The Godfather* portrays our ability to separate what we do and say in the sacred place or church and what happens in the nonsacred place. Michael Corleone, the head of a Mafia family, is to be his nephew's godfather. During the Catholic ceremony of baptism, Michael answers yes to each of the baptismal vows. But as he responds, the scene changes to another location in New York where under the Godfather's order, death is carried out. Michael believes the church to be sacred and can boldly defend his belief and answer Yes! to the baptismal vows because he believes they have nothing to do whatsoever with what goes on in his daily life.

But everything in creation is sacred; with this vow we affirm that we will see the entire world as a place where we practice and live out our statement of faith.

PRAYER: Most gracious and good God, help me remember my vow to represent Christ to the world—to be a little Christ. May I express my overflowing love to all my sisters and brothers, your children. Amen.

SATURDAY, MARCH 11 • Read Psalm 25

Immediately after the faith community's affirmation of support, the United Methodist baptismal covenant requests that the entire congregation "join together in professing the Christian faith as contained in the Scriptures of the Old and New Testaments." This request presumes that we know what the scriptures contain, acknowledging their primary role in our ability to turn from evil, to declare Christ as Lord, and to be representatives of Christ in the world.

For the Bible to become alive, dynamic, and exciting, we must see the Bible as a book that reads us. We call it the *Holy* Bible, not because it is holy in and of itself but because it contains God's communication to us through human beings like us. The revelation of God in scripture lets us know what the holy is like. And we can read ourselves in the Bible. Our story is there. It will read us once we begin to read it. The Bible validates all our experiences—it reads us. We are in there and when we see ourselves, when we read ourselves, we allow ourselves to hear the word of God speak to us. Then we begin to know the scriptures and can profess the Christian faith.

A form of drama flourished in sixteenth-century Italy called *commedia dell'arte*. Those watching the drama were asked to put themselves in the story. That is what happens with us and the scriptures.

The Great Dramatist, the Holy One, is apt to lure us from the spectator's balcony and put us into the act when we read and study the Bible. We then will be confronted with ourselves, and we will find out that God knows us and knows us well. We will be read by the scriptures and find God's grace in our lives so we are able to profess that grace to others.

PRAYER: O Holy One, help me read, study, receive, and profess the Christian faith as contained in the scriptures. With the psalmist I ask you to guide me by your truth and instruct me by your word. Amen.

Sunday, March 12 • Read 2 Corinthians 6:3-10

First Sunday in Lent

In my faith tradition, the entire church takes part in every baptism when the clergy addresses this question to the congregation, "Will you nurture one another in the Christian faith and life and include these persons now before you in your care?" And the members respond, "We will surround these persons with a community of love and forgiveness, that they may grow in their trust of God and be found faithful in their service to others. We will pray for them, that they may be true disciples who walk in the way that leads to life." Of course we will nurture, support, be there for, struggle with, and love them through their journey—just as they will with us!

Jesus did not call just one person to take his place here on earth. He gathered together a group of followers who called others into fellowship.

In a wind tunnel, engineers have calculated what happens in the V formation in which Canada geese fly. Each bird creates an upward lift for the one behind. This upward lift helps all the birds conserve strength and gives them a seventy-one percent greater flying range than if each bird flew alone. If one goose begins to fall behind the system, the others "honk" it back into place. And that is how we as church members are meant to be. When we feel tired, confused, discouraged, we are called back to remember the vows we took at baptism and be loved by those who took those same vows.

Often people ask if you can be a Christian without being part of a church family. Why would you not want to be with a family who is called together to support and love and pray you through your journey of faith and encourage you to go on… and on…and on…?

Suggestion for meditation: Remember who you are as a child of God and remember the church family who encourages you to live out your life's journey.

God's Dream for the World

March 13–19, 2000 • Joe E. Pennel Jr.

MONDAY, MARCH 13 • Read Genesis 17:1-2

The God of Hebrew Scriptures is not passive and far removed. This God acts, initiates, and intervenes in the life and thought of people. In today's reading God takes the initiative; not only does God "appear" to Abraham, God also speaks.

I believe that God continues to speak to us through listening prayers, through the reading of the scripture, through public and private worship, through the poor, through the pain and beauty of the world, and through other people whom we know and do not know. We must remember that God's voice is more like a whisper than a shout.

To hear God's voice requires a listening ear. Listening is hard work that demands great concentration. Every now and then I will ask my wife a question, and she will say, "You don't listen to me. I answered that question thirty minutes ago." If it is difficult to listen to others, how much more arduous is it to hear the talk of the Holy One?

We cannot invoke the voice of God. It comes to those who listen. By listening we can hear the voice behind the many voices that call our name. Behind the multitude of voices that beat against our ears is a word that yearns to be heard.

Listening is not conditioned by age or circumstance. Today's text reminds us that we are never too old to listen to God: Abraham is ninety-nine years old when God speaks to him about a covenant and a son. Every person can listen to the voice that is both deep within and far beyond. God's dream is that we listen.

PRAYER: GOD, help me listen with the depths of my soul so my heart will be entirely directed toward you. Amen.

---

*Bishop of the Virginia Conference of The United Methodist Church.

TUESDAY, MARCH 14 • Read Genesis 17:3-7, 15-16

The God who takes the initiative and speaks to Abraham also enters into covenant with him. Not a business deal where two people sign a contract nor a handshake over a fair exchange, a covenant is more profound than either of the above. A Bible covenant unites people to God and to one another. Accounts of covenant making between God and Israel show three aspects.

First, God offers a covenant as a gift to people. The covenant comes about only through God's initiative; it in no way rewards Abraham for his merits. Abraham, like all humanity, has flaws. Yet God chooses to enter into a special relationship with him. Likewise, the new covenant in Jesus Christ comes as a sheer gift, not because we earn it or deserve it but because God chose to come in human form.

Second, through the covenant God comes into relationship and creates with God's people a bond of communion. A human analogy would be that of marriage. The joining of two persons in holy matrimony creates a unique and sacred bond. Marriage establishes a mutual covenant of love and trust. Likewise, when God brings people into a sacred relationship, God does not record it on stone or paper but on the heart—or in the instance of Jesus of Nazareth, in human form.

Third, the covenant creates obligations that take concrete shape in word and deed. A covenant is not established and forgotten. Individuals and the faith community live it out. Israel sins when it forgets the covenant. Abraham's descendants begin worshiping other gods, thereby turning their backs on the covenant that God had established.

Keeping the covenant is God's dream for us.

PRAYER: God of covenant relationship, help me keep the covenant and call it a delight so that I might be strengthened and gladdened by your goodness. Amen.

WEDNESDAY, MARCH 15 • Read Psalm 22:24

Words have power to shape reality, to hurt or to heal. They can make "this" look like "that." One word can bring discomfort and discord. Likewise, one word can bring hope and healing.

Human speech may be powerful, but it inadequately expresses the deepest feelings of the human heart. Words, for example, cannot express what we feel at the baptism of our child or at a grandchild's wedding or when we say good-bye to an offspring who is going away to college. Words inadequately express the pain we feel when someone close to us disappoints us or when we feel proud of one we love. Nor can words adequately express what God is like.

God must have realized the limitation of words because wanting to speak in a definitive way, God made the word become flesh. Jesus displayed the word in human form. When God wanted to say, "I love you," God did not write a note; God said it with a human being.

Though words are inadequate, the church must use words to speak about the Word made flesh. Searching for the best word becomes an important task for every Christian. The psalmist did not have the advantage of seeing the Word made flesh, but he could say that "God did not hide his face from me"—nor does God hide the divine face from us.

God's dream is that the Word will become flesh through all who believe.

PRAYER: Incarnating God, open my heart to your word that the Word might become embodied in me. Amen.

THURSDAY, MARCH 16 • Read Psalm 22:23-31

Glory and splendor mark the beginning of time. All that God made was glorious. All of creation, including humankind, pointed to a God whose nature was thought to be glorious.

God intended that all of creation cooperate with that splendor. Adam, according to Genesis, chose to exalt himself by placing his will over God's intention. He used the glorious garden of Eden to bring beauty, honor, and splendor upon himself. Thus he tarnished the glory of God by turning away from the Creator and toward himself.

The psalmist holds a lofty view of God's intentions. So he urges the offspring of Jacob to glorify God. His poem reminds us that we glorify God by reflecting the glory of the Holy One.

It is easy to be like Adam. Like him, we also succumb to the temptation to magnify ourselves by putting ourselves at the center of life. Our culture has taught us to reflect our glory rather than to reflect God's glory. As Christians, we reflect the glory of God when our lives are governed by the kind of love we see in the second Adam, Jesus of Nazareth.

God does not will our efforts at self-glorification. Such efforts do not join people to one another and to God. Self-glorification divides people, erects walls, and does not create community. The Holy One wills something very different for us. God's dream for the world is that we be liberated from the pharaohs of self-glorification.

PRAYER: God of steadfast love, uphold my faith that I might glorify you and serve you forever. Amen.

FRIDAY, MARCH 17 • Read Romans 4:13-25

During the early 1940s my grandfather on my mother's side spent one month out of every four with our family. He spent the other three months with my aunt and two uncles. Life shifted when he came to our house. Room at the table and in the house had to be made for one more person. It was not easy, but it had its positive side.

As a five-year-old child, I was pleased when our turn came. Grandaddy's being at our house brought me pleasure, because when he was there, I had someone to intercede for me. No matter what I said or did he was always in my corner. When my mother threatened to discipline me because I had acted out, he was sure to come to my defense. When I was a good boy, he was the first one to give me praise.

In Romans 4:13, Paul says that God gave Abraham a promise and that "this promise wasn't made because Abraham had obeyed a law but because his faith in God made him acceptable" (CEV). Maybe that's how I felt with Granddaddy around—acceptable. Because of his intercession for me and his advocacy on my behalf, I wasn't always subject to parental punishment—to the law. For me, Granddaddy was the embodiment of God's grace, which moves beyond law to love. And that love, because of the work of Christ, makes us "acceptable to God" (CEV). Later in his letter to the Romans, Paul reminds us that the risen Christ intercedes for us when we are weak (Rom. 8:26-27). Thanks be to grandfathers and all others who embody our loving advocate, Jesus Christ, God's ultimate dream for the world!

PRAYER: As you taught our ancestors through the words of our advocate, so may your advocate teach me to follow the paths of goodness, kindness and love. Blessed is the Lord, shield of Abraham, Isaac, and Jesus. Amen.

SATURDAY, MARCH 18 • Read Mark 8:31-33

God has a great dream for the human family. Scripture makes this dream plain. A portion of God's vision is that we would practice sacrificial, suffering love for one another.

If everyone in the human family embodied sacrificial love, there would be no war, no hunger, no strife, no abandoned children, no racism, no sexism, no exaggerated nationalism, no greed, no exploitation, no homeless families, and no people cursed with overabundance.

Only sacrificial love has the power to bring down the walls that isolate and divide. Suffering love is the only force that can reconcile people to God and to one another. Nothing, absolutely nothing, has that strength. We must remember the power of sacrificial love because the church exists for the purpose of reconciling people to God and one another through Jesus Christ.

When Jesus speaks about sacrificial love, Peter rebukes him. Peter wants a Messiah who will be victorious without suffering and rejection. Peter is hesitant to believe in one who speaks about losing one's life for Christ and for the gospel in order to save it. He does not want Jesus to forecast his death at the hands of elders, priests, and teachers. In a word, Peter wants the fulfillment of God's dream without sacrificial love.

God's dream is that we will practice sacrificial love toward one another. Therein lies the hope for the human family.

PRAYER: **Loving God, set the meaning of sacrificial love on my heart that I might live faithfully and in service to you and to all humankind. Amen.**

SUNDAY, MARCH 19 • Read Mark 8:34-38

SECOND SUNDAY IN LENT

"Following Jesus" is a familiar Christian phrase. Those of us who grew up in church recall "following Jesus" as an important teaching. To tread on the heels of Jesus does not mean to believe in a prescribed set of doctrines or teachings about a man from Galilee. It means "to give one's heart to." The heart, according to scripture, is the self at its deepest level. Following requires more than giving mental assent. It requires more than believing doctrines about Jesus. Following Jesus means to give one's heart, one's self at its deepest level to the man who turned his face toward the cross. And beyond that, it means to come along after Jesus, the human face of God turned toward us.

In today's text Jesus invites the crowd to follow after him. It will not be easy. It will be the way of cross bearing and the way of losing one's life. Oddly enough, those who are willing to lose life will be the very ones who will gain new life.

A sincere desire to follow Jesus in word and deed moves us from secondhand religion to firsthand religion, from reading about Jesus to being in relationship with the spirit of the living Christ.

Jesus Christ is not an antiquated, historical figure confined to the past. His spirit lives today, and he continues to invite people to give their heart to him—to follow him.

God's dream is that we would give our hearts to Jesus Christ.

PRAYER: O God, give to me the faith and strength to follow Jesus. Amen.

Let God's Law of Love Be Our Guide

March 20–26, 2000 • Susan Muto*

MONDAY, MARCH 20 • Read Exodus 20:1-11

The Ten Commandments are not debatable suggestions but divine directives leading to a lifelong course in character formation. They are floodlights in dark nights of self-inflicted confusion. The first commandment calls us to adoration by reminding us that we are not gods, though pride may prompt us to play this illusory role. Any idol we place before God, be it power, pleasure, or possession, is bound to disappoint us. God wants the only object of our worship to be God's glory, never our own grandiosity. Adoration leads to veneration. To revere God's name is to show our desire for a life of intimacy with the divine. The second commandment invites us not only to proclaim the holiness of God's name but to venerate the Lord as our maker and creator. The dispositions of adoration and veneration inspire in us the zeal and dedication to keep holy the day of the Lord and to remember that we are people blessed and consecrated for a finer purpose, a nobler commitment. The third commandment reminds us, amidst the frenetic pace of life, that we are called to rest and restoration. Now is the time to greet the Lord with a joyful song and to practice the art of contemplation so that all our actions will unite us to God.

PRAYER: Holy and blessed Lord, remind me of the importance of bending a knee to your majesty, venerating your name, and accepting your invitation to peaceful intimacy. Let your laws of love shine like beacons guiding my passage through perilous seas. Let them be the keys to what alone can make me happy. Amen.

---

*Executive Director of Epiphany Association, Pittsburgh, Pennsylvania; professor of literature and spirituality; speaker, writer, and consultant in the field of Christian formation.

TUESDAY, MARCH 21 • Read Exodus 20:12-17

When we obey the first three commandments of the Decalogue, we follow the first part of the Great Commandment; we obey the second half of the Commandment by loving our neighbor as we love ourselves. We begin this loving of neighbor by honoring our parents and those in authority over us. The Giver of all life then commands us not to kill but to fulfill the plans God set in motion for us from the beginning. Just as we have no right to take another's life physically, so we are forbidden to destroy another spiritually. It follows that adultery kills trust and fidelity, pulverizing one's sense of self-worth and demeaning the sacred nature of human sexuality.

The seventh commandment seems not only to forbid the theft of another's property and possessions but includes the prohibition not to steal another's trust. The eighth commandment forbids deceit and the wicked injustices it spawns. False witness distorts the truth. Love of self is swallowed up in self-deception. And who suffers? Our neighbor. Thus the ninth and tenth commandments reveal the result of dishonor, destruction, infidelity, stealing, and lying rooted in the sin of covetousness. All such forms of possessiveness and impurity make avarice and lust, not generosity and love, the ruination of personal relationships. No wonder we pray for release from these gross aberrations that are so contrary to our being guided by God's liberating law.

PRAYER: Merciful God, melt humanity's malformation, Eden's usurpation of authority belonging to you alone. Soften my heart of stone as I stand bitter and alone in a sinful prison of my own making. Save my limping life, however undeserving, by the meritorious outpouring of your forgiveness from the cross. Mine only is the loss if I do not bend a knee to your victory. Amen.

WEDNESDAY, MARCH 22 • Read Psalm 19:1-8

Contemplative souls see in nature an epiphany of God's forming, reforming, and transforming mystery. They read the divine law in the stars' glimmer at night, in the light of dawn, in the brightness of the sun. This law is not only etched on our hearts; it is also penned on and proclaimed by every iota of creation. The question is, Do we see it, or are we too busy to notice its splendor?

Against this backdrop of nature's serene attunement to the laws set in motion by God, the psalmist celebrates the victory of the Lord over unbounded chaos. Using a familiar comparison, he looks to the sun, the organizing force of our solar system, and compares it to a bridegroom (like the Son of Man), to a champion (like the faithful soul who finishes the race), to a lawgiver, who puts into motion a course of action that is life-giving.

Similarly, the law of God is absolutely trustworthy. It builds character. It revives drooping spirits. It makes simple souls wise. It evokes joy in the hearts of believers. Where the darkness of ignorance once resided, God's law brings light. In a few phrases the psalmist succeeds in summing up the eternal value of the Decalogue, announcing to a world at risk of losing its moorings and missing the mark that the Lord's commands are radiant, perfect, and right.

SUGGESTION FOR MEDITATION: Take any daily newspaper and list the number of reports that reveal our refusal to obey the commandments of the Lord. Do not be surprised by the instances recorded of idolatry, blasphemy, and the flaunting of authority, to say nothing of killing, stealing, lying, and coveting. Ask God what you can do today to offset the dire effects of disobedience. Begin by beholding in awe the natural law.

THURSDAY, MARCH 23 • Read Psalm 19:9-14

The rest of this psalm directs our attention from the universe at large to the heartfelt longings of a soul who, despite sin, wants to obey. The first disposition we need to cultivate is awe or fear of the Lord. We need to abide with and attend to the Lord's commands. Once we taste the honey of obedience, the vinegar of disobedience has no appeal.

Keeping the law of God is not a burden imposed by a stern judge, nor are we motivated to obey out of fear of punishment. Rather, our "yes" to God brings with it great rewards. Conviction that this law is nothing less than the will of God inspires in us a series of prayerful petitions. The first is an appeal for forgiveness: *God, wipe out not only my willful transgressions but also my hidden faults.* We seek liberation from the imprisoning power of original and actual sin.

The psalmist's prayer reflects a longing to return to the blameless state of primordial innocence when male and female walked hand in hand with God in the garden of Eden. Alas, disobedience changed this pristine intimacy forever. Yet through the grace of repentance we can escape from the prison of gross faults. We can speak with reverence of the ways of the Lord and grow more pleasing in God's sight.

PRAYER: Holy and blessed Lord, God of all creation, my Rock and my Redeemer, come and dwell within this wounded heart of mine. Heal the scars of sins—their great gashes and pinpoint pricks. Protect me with the shield of your mercy from demonic seduction and willful transgression. Make me today and all the days of my life a servant, the very sight of whom brings joy to your heart. Amen.

FRIDAY, MARCH 24 • Read 1 Corinthians 1:18-25

Compunction and the longing for redemption bring us to the foot of the cross. We know that no work can save us. Only faith in the foolishness of the crucified Christ, who loved us to the point of death, can break the bondage of sin and make us worthy to receive the grace of salvation.

Human wisdom might be inclined to scoff at the saving power of humility, but the last laugh, as Paul says, belongs to people faithful enough not to seek proof of Christ's power in anything other than the foolishness of the cross. The cross threatens unbelievers because it seems so contrary to the wisdom of the world. Indeed, as the prophet Isaiah warned, God often will thwart worldly expectations. (See Isa. 29:14.) The mystery of suffering for the sake of love calls for a new set of laws that transcends the old law's demand of an eye for an eye and a tooth for a tooth. (See Matt. 5:38-42.)

Jesus writes a new law of love as he hangs in helpless abandonment on the wood of the cross. This event evokes wonder in Paul who once persecuted Christians. No longer can he—or we—consider suffering to be punishment for sin, for Christ had no sin. Suffering must have a greater meaning, that of atonement! And this is good news!

SUGGESTION FOR MEDITATION: **Pause in the midst of whatever you are doing and feel the full weight of the cross in your heart. Consider your image of the church. Do you view it as a worldly power frustrated before its foolishness? Consider your self-image. Do you need signs and wonders to bolster your faith, or is it enough to stand in wonder before your crucified Lord? Rather than resent the weakness you experience, let it lead you to rely on the strength of God.**

SATURDAY, MARCH 25 • **Read John 2:13-17**

To understand Jesus' display of righteous anger when he casts the money changers out of the Temple and castigates them for turning his Father's house into a marketplace, we need to focus again on several commandments. We need to revisit the first commandment's prohibition against any form of idolatry, the second commandment's condemnation of blasphemy, and the third commandment's recognition of the Sabbath and therewith the holiness of sacred spaces like the Temple.

The lying and cheating that go together with so much buying and selling must offend Jesus to the core. He sees this edifice as the center of worship and authentic sacrifice, as the site of God's presence, and as a symbol of God's fidelity to Israel. Here people should come to pray, not pay; to gather alms for the poor, not to collect money. Such avaricious behavior arouses the man of forgiveness to castigation. What consumes Jesus is not only an aversion to consumerism but zeal for his Father's house. His fury is an expression of his faith and the purity of his sense of mission.

This explosive, prophetic gesture, though a sign of Jesus' fidelity to the Father, becomes a final straw—at least in the Gospels of Matthew, Mark, and Luke—that leads to his condemnation. Once he becomes the brunt of his enemies' antagonism, there can be no turning back from his own Passover supper.

PRAYER: Jesus, help me. I often lack the courage to stand up and fight for what I believe. Don't let me succumb to the tempting complacency of popularity or to the lure of money. Give me the gift of zeal with all the bravery and devotion it requires. Teach me to conform my life to yours. Make me a worthy dweller in your Father's house, a worshiper in spirit and in truth. Amen.

SUNDAY, MARCH 26 • John 2:17-22

THIRD SUNDAY IN LENT

As a lawbreaker in the legalistic sense, Jesus has to answer to people who already hate and fear him. They dare him to justify his actions by explaining to them the authority under which he operates. In fact, they try to tempt him to produce a sign to show that this is his Father's house.

Jesus reads their hearts and rises to the challenge. They understand nothing beyond literal proof, so what does it matter if he speaks on another plane of reality? The temple he dares them to destroy is his own body. They can kill it, but they cannot control the miracle of his rising up in three days. With minds as opaque as that of the Samaritan woman who thought Jesus could conjure up a bucket of water that would never dry up (John 4:11-15), Jesus' adversaries scoff that it took forty-six years to build the Temple. Is he foolish enough to believe he can rebuild it in three days?

Only after the Resurrection do his disciples remember this prophetic moment. Only after they behold him as their risen Lord do they realize the significance of what he has said. Only then do they come to believe in the true miracle of his glorified body.

SUGGESTION FOR MEDITATION: **As this story unfolds, be honest about your own lack of belief. Haven't you felt at times that God's fidelity to us is almost too incredulous to take seriously? Many today challenge the truth of the Resurrection, yet to claim that "Christ has died, Christ is risen, and Christ will come again" is the central tenet of our faith. Let all these doubts come to rest at the altar of the risen Lord, for you have become a temple of the living God. (See 1 Corinthians 3:16.)**

For God So Loved

March 27–April 2, 2000 • *James K. Wagner**

Psalm 107 offers a wonderful word of encouragement in the midst of personal troubles and unresolved problems. When we face difficulties that defy solution, the psalmist lays out a helpful prayer format.

Begin by giving thanks to the Lord in advance of deliverance and personal help. Why? Because God is good and God's love endures forever. The New Revised Standard Version of this psalm describes God's love as being steadfast. Notice this same teaching in verses 8, 15, 21, 31, and 43.

Unlike human love that tends to be fickle, unstable, and unsteady, God's love is constant, enduring, and faithful. This understanding leads to the next step in the prayer process: Recall troubled times in the past that turned out OK. This psalm names specific categories of problems: traveling in the desert without enough food and water, getting lost, being imprisoned, being so sick that death is welcome, detailing the perils and disasters associated with sea travel.

This recollection leads logically to the last line: "Let those who are wise give heed to these things, and consider the steadfast love of the LORD" (v. 43).

SUGGESTION FOR MEDITATION: **Reread Psalm 107 slowly, ponderingly. In an attitude of prayer, affirm God's goodness and steadfast love in your life. Recall and write out several troublesome situations in your past and the result of each one. List any present dilemmas or personal problems. What positive difference could knowing God's desire to help you make in your prayers, attitudes, and actions?**

---

*Author; National President of the Disciplined Order of Christ; United Methodist minister, West Ohio Conference.

TUESDAY, MARCH 28 • Read Psalm 107:1-3, 17-22

Among the various kinds of troubles and distresses in Psalm 107, the psalmist lists the universal problem of human sickness. When illnesses come into our lives, we automatically join the unorganized, all-inclusive fellowship of sufferers.

Sometimes we bring on our personal sickness through unhealthy lifestyles. Other illnesses can lay us low through no fault of our own. Whatever the origin of our lack of health, the psalmist states boldly that God not only wants us to be healed but also wants to provide therapy in the healing process. Verse 20 reminds us of the Roman centurion who came to Jesus requesting healing for his servant. When Jesus offered to go home with him, the soldier said, "Lord, I am not worthy to have you come under my roof; but only speak the word, and my servant will be healed" (Matt. 8:8).

Consider this evidence that God sides with our desire for good health:
- God's good creation as described in Genesis 1–2
- The natural ability of the body to heal itself
- The intentional healing ministry of Jesus, which dealt with the whole person
- The discoveries and resources of the health-care profession

SUGGESTION FOR MEDITATION:
Taking your cue from Psalm 107:21-22:
- **Thank God for the healing love you have experienced in times of past personal illnesses.**
- **Thank God for creating your body with built-in systems of renewal and regeneration.**
- **Thank God for the healing Christ who actively participates in your quest for health and wholeness in body/mind/spirit and in all your relationships.**
- **Be open and receptive to God's therapies in dealing with any present or future illnesses.**

WEDNESDAY, MARCH 29 • Read Ephesians 2:1-5

Do you remember all those childhood tales that began, "Once upon a time…"? We liked these stories because they ignited our imaginations and helped us enter the world of "let's pretend."

In the opening lines of Ephesians 2, the writer asks his Christian readers to remember "once upon a time" in their former lives, before they met Christ. Can you recall how that was in your past? In what ways can you identify with living "once upon a time" by the passions of your temptations, disobedience to God and other authority figures, following your natural desires without paying attention to the consequences of your actions?

The writer goes on to state that God "who is rich in mercy" and who consistently operates out of great love, has rescued us from all that in and through Jesus Christ. Does that mean we are home free from sinning?

No, but we should be making some progress. Even though all Christians may not have a notorious, rebellious past, all Christians do fall short of God's glory. We find ourselves in the process of becoming new creations in Christ. We sometimes call that process *sanctification* in Christian spiritual maturity.

Truthfully speaking, we tend to waffle, reverting at times to our pre-Christ days while living at other times in the mind and spirit of Christ.

SUGGESTION FOR MEDITATION: Recall your pre-Christ days—your attitudes and actions from "once upon a time." Comparing your pre-Christ days to your present level of commitment to Christ, how have you become more Christlike? Do you consider yourself to be on the road toward spiritual maturity, or are you still in the spiritual nursery?

THURSDAY, MARCH 30 • Read Ephesians 2:5-10

Notice how the author of Ephesians ties together grace and good works. Without acknowledging God's grace in our lives, our so-called "good works" lack divine purpose and staying power. Humanly motivated good works often lead to burnout. On the other hand, when we ignore or refuse to do good works, we receive and enjoy God's grace selfishly.

The text clearly states that by grace we have been saved through faith. All of this comes to us as unearned gifts from God, "not the result of works, so that no one may boast. For we are what he has made us, created in Christ Jesus for good works, which God prepared beforehand to be *our way of life*" (vv. 9-10, *italics added*).

Christ's experience becomes realized in the lives of believers. In the Greek, the three verbs "made...alive," "raised up," and "seated" combine with a particular preposition to imply that this is not an individual experience but a *shared* experience. We are not made alive, raised up, and seated independent of Christ and our Christian brothers and sisters.

The only acceptable response on our part is to adopt a good-works lifestyle. Some of us do this more easily than others. Some of us have to work at it. How is it with you?

SUGGESTION FOR MEDITATION: **Look closely at your personal lifestyle, specifically the last seven days. Write out everything you believe comes under the heading of "good works." List good works that fall within your capabilities and good works you could do if you so desired. Consider placing prayer for others every day by name (intercessory prayer) at the top of your good-works list. Ask God to guide and motivate your intentionality in doing good works in response to God's grace.**

FRIDAY, MARCH 31 • Read Numbers 21:4-9

Have you ever heard anyone play a game called "Yes...but"? Basically it has to do with faultfinding in the midst of some good or positive happening: "Yes, I liked the sermon, but the preacher spoke too softly (or too loudly or too long...)."

"Yes, our membership is growing but maybe too fast."

"Yes, the weather is not bad today, but it could get nasty tomorrow."

Who invented this universal game of "Yes...but"? It could well have been the children of Israel on their exodus trek from Egypt to the Promised Land. Just a few days into the wilderness, and they begin complaining—first about the water, then about the food and harsh living conditions.

The Book of Numbers contains six of these "yes...but" or murmuring stories. However, in today's verses, the Israelites not only complain to Moses; they speak out against God, which prompts God to send divine punishment in the form of snakes.

Before long, the "yes...but" game players repent and plead with Moses for help. Moses intercedes. God listens, then instructs Moses to prepare an antidote that will counteract the snake bites. The cure? Moses fashions a bronze snake, places it on a pole, and whoever looks at it lives.

We may question the harsh punishment and the strange cure, but it worked. To this very day, the symbolism of the snake has a double meaning: punishment and evil, as well as creativity and healing. Today two intertwining snakes on a staff serve as a symbol for the medical profession.

This story's message is clear. Murmuring, complaining, and constant grumbling do not please God, who is in charge and who desires health, wholeness, and salvation for all.

SUGGESTION FOR MEDITATION: **How do I play the "yes...but" game with God, my family, and my church? Do I tend to murmur and complain even in the midst of good things that happen in life? Do I need an antidote from God that would turn my "yes...but" into "yes...yes and praise the Lord"?**

SATURDAY, APRIL 1 • **Read John 3:14-21**

The author of John's Gospel certainly knew the traditions and stories of the Hebrew Scriptures. The third chapter contains some of the most-quoted, best-loved teachings in the New Testament, especially verses 3 and 16. But what shall we do with verse 14, a direct reference to Numbers 21:4-9?

And just as Moses lifted up the serpent in the wilderness, so must the Son of Man be lifted up.

Jesus had an uncanny way of connecting with his audience, so we must assume that this Old Testament reference somehow relates to the famous nighttime conversation between Jesus and a Pharisee named Nicodemus. Nicodemus would have known the story about the Israelites and the bronze serpent.

What does Jesus' identification with this bronze serpent mean for Christians and non-Christians today? Just as God offered love, mercy, grace, and power to heal and save the Israelites, so today God's Messiah Jesus offers the same love, mercy, grace, and power to heal and to save.

God did not choose a bronze, artificial image but rather an old, rugged, despised cross on which God's beloved son gave up his life so that the entire world could receive forgiveness, healing, and salvation.

Notice in these verses from John's Gospel that Nicodemus fades from the picture and the spotlight centers on Jesus. Even though we do not understand all the workings, we can, by faith, accept all of God's promises in the Bible, especially John 3:15: "Whoever believes in [God's son] may have eternal life"—eternal life that begins now.

SUGGESTION FOR MEDITATION: What names can you give some of those pesky, frightening "snakes" that disrupt and poison your life and attitude? What attitudes do they generate within you? How can you keep the eyes of your spirit, heart, and mind focused on Jesus, who came not to condemn but rather to forgive, to heal, and to save?

FOURTH SUNDAY IN LENT

An invalid mother's newly ordained minister son came to see her on the Sunday afternoon following his first sermon. After sharing with her some of the complimentary comments he had received about his message, his saintly mother said, "That's wonderful, son, but did you put in a good word for Jesus?"

The third chapter of John's Gospel is the very heart of the New Testament, offering life-giving blood and nourishment to the Body of Christ. Verses 14-17 challenge all Christians to keep priorities straight in the local church. This passage reminds those who have the privilege of being in leadership positions, especially teachers and preachers, to put in a good word for Jesus without apology and without ceasing.

We are too easily tempted to make secondary issues the main purpose and work of the church. Building maintenance, financial matters, community problems, doctrinal debates, internal controversies, differences of opinion among the church members, social and political issues—all have their place on the agenda of the church but not the place of highest priority.

Early into my first pastoral appointment, a retired college professor in the congregation took me aside one Sunday after morning worship and said, "Brother Wagner, that was a fine sermon you gave us today, but always remember in the pulpit not to blow your own horn; rather, sound the trumpet for Jesus!"

SUGGESTION FOR MEDITATION: Do you consistently put in a good word for Jesus in your family, with your friends, and at church? When have you put in a good word for Jesus with strangers or with unchurched persons? What seems to be the main agenda of your faith community?

Bound for Glory

April 3–9, 2000 • *Blair Gilmer Meeks**

MONDAY, APRIL 3 • **Read Jeremiah 31:31-34**

"I invite you to make a right beginning of repentance." These words, found in many worship books, are a time-honored way to begin Lent. For some people, however, talk of discipline and repentance serves as a stumbling block rather than an invitation to new life. The words spoken in the Passover Seder carry more vibrancy: "Once we were slaves; now we are free." Jeremiah reminds the people of that story: "I took them by the hand to bring them out of the land of Egypt." The people fail to keep the covenant, but God gives them a new way to live in tune with God's will.

The expectations of the law—the Torah—remain the same for Jeremiah, but Israel receives a new reason to obey. God's law brings freedom, not restrictions imposed from outside. Because the people now internalize the law—it is written on their hearts—they will live in the covenant joyfully with no excuse for rebellion.

God makes obedience a pleasure. First, God takes us by the hand; God strengthens our hearts in holiness (1 Thess. 3:13). Second, God creates a people who know God, from the least to the greatest (Jer. 31:33-34). God therefore makes us a people who can live together in faith.

Joyful obedience marks our Lenten journey to Easter. We remember the promises of our baptism and rejoice that we know God through Jesus Christ.

PRAYER: God of grace, take me by the hand and bring me out of fear and illusion. Teach me the obedience of caring for others and of living in harmony with creation. Grant me the joy of knowing you through Christ Jesus. Amen.

---

*Former editor of *Liturgy*; editor and writer now living in Nashville, Tennessee.

TUESDAY, APRIL 4 • Read Psalm 51:1-7

Psalm 51 has long been associated with the confession of wrongdoing by public figures. President Bill Clinton, for example, used phrases from this psalm on several occasions to ask forgiveness from the nation. King David is the first political figure to be connected with this prayer. The composer of the psalm intends that it recall the words of David, seeking forgiveness for his adultery with Bathsheba. Nathan assures David of God's forgiveness: "Now the Lord has put away your sin; you shall not die" (2 Sam. 12:13). But the terrible consequences of David's act remain and bring suffering to him and his nation.

We also associate Psalm 51 with Ash Wednesday services; various faith communities have read or sung this psalm during Lent for centuries. Once on Ash Wednesday, I heard the Men and Boys' Choir at King's College, Cambridge, sing it; the psalm seemed to reverberate from every arch and penetrate to the bone. The clear voices echoing from the stone vaulting were inescapable. I wondered what Henry VIII, another ruler known for his failings, might have thought when he heard it sung in the magnificent Gothic chapel he had built.

This psalm, whether read or sung at communal worship, is meant for us. We may not need to confess on as grand a scale as prominent political figures, but our sins also have consequences for us and for our community. The first step is to seek forgiveness. The gift of Jesus' death and resurrection assures us of God's power to forgive and offers us reconciliation with one another and with God.

PRAYER: **God of mercy, when my own failings stare me in the face, grant me the grace to come to you. Hear me, tender God, and wash me with fresh water. Let your truth be my center; teach me the secrets of your wisdom. Amen.**

WEDNESDAY, APRIL 5 • Read Psalm 51:8-12

This psalm that speaks of sin and forgiveness can bring comfort to another kind of human suffering as well. A friend recently told me that his sister had discovered this psalm in a new translation and that she relied on its words during her treatment for bone cancer.

> *Fill me with happy songs,*
> *let the bones you bruised now dance.* *

These words from verse 8 became her daily prayer and brought her strength throughout her painful ordeal.

Psalm 51 has medicinal references ("purge me with hyssop") and testifies to God's willingness to create us anew. Can we hear it as a prayer for health? Certainly the health of God's community was at stake when the psalmist wrote.

Paul knew Psalm 51 and quoted it to address conflicts in the churches of his day. In 1 Cor. 5:17-20, Paul relates Psalm 51:10 to the new creation in Christ and urges us to accept our "ministry of reconciliation." Paul, who knew firsthand the pain of physical suffering as well as the hurt caused by conflict, tells us that the key to our health is our acceptance of God's gift of reconciliation. God, Paul says, does not count our trespasses against us and calls us to be ambassadors for Christ in his mission of reconciling the whole world to God.

God's new act of recreation brings wholeness and joy: "Restore to me the joy of your salvation" (Ps. 51:12).

PRAYER: God of mercy, send your healing streams to all who are sick and in pain. Teach me to find my health in your presence; comfort me with the nearness of your Spirit. Heal and reconcile your church so that it may show love to your hurting world. Amen.

---

*From *The Psalter*, copyright © 1994 International Committee on English in the Liturgy, Washington, D. C. Used by permission.

THURSDAY, APRIL 6 • Read Hebrews 5:5-6

What does it mean that Jesus is a priest? In these verses, we meet Melchizedek, a minor character from Genesis who blessed Abraham. What link does Jesus have with Melchizedek? Perhaps one link is that Jesus' priesthood is ancient in origin, predating even the levitical priests. Both Jesus and Melchizedek serve as priest and king. Melchizedek, king of Salem or "peace," reminds us of Jesus' kingship. Hebrews 5:5 echoes Psalm 110, which expresses Israel's hope for a messiah and celebrates the priest/king (in fact, the whole people of Israel) as anointed directly by God.

It is God who says, "You are my Son; today I have begotten you." These words resemble those spoken by the voice from heaven at Jesus' baptism. They relate Jesus' identity and connect his sonship, baptism, and priesthood.

This connection of priesthood with baptism seems especially significant for Lent, which, since the early church, has been the time of preparation for baptism or for the reaffirmation of baptismal vows on Easter. Our baptism authorizes our ministry as God's church. We believe in the priesthood of the baptized. If we follow Christ, we will accept the priestly responsibilities our baptism confers on us. We will stand up to serve as God's priests—as representatives of Christ—taking part in the ministry of reconciling the world to God.

Do you have pictures taken at your baptism? If you were baptized as an infant, has someone told you about that day? Some families celebrate the baptismal anniversaries of their children. If you don't remember the exact date, celebrate now during Lent. "Remember your baptism and be thankful."

PRAYER: God of love, prepare me for the coming celebration of Jesus' death and resurrection. Teach me to bring his power for life to the world you loved enough to send your son. Amen.

FRIDAY, APRIL 7 • Read Hebrews 5:7-10

As we near the fifth Sunday of Lent, these verses from Hebrews 5 turn us toward the events leading to Easter. Verse 7 reminds us of Jesus' prayer in Gethsemane, and the remaining verses echo the great hymn of Philippians 2 that we usually read on Palm Sunday. Jesus, though God's son, humbled himself to become an obedient slave—obedient even to death on a cross (Phil. 2:8).

The astounding thing about the way the Bible tells the story is this: The low points are always the high points. A baby's birth in a stable is announced by angel choirs. A boy whose parents are worried sick over him teaches elders in the Temple. Jesus is first revealed as the giver of unbelievable abundance when the wine runs out at a wedding. Jesus' best-known parable is about a malodorous ne'er-do-well whose father throws him a party.

The stories of reversals fill the Gospels, leading us to the story we will hear again in the coming days. Jesus rides into the city on a lowly work animal and is proclaimed king. He is led away to an excruciating execution and lifted up for all the world. He is buried in a borrowed tomb and rises to the brightness of an Easter morning that will never fade. The one who was humbled to death is raised to glory. "Therefore God also highly exalted him and gave him the name that is above every name" (Phil. 2:9).

Where might we look for God's reversals in our time?

PRAYER: God, I thank you that the one who was with you from the beginning came to be one of us. Guide me to the places you live: with the hungry, the homeless, the sick, the imprisoned, and the sorrowing. Prepare me for the coming celebration of Jesus' victory. Amen.

"We wish to see Jesus" is the request of the Greeks in verse 21, reminding us of words from the much-loved hymn: "We would see Jesus...God made flesh, in loving service met." In John's Gospel, seeing is believing, so these outsiders make an astonishing demand of Philip and Andrew. They ask not only to be brought into Jesus' presence but to be brought into the faith. The request gives Jesus the opening to prepare his disciples for what soon will happen to him and, because whoever serves him must follow him, what will happen to them also.

The time has come for Jesus to be glorified; and to be glorified, Jesus must die. Is it any wonder the disciples can't comprehend Jesus' words? Jesus therefore offers them a parable from farming: "Unless a grain of wheat falls into the earth and dies, it remains just a single grain; but if it dies, it bears much fruit." His death, Jesus seems to say, is necessary because it would be unthinkable to remain one solitary grain when the possibility exists for a plentiful harvest. Jesus' life, death, and resurrection will serve this purpose: to gather an abundant harvest; in other words, to gather all the peoples of the earth to God. The single grain is Jesus; the fruit that follows is the church, working to reconcile the world.

Jesus' ministry, culminating with Good Friday and Easter, brings God's people to life. The community that recognizes Jesus, broken and risen, in the sharing of bread and cup begins with the death of the solitary grain of wheat.

PRAYER: Living God, you made me your new creation by water and word. Give me courage to embrace the world in your name and bring Jesus' gift of life to those who live in the shadows. Bring me joyfully to Easter. Amen.

SUNDAY, APRIL 9 • Read John 12:27-33

FIFTH SUNDAY IN LENT

The African American spiritual "Nobody Knows the Trouble I See" tells of unbearable burdens; yet the final words in the song are "Glory, hallelujah!" How can anyone speak of glory in the face of injustice, sorrow, and pain? John's Gospel raises the question, How can we talk of anything else?

The word *glory* connects Christmas and Easter, yet it's a word that defies definition. We sing both "Glory to God in the highest" and "In the cross of Christ I glory." Glory includes all the wondrous blessings of God's presence. John's Gospel uses the word *glorify* ("to give glory to") as an indicator of God's relationship to Jesus, which amazingly includes us in communion with God. In verses 23-24 Jesus speaks about his death, and verse 28 implies that by dying and rising again, he will glorify God's name. Later the writer of John will give us the remarkable prayer of Jesus, in which he asks that the glory he shares with God be given to us so that we might be one with Jesus just as Jesus and God are one (John 17:22). God and the world will live as one in the glorious community.

Jesus' death and resurrection will create this community: "And I, when I am lifted up from the earth, will draw all people to myself." Jesus had told Nicodemus much the same thing in John 3:14-16. The phrase has an imaginative double or triple meaning. "Lifted up" connotes the crucifixion (lifted up on the cross), the resurrection, and ascension. Jesus' crucifixion, resurrection, and ascension are one glorious act of God. Jesus was lifted up so that the world could be uplifted to God. This is the glory of God.

PRAYER: God, I lift up my heart to praise you for your gift of Jesus Christ. Bless me in the days to come as I remember Jesus' death and resurrection. Teach me to show your great love for the world. Amen.

Bells and Balloons

April 10–16, 2000 • *Phyllis Tickle**

MONDAY, APRIL 10 • Read Philippians 2:5-11

I have a close friend who is dying of cancer. Her diagnosis came three months ago; she will probably be dead before you read this. "You know what I hate most?" she asked me after the first surgery. "It's the loss of control. I'm not in charge of where I go and what I do any more. The doctors are."

Now, four surgeries later, she lies in a hospital bed with an IV in one arm and wired to the wall monitors with the other. Tubes come out of every part of her. Speaking for more than a minute or two exhausts her. She's quit fighting her illness and simply awaits its conclusion.

Every time I look at her or struggle to understand what she is trying to say to me, her situation shocks and sickens me all over again. This is what it means to be human, what it means to die as a human being—without control over your own movements and decisions, without basic privacy, without the shield of any dignity.

That, of course, is what Jesus elected to do. And this morning I am almost unable to bear my newfound understanding of that single fact, just as I am hushed before the gifts of love that death can bring us.

PRAYER: Son of God, Son of Man, forgive the smallness of my imagination and my great fear of using it. I can't grasp what you have done for us and don't have the courage to try. I pray instead for grace and mercy and the time here in which to become, if nothing more, at least truly compassionate. Bless me, Lord, for I am too weak to bless myself. Amen.

---

*Contributing Editor in Religion to *Publishers Weekly*; lay eucharistic minister and lector, St. Ann's Episcopal Church, Millington, Tennessee.

TUESDAY, APRIL 11 • Read Mark 14:26-51

Over the years, I have made a kind of hobby of collecting the asides and sudden, almost disparate, details that now and again interrupt Holy Writ. For me, these deeply human additions lift the record from history and set it firmly into some human being's reality. Because Judaism holds respect for the individual as integral, the Hebrew Scriptures are full of such artifacts, little pieces of story that give texture to the bigger tale: the tar pits in the valley of Siddim where the kings of Sodom and Gomorrah met their first retribution; the midwife's naming of Perez after he yanked his twin back into Tamar's womb so he could be her firstborn (and thereby, the forebear of the Messiah); the detail of the lattice in the window through which Sisera's mother looked as she mourned her son. They are all there and dozens more, but in the New Testament Gospel stories, I have found only one (and it occurs only in one Gospel) that adds such a lovely and accessible detail.

In the garden on the night of Jesus' arrest, "a certain young man was following him, wearing nothing but a linen cloth. [The soldiers] caught hold of him, but he left the linen cloth and ran off naked." Like a strong mast in a whirlwind, like a tunnel through a wall, like an angel in an illness, that one image leads me into the vividness and immediacy I need if I am to feel, as well as worship, the events of these next few days.

Real people with real problems like clothing and real vulnerabilities like nakedness participated in real but horrifying events. They had seen and known, however imperfectly, divinity among them...and at least one of them left the imprint of his embarrassment upon their story.

PRAYER: In the small world of my life, Lord, let me honor the details—both those I leave behind me for others and those I discover in what you give me. Amen.

WEDNESDAY, APRIL 12 • Read John 12:12-16

My husband and I have a son getting married this spring. It's time—he's been gone from our house for over three years now. We love the girl almost as much as he does, albeit for different reasons. So we experience none of the usual anxieties of "too young," "too unsettled," or "wrong girl." It is not my anxieties that bind my thoughts to my son this week. In fact, my dreams more than my thoughts seem to be traveling these days of Passiontide heavy with the memories of him: his intense, dark eyes set so deep in that small face that to see them was to enter into his dreams, to see his sights; the soft pork-pie hat that he wore everywhere as a little fellow, calling it his "fishing hat" and refusing to give it up except to go to bed; the penchant he had for climbing all the way to the top of the huge magnolia tree in our front yard and sitting there for hours on end, riding the wind-swayed branches as confidently as would a sea captain his deck.

So as I dress for yet one more prenuptial party or go over yet one more list, I have trouble imagining his going down that aisle in two weeks and laying claim to this new life he is taking on. I keep seeing instead the dark eyes and the pork-pie hat and the little captain secure in the high cradle of an old tree. And more than any other thing about this strange season, I wonder what Mary was imagining as she watched her boy move through the events of this climactic week in his life.

SUGGESTION FOR MEDITATION: Sometime this afternoon or evening when you are alone, repeat quietly to yourself the great festal shout of, "Hosanna! Blessed is the one who comes in the name of the Lord—the King of Israel!" Consider what this sure invitation to execution as an anarchist must have meant to Jesus' parents.

THURSDAY, APRIL 13 • Read Isaiah 50:4-9a

Five years ago, after months of being without a pastor, our small, rural parish finally found one. We were all delighted with him and he with us, which is why nobody expected anything like his first Easter morning with us.

As we entered the nave, we discovered dozens of helium-filled balloons taped to the ends of the pews. In the pews themselves we found dozens of little dime-store bells tied together in bunches with bright wool yarn. Stunned, we couldn't believe it when our new pastor instructed the children to shake the bells every time they heard the word *alleluia*. The children loved it. Most of the longtime parishioners did not.

"How dare you!" was the greeting of one senior vestry member immediately after the service. "You took a holy thing and made it into an event, a celebration—like we'd won some kind of game or something!"

"Precisely," our new rector replied.

The pastor's answer was good theology on his part, of course—sound theology, in fact. We've had balloons and bells on Easter ever since. But the new rector's reply offered more than intellectualized theology; it offered hope and a new wakening of the ear to listen to God.

So now we fill the helium tanks and stock the parish closet with new bells and balloons during Lent each year, just as regularly as we prepare the little palm crosses or clean the larger ones for flowering. The more celebratory bells and the far more jolly balloons help us remember during these sad days that because of Easter we are going to win the game—and that hope, after all, offers the best theology.

SUGGESTION FOR MEDITATION: How can you avoid the spiritual danger of letting the historic, life-changing parts of your faith slip over into being "holy things"? How can you discuss and present the historical events of the faith so as to expose the immediate, living heart of their truth?

FRIDAY, APRIL 14 • Read Psalm 118:1-2, 19-29

It is impossible for me, even sixty years later, to hear the psalms read without hearing as well the sonorous, slightly British voice with which my father read them—especially the mighty psalms of Passiontide. "The stone that the builders rejected has become the chief cornerstone. / This is the Lord's doing; it is marvelous in our eyes. / This is the day that the Lord has made; / let us rejoice and be glad in it." And then, two verses later, the great shout, "Blessed is the one who comes in the name of the Lord..../ Bind the festal procession with branches, up to the horns of the altar..../ O give thanks to the Lord, for he is good, / for his steadfast love endures forever."

"You see," my father would say to me every Palm Sunday, "what we are doing is looking back to something the psalmist looked forward to." Then he would add, "Don't ever forget that you're only a part of a pattern, a river of history set down before time and moving to its full completion beyond time—what is, was, and is to be."

I think of those words today as I begin the baking for our Palm Sunday lunch—not a single moment sealed in the first century of our era but an act within that vast flow of history that connects me to the psalmist as well as to a triumphal entry.

SUGGESTION FOR MEDITATION: **Psalm 118:1-2, 19-29 is one of the appointed readings for this week for obvious reasons. Try reading it aloud over and over again as if you were an actor or actress about to perform it for a theatre audience. How does the vibrancy and urgency of the words change with this type of presentation. How much nearer to the vibrancy and urgency of their actual meaning as originally intended do they seem?**

SATURDAY, APRIL 15 • Read Psalm 31:9-16

Passiontide would be halfway over today, if such a season still existed. The great wave of liturgical tidying up that swept the church over thirty years ago took care of that. But until that work of liturgical reform, Passiontide stretched from the fifth Sunday of Lent through Holy Saturday.

Passiontide was always a strange time. Perhaps the exotic nature of its observances brought about its demise. A full-of-mystery time for children, Passiontide was that season in the church year when all the pictures, mirrors, and crucifixes were draped in purple—or sometimes turned to the wall and then draped. Lent became a time when adults stayed home at night, when one's house was robbed of its usual consolations; and we could count on nothing to be as it had been.

Perhaps it was all too spooky, too interruptive, too literally suggestive of the approaching death. Perhaps the church removed Passiontide and its doleful practices from our calendar for those reasons. But in this time of millennium, of the mysterious and the deeply suggestive, for the first time in years I feel bereft of the rituals of Passiontide.

Tomorrow, as every year, I will worship the ambivalence of triumphant sorrow and grief-filled joy. Today, however, I am simply lonesome for the habits and gestures that used to give form to that confusion. Today I am restless with a need to drape my pictures, or barring that now suspect exercise, to bring into my hearing the Messiah's approaching lament: "I have passed out of mind like one who is dead; I have become like a broken vessel." Even so, come, Lord Jesus.

SUGGESTION FOR MEDITATION: Join me in selecting one picture or mirror and turning it toward the wall until next Saturday. Jewish custom, from which this practice comes, calls for mirrors to be turned in a house of mourning. Choose a picture or mirror that is either dear enough or employed often enough that you will feel the absence keenly.

SUNDAY, APRIL 16 • Read Mark 11:1-11

PALM/PASSION SUNDAY

On this day the Gospel of Mark tells us that people cut branches in the fields and spread them, along with their cloaks, in the path of the Messiah's colt, making a kind of noble highway. And they sang and shouted, just as the psalmist had said they would, saying, "Hosanna! Blessed is the one who comes in the name of the Lord!"

But after that spontaneous parade of country folk on holiday, after that brief, wild dance of freedom and celebration, Jesus "entered Jerusalem and went into the temple; and when he had looked around at everything, as it was already late, he went out to Bethany with the twelve." Just another "day at the office," in other words—and perhaps the strangest piece of the whole passion narrative.

As a teenager I thought the triumphal entry was the most exciting story in the Gospel narratives, far exceeding even the angels' singing at Christmas or the dove's descent at the Jordan. Looking back now, I think I viewed those affirmations of Jesus' messianic role as somehow external to him. The Christmas angels and Jordan's dove were "given," but Jesus has earned the hosannas of the triumph. The hosannas prove that he has done his job on earth well.

The only flaw in my theory comes in this distressing verse from Mark that indicates rather clearly that the crowd's acclaim was of no moment to him; it was just another piece of the job he had to finish. Now that I am older, I have learned that he was right and that keeping one's attention on the kingdom rather than the crowd is the most Christlike of the spiritual disciplines.

PRAYER: God of the Passiontide and the Triumph, giver of all grace and all virtues, bathe my soul and my understanding with your great peace and fix my heart and my doing always on your most beautiful and eternal will. Amen.

The Secret Is Out

April 17–23, 2000 • Heather Murray Elkins*
William Wesley Elkins**

MONDAY, APRIL 17 • Read Isaiah 42:6b-7; John 12:1-11

John Calvin, the great reformer, taught that the purpose of studying scripture is to view truth through the "eye/I" of Christ. Seeing is not believing, unless what we see in Christ through scripture corrects the distortion of our hearts. Through the insight of the Spirit, the word heals our distorted "I" and teaches us to read God's will for our lives.

The Gospel of John is a Gospel of incongruous meals and table manners. Here's Lazarus, "raised from the dead" and sitting with Jesus at dinner. This illuminates the prophecy of Isaiah: The captive has been released from the darkness of death. Here's Mary, extravagant in her freedom, publicly proclaiming Jesus as messiah, Christ, the anointed one. And here's Judas, objecting to the guest list, the hospitality, the host. Poor Judas. He suffers from a poverty of God. The economics of grace are never practical; they rarely add up.

Jesus deepens the conflict by predicting his passion and death. In this act of costly love, we are redeemed, purchased back from slavery, set free. Our debts are forgiven. We owe everything to God. We're invited to Christ's table as free women and men. We have passed over from death to life. What a meal —living the life of Christ, being rich in God and famous for our hospitality, sharing the living Word.

PRAYER: Holy One, may I see the world through Christ's "I." Teach me your economy of grace. Amen.

---

*United Methodist elder; Academic Dean of Drew Theological School, Madison, New Jersey.

**Assistant Professor of Pastoral Theology, Drew Theological School, Madison, New Jersey.

TUESDAY, APRIL 18 • Read Isaiah 49:1*b*, 6*b*; John 12:20-36

"Sir, we wish to see Jesus." But what do we see? A good teacher. And like all good teachers, Jesus brings the situation into his teaching. The Greeks, the Gentiles, the outsiders have arrived. This is a sign. Those who have faced division by religion and region have heard of "the light to the nations" and have come to see Jesus. But "seeing Jesus" involves more than just evaluating his teaching style, his dress, and his demeanor. Seeing Jesus is to discern his truth and to imagine our lives differently. Seeing Jesus takes time—time to adjust our focus, our unwillingness to let in "the light to the nations." We have to correct our perceptions. We have to learn to stop squinting.

We will need help. We learn slowly as Jesus teaches us to observe. The first thing Christ teaches us is to ignore the obvious. Power and authority do not headline the "glory of God." The Holy One of God does not "lord it over the world." This is the glory of a seed that falls deep within the world, dies, and bears new life for all the nations. This energy overcomes despair and corrects our distorted world vision.

Do we have a problem with this? Yes, but the one named Teacher knows the difficulty of this vision test. He knows we love what we know and serve what we recognize as being ours. Region, race, human condition, and religion limit our range of insight into the world. No one is as blessed as those who think and act as we do. But Christ calls us to "lift up our hearts"; and in this vision, we will see a new heaven and earth. "And I, when I am lifted up from the earth, will draw all people to myself."

PRAYER: Giver of life, may I rise with you. Teach me your vision for the sake of those who have eyes but refuse to see. Amen.

WEDNESDAY, APRIL 19 • Read Psalm 70:5; John 13:21-32

Jesus says, "One of you will betray me." That's something hard to hear and even harder to admit. It's natural to see ourselves as the disciples, harder to see ourselves as betrayers of Jesus. The disciples do not understand Jesus. We don't understand why they don't understand. It seems so clear to us. Jesus offers a special sign: He takes a piece of bread, dips it, and gives it to Judas. After taking it, Judas "immediately" goes out into the night. He has become part of the darkness that will betray the Light of the world. "And this is the judgment, that the light has come into the world, and people loved darkness rather than light because their deeds were evil" (John 3:19).

So the cold, hard truth of this text is that we will betray the Light of the world. But given these facts of our fallible faith, can we find any light and warmth in this scripture? Given the decaying scent of betrayal and the cold chill of loss—"I will be with you only a little longer"—where is the balm of Gilead, the cure for our dis-ease?

This scripture both wounds and heals. We receive God when we really need God. What do we see and hear when our love for Christ fails? God will glorify the one who has been faithful, the human holy Son. The powers of the world constrain and constrict justice and mercy. The glory and power of God will break through any barrier to set the Beloved free. God will do what God wills done. "There are only wounded in the army of the Lord" is one way to describe the company of Christ. We, wounded healers, will be charged with the work of witnessing to this transforming Light of Light.

PRAYER: Lord, when I falter, fail, and fall, let the One who loves the world lift me up as he was lifted. Amen.

THURSDAY, APRIL 20 • Read Psalm 116:12-13;
John 13:1-17, 31b-35

MAUNDY THURSDAY

There is no way around it. We've got to pass through this night of cups. The cup of the Passover of God. The cup of the New Covenant. The cup that Jesus prayed to put down. He offers the cup to the friend who is his betrayer. Judas turns and disappears into the night. These are dangerous times. Be careful with whom you drink. When Jesus and Judas meet again, the bitter cup has been lifted. Betrayal will lead to arrest, then interrogation, then torture, then public shame, then the cross and a lonely, thirsty death.

How can we follow Jesus when he tells us, "Where I am going, you cannot come"? What is in the cup? Something terrifying. Who can blame us if we try to escape this nightmare by falling asleep?

This Gethsemane night of the soul is not unlike the night of the first Passover. After a meal of cups and bread, there is darkness and waiting and fear and prayer. The angel of death, the judgment of God, passes over the people of God as they wait through the night. On that night in Egypt, judgment passes over those who have been marked by the blood of a lamb. On this night in the garden, the judgment will pass over us because of the One who is the Lamb of God.

It is the Lamb who lifts a cup and gives us a new commandment: "Just as I have loved you, you also should love one another." And even though we cannot follow him now, we will follow him later. Even though we gather darkness around us now to hide how our lives betray the light, we will stand in the open in the broad light of day to proclaim God's mercy. Even if we cannot lift the cup now, there will come a morning when we, like the psalmist, will pray, "I will lift up the cup of salvation and call on the name of the Lord."

PRAYER: Pray Psalm 23.

GOOD FRIDAY

Who remembers the words to songs for thousands of years? We know that some of the oldest passages of scripture are the Exodus songs of deliverance. What possesses a people to sing love songs, fight songs, protest songs, and even the blues in honor of God? The psalms record the ancient sounds of a people who remembered by singing. They wrote songs in honor of prophets they betrayed or failed to believe; and through the songs, the words of the prophet came to life again. The songs of the unknown suffering servant from the years of exile became the songs of the early church's praise of Christ.

We know enough about the workings of human memory to know that what we learn earliest lasts longest and that what we link to rhythm and melody is most memorable. Early Methodists learned their theology through their hymns and sang those hymns by heart. Moving accounts attest to those who died singing, pressing their last breath into a sound of praise. John Wesley's final hymn, "I'll praise my maker while I've breath," provides a classic source of spiritual discipline. But at the center of Christian memory there is another singer, an older song.

"My God, my God, why have you forsaken me?" is the sound of agony. It is the cry of an abandoned child, of a human without hope. No lonelier sound exists in human language. It silences all our easy promises and gospel gossip. In the midst of the silence—God's and our own—we remember that these words are also those of a song. The one who dies in silence after speaking these words is the One who rises and turns our mourning into song.

PRAYER: "To him, indeed, shall all who sleep in the earth bow down; before him shall bow all who go down to the dust, and I shall live for him."

HOLY SATURDAY

"I've got a secret. I've got a secret." This is the triumphant chant of a child's game. It also expresses a mystery of faith by which God maintains the church until the end of time. This is a mystery, a story with a twist. When the faithful turn faithless, secret disciples will do what God deems necessary to keep the faith for the future. We know that the never-ending story of salvation must continue. The question is, How?

We know that the main characters, those who have been center stage, those who have spoken the best and bravest lines and have shone in the limelight, have disappeared. They are not there. They've scattered. They are keeping their knowledge of Jesus secret, avoiding the paradoxical glory in the dying of the light.

And the dying of the light reveals the mystery, the secret. When the Light of the world is extinguished, when the darkness is the deepest, then the fire is rekindled. The silence is broken. Surrounded by death, we are reborn through water and the Spirit. The ancient church practices of fasting and prayer, telling the story of salvation and baptism, and the celebration of the paschal mystery took place on this night. Those who betrayed or deserted were reconciled and forgiven.

The rising Son reveals the secret of God's story. The mystery is not solved but sealed in the lives of those who discover the empty tomb.

What the darkness has concealed, the light reveals. What has been whispered behind closed doors will be shouted from the rooftops. We've a story to tell, a secret to share: The light encountered darkness and was not overcome.

SUGGESTION FOR PRAYER: Softly sing "This Little Light of Mine."

Sunday, April 23 • Read Psalm 118; John 20:1-18

EASTER

At the beginning and end of Jesus' story, we find men named Joseph. One man assists at Jesus' birth; one man assists at his death. One watches as wise ones give myrrh to a child wrapped in swaddling cloths, lying in the shadows of a manger. At sundown the other wraps Jesus' body with spices in linen cloths and places him in a tomb. One man is poor, one wealthy. One has social and religious authority; the other has the dignity of his calling as a carpenter. Very different—yet both men share the same name, love the same God, and in the end, serve the same Messiah.

Joseph of Nazareth risked his reputation for an unborn child he could not name as his own. Joseph of Arimathea risked his reputation to defend a man he did not publicly proclaim as Messiah. The first Joseph protected the holy child with his own life, guided by dream and using the darkness of night to cover their escape into Egypt. The second Joseph sat in the shadows of power at Jesus' trial and risked exposure after he witnessed the death of a man he could not protect. For both men there was a time for secrets and a time to witness to the truth of God revealed in Jesus the Christ.

What we do in the light of Easter reveals what we have chosen to be in the darkness. What the Spirit reveals in the privacy of prayer is to be lived out in the public square. The living Christ calls us to proclaim from the rooftops what we have whispered in the dark. The Risen One invites us to abandon our margins of safety and to witness to God's will to love. Nothing is to be kept hidden now. As disciples we are to live such lives of public abandon that the world will always wonder what really happened in that garden. The secret is out, "Christ is risen. Christ is risen, indeed."

PRAYER: Risen One, be our wisdom, our vision, our life. Amen.

Walk in the Light

April 24–30, 2000 • Cecil L. Murray*

MONDAY, APRIL 24 • Read Acts 4:32-35

Being *almost* persuaded falls short of being *fully* persuaded. Both elements are present in the early Christian community, a waiting community, seeking ways to abandon poverty through equitable distribution of food while waiting for the Lord's return. The community decides to sell all properties and to give the money to a common pool for benevolences.

This approach is not an economic formula any more than is Jesus' advice to the rich young ruler to sell his possessions and follow him. No, this is a spiritual formula, a call to common love, to collective love; a call to remove anything that keeps us from going over the edge.

We own nothing. Everything we have is lent to us for a purpose—to share it, even to share it with God. Failing to see that we own nothing blinds us to seeing that what we own owns us.

When our property owns us, we do not sell it, which is the response of the rich young ruler. Or perhaps we do sell it but give only *part* of the income to the people's fund.

When it comes to true ownership, we receive the invitation to go over the edge and to see that we do not belong to the things that belong to us. We belong only to Jesus.

Jesus owns us. This ownership leads us to go over the edge, not to stop at it. When full, we go over the edge to give bread to those who have none. Our spiritual table manners attune our ears to hear the divine appeal: "Pass the blessing, please."

PRAYER: God of all, may I allow you to be Lord of all. Amen.

---

*Senior Minister, First African Methodist Episcopal Church, Los Angeles, California.

TUESDAY, APRIL 25 • Read Psalm 133

You may ask, "Can't we all just get along?" And the reply comes back, "No, we never have; we never will." In the last 6,000 years of history, we have had less than 300 years of peace. We human beings will fight about anything. When there's nothing to fight about...well, we'll fight about that.

Yet the psalmist rises above the understanding of history as our-story to focus on the story of God's unifying love: "How wonderful it is, how pleasant, for God's people to live together in harmony" (TEV). The ultimate then is the harmony of God's people, all God's people, getting along with one another.

Love's getting along offers leeway. Love teaches us to get along in *community*, not simply in unity. Unity depicts the melting pot where everyone is melted down and blended with the predominant ingredient. The salad bowl, on the other hand, extols diversity. Each element freely contributes of itself to the whole: green olive, black olive, red pepper, yellow pepper— they all give their best.

As kindred we are not of one mind but of one goal. Minds differ; goals are fixed. Goals are fixed by different minds who then feel obligated by ownership to accomplish them.

Love's getting along gives life. The psalmist defines the essence of life as the oil of gladness, fragrance, and comfort that involves everyone in a trickle-down effect: the abundance of the Lord in a fellowship of love.

As the dew nourishes and gives life, so the divine refreshment of our Lord takes the dew from Mount Hermon far to the north and sprinkles it on Mount Zion far to the south—a miracle linked by love. Love bridges. Love gives. Period.

PRAYER: Dear God, may I come to value the diversity within community. Amen.

WEDNESDAY, APRIL 26 • Read 1 John 1:1-4

How do you know what you say you know? This is a most responsible question. A most responsible answer is, "I'm an eyewitness. I saw it myself." Now that unimpeachable testimony becomes an immovable confession when combined with the courage of conviction.

The writer of this epistle (let's call him John) insists, "My soul is a witness to wonder." A real witness, John. A real wonder, Jesus. If you haven't seen anything, heard anything, felt anything, then you can't witness to anything. But if you have seen, heard, felt—then the experience explodes out of you to anyone willing to listen.

The head learns from the eye, the ear, the heart. How else could John know that Jesus comes from the Father to us, unless Jesus has communicated this directly? John's Gospel refers to Jesus as "the life," or the lifeline, if you will. Jesus becomes the tie that binds us to one another and to God.

Now if that tie binds us together and as believers we form a circle, that completed circle is the circle of joy. The circle perfectly symbolizes God's love: It has no beginning, no middle, no ending. Like God's love, the circle of joy has always existed. To be in the circle is to be in the know, for to be in the circle is to touch, to feel, to see the humanity of Jesus for yourself.

Jesus is real! Come and experience for yourself that Jesus is no ghost. Hear John calling to you and me to join the circle of life, the circle of love. Jesus remains at its hub, its beginning, and its ending.

John sows, John the initiator. You and I reap. You and I, those who gather. Sower and reaper rejoice together as our circle of joy is being completed.

Prayer: Loving Advocate, I rejoice in your love for me. Amen.

THURSDAY, APRIL 27 • Read 1 John 1:5-10

You have a choice: light or darkness. Only you can make that choice; and once you have made it, you must live with the consequences of your choice. Don't blame anyone except yourself, for the true light has come into the world; and no matter how dark your cave, you have been exposed to the light of Christ. Now choose!

If you say you choose friendship with Christ, yet continue to live in darkness, you lie. If you choose to live in the light, then you have fellowship and joy with one another and with Jesus Christ the Lord. Thus states the epistle writer.

Whoa, John, that's pretty strong language, isn't it? I mean, calling me a liar just because I'm human and slip back into darkness from time to time? Does that make me a sinner?

If we say, "We are not sinners," we lie. We are all sinners. We occasionally sin in the darkness and then come to the light singing psalms and hymns, even pointing the finger at other sinners who differ from us only in that we haven't been caught yet. The test: Anyone who says, "I am a Christian," should live as Christ did. That's the acid test, and you can't fool people easily. They know an actor when they see one.

Then where's the hope, John? Where's the hope?

Glad you asked. If you say, "I am a sinner; I confess my sin; I want to change my ways and will change my ways," then you are forgiven. So it's your call—light or darkness, lies or truth. Which will you choose? You have a night-light that will guide you step by step to the source of light—Jesus. Turn on the light and live!

PRAYER: God of light, turn me on and give me hope, that I may walk in light rather than darkness. Amen.

FRIDAY, APRIL 28 • Read 1 John 2:1-2

An ounce of prevention remains the essential ingredient of common sense. Most of our wisdom, however, is hard won. We learn mainly through personal pain. We acknowledge the heat of the fire only after feeling its searing sting.

John would save us from the fire: Don't sin. But John knows that love always provides a back door. God in creation foresees the need for re-creation, providing the second Adam (Jesus) at the same time God conceives of the first Adam. The One who sits high and looks low also looks way down the road to see the need and provide the solution before it's needed.

In theory, sin is preventable, but we human beings haven't subscribed to the theory yet. So instead of being preventable, sin seems inevitable, like crime in a community, even a gated community—even angels on guard can't keep sin out.

Our salvation comes when we find ourselves hauled into court. There we discover that we have a defense attorney, an advocate with the chief judge, sent to us by the chief judge. Our defense attorney has a unique relationship with the judge, but this relationship does not cause the court to set aside justice in forgiving. We are found guilty.

But glory be to God, love does not set aside mercy either. After the sentencing, the judge gets up, takes off the robe of judgment, goes down and stands with the accused and then stands for the accused, accepting the sentence in place of the accused. Jesus provides the bridge to the Father. So we are "at-one" in the atonement (at-one-ment). God's wrath against sin is removed. The magnet of God's love then compels the whole world to come to the mercy seat, a way in after a way out.

PRAYER: O God of mercy, offer me a way in when I have locked myself out. Amen.

SATURDAY, APRIL 29 • Read John 20:19-23

Like the disciples hiding in fear that Sunday afternoon of the Resurrection, we are often locked up tight with our fears. This deadbolt delirium gives us tunnel vision so we can't see beyond this place or time.

Our deadbolt delirium provides an excellent medium for the Master: opportunity. Importunity and opportunity—how often the two combine to make for the divine moment! At the darkest hour, the light of God comes unbidden into our midst.

"Peace be with you"—a most common greeting, much like our "good morning," "good evening," "good-bye." A most common greeting for the most uncommon occurrence. Jesus is gone. Sunshine is gone. Hope is gone. Purpose is gone.

But God is not gone. Do you not remember Jesus' stressing this point when he walked and taught and healed and counseled and loved? As long as there is a way to God, there is a way to life. The grave cannot destroy what God has created. Even as good morning means "God's morning" and good night means "God's night," so good-bye means "God by you." "Peace be with you."

God always validates those who believe; Jesus receives validation no matter what the odds. God's validation of Jesus is a response to a world that asks, "Show us your scars." Apparitions don't have scars. Novices don't have scars. Veterans have scars. God's noble ones have scars. Calvary's scars are God's chief advertisement.

Then Jesus, God's validated one, gives us our anointment and our appointment: Receive the Holy Spirit; go get your scars. We accept the charge to combat sin with the instrument of forgiveness, knowing that we move in the strength of Jesus and not in our strength alone.

Life's choice: scared or scarred?

Scarred, Jesus, scarred!

PRAYER: God, validate me, anoint me, appoint me. Amen.

SUNDAY, APRIL 30 • Read John 20:24-31

Thomas doubted. Cursed be Thomas for doubting! Blessed be Thomas for doubting! Now every Thomas who comes after him will know that Jesus has passed the litmus test. Testimonials don't work for some; they demand to be in the loop where seeing is believing.

Or so they think. Perhaps some Thomas will realize that the really important things in life can't be seen. Invisible is faith. Invisible is hope. Invisible is love. In John 3, Jesus points Nicodemus to the wind that moves through the trees. You see the movement but not the mover. You see the effect but not the cause. The things you see are often not worth seeing, let alone worshiping.

The empiricist serves a purpose, of course, proving that truth can stand up on its own without props. The proof about Jesus: Jesus is Lord; Lord of death and Lord of life, Lord of negativism and cynicism and escapism and me-too-ism and materialism. Touch him and see.

Jesus offers Thomas not only the proof of sight but the proof of touch. Nothing leads us to believe that Thomas accepts the invitation. Thomas has had enough: "My Lord and my God!" All his life Thomas has learned to ask the right questions. Now Thomas learns that some questions are irrelevant.

Thomas, through your optical nerve you have opened up blessings for those with spiritual nerve: believing without seeing. Blessed are those who believe what faith receives. Faith has an eye of its own. Faith has a touch of its own, a certainty of its own.

PRAYER: Lord, I believe. Help my unbelief! Amen.

*May 1–7, 2000 • Danny Dickerson**

MONDAY, MAY 1 • Read Acts 3:12-16

As we begin our meditations this week, let us remember the overview of God's work in the world. Throughout God's covenant relationship with the descendants of Abraham and Sarah, God demonstrated not only love for the chosen people but also authority over all the earth.

In today's scripture, Peter asks the crowd assembled at the portico of Solomon why the miracle of healing surprises them. Simultaneously, Peter reminds the crowd that it is not the power or piety of the disciples that healed the lame man but the man's own faith in Jesus' name.

Where have we heard similar words in other stories about Jesus' work? Didn't Jesus himself question the crowds and the disciples about their "surprise" at miracles, given their sincere belief in God's authority over the world?

This week's themes focus on three issues. First, we remember that God acted (and continues to act) with compassion and authority over the world. Second, God's actions through Jesus fulfill the promises made through the covenant relationship with the descendants of Abraham and Sarah. Most important, we pray to understand our personal responsibility to the world, as well as to whose authority we answer.

PRAYER: O God, I pray for your help in living in the world as I attempt to bear witness to your promises. Help me reconcile your authority in the world to the world's attempts to assert its authority over me. Amen.

---

*Retired musician; now a practicing certified public accountant, Nashville, Tennessee.

TUESDAY, MAY 2 • Read Acts 3:17-19

Several times in the New Testament, Peter and Paul explain to various groups the basics of the Christian faith: who these Christians are and what the basis of their faith is. This explanation often includes a description of Jesus' ministry and crucifixion, emphasizing the involvement of the Jerusalem authorities who put him to death. In this passage, Peter uses the personal pronoun "you," implying that some members of the crowd assembled at the portico of Solomon belong either to the political and religious elite who sent Jesus to die or to the masses who did not protest that decision. "You acted in ignorance, as did also your rulers," Peter tells his audience. He then explains that Jesus' suffering and death were necessary in order to fulfill the prophecies of the Hebrew Scriptures.

How often do the authorities of our world also act in ignorance? In what areas do the secular powers of the world evidence a willingness to recognize God's presence and grace whenever manifested? In Roman-occupied Palestine, the Hebrew people sought a messiah like the great King David, who would banish the Roman oppressor and unify the kingdom once again. Because the people looked for a warrior king, many could not recognize the Son of Man as their Savior.

If Jesus appeared among us today, would we recognize him? Or would we, like the people of Jerusalem, fail to see beyond the clothes he wore, the car he drove, or the neighborhood where he grew up? Would we also seek a warrior to take care of our enemies, or would we seek a person of peace and reconciliation?

PRAYER: Lord, help me see beyond those qualities that the world calls "good." Help me look beyond the possessions that the world insists are necessary to happiness and to focus instead on the unseen qualities written on the human heart. Amen.

WEDNESDAY, MAY 3 • Read Psalm 4:1-3

How often have we turned to the psalms in time of trouble? Even individuals who do not attend church regularly find comfort in the words "The Lord is my shepherd," recorded in Psalm 23. Many of the other psalms bring comfort in times of pain and tribulation.

As we read this psalm attributed to David, let us consider the context of its writing as reflected in David's life. Enemies often pursue David: members of his own family or former allies. We may have a hard time imagining the pain and fear of pursuit by enemies. David invokes the presence of the Lord in his prologue when he exclaims, "Thou hast given me room when I was in distress" (RSV). No matter what trouble David finds himself in, he always proclaims the Lord's authority and asks for mercy.

Like David, we also acknowledge God's power over us when we pray for help or relief, particularly when our choices generate the trouble. Even David sometimes creates his own problems through poor choices. Yet David confidently believes that God is present for him and hears his prayer. He states, "The Lord hears when I call to him."

Although we cannot claim to be a great king or warrior like David, we face many of the same problems he did: victory, defeat, desire, and betrayal. In a way, David's story becomes a metaphor for our own struggles with the world. And like David, may we never fear or feel ashamed to call upon God, because God hears our cry of distress.

PRAYER: O God of David, help me remember to turn to you in times of trouble. Help me remember that your only son also intercedes on our behalf in times of fear, isolation, and pain. Amen.

THURSDAY, MAY 4 • Read Psalm 4:4-8

Having turned again to God in verses 1-3 of this psalm, David continues his prayer by naming several specific steps to follow for those in covenant relationship with God.

Verse 4 states, "Be angry, but sin not" (RSV). While this command may seem strange to Christians, we need to place it within the context of David's time. David has many enemies, both within the kingdom and without. He faces a seemingly endless series of power struggles, wars, and intrigues. Obviously David cannot avoid anger entirely. Probably David is seeking to follow his own advice, as well as to give it to others. If anger is unavoidable, David wants to purge the desire to sin from his own heart and those of his people. He then advises us to "commune with your own hearts on your beds" (RSV).

Centuries later, Jesus emphasizes that the deeds written on one's heart may cause the faithful to stumble, even if they never really complete the sinful deeds. Likewise, does not God interpret the desires of the human heart like an open book? David knows, as did Jesus, that the will to sin begins in the heart before the flesh takes action.

David completes his prayer with a thought on "fair-weather faithful," who pray for good things and whose primary concern is material wealth. The Lord has brought David more joy through covenant relationship than those primarily concerned with the bounty of their harvest will ever know. Then how much more joyful should we be, having received not only the gift of God's covenant relationship but the final fruits of this relationship in the gift of Jesus' life poured out for us!

PRAYER: God of relationships, help me be mindful of the seeds of sin sown in the heart and of covenant relationships that help me bear fruit worthy of your gifts. Amen.

FRIDAY, MAY 5 • Read 1 John 3:1-7

Jesus told us to give to Caesar that which belongs to Caesar and to God that which belongs to God. Discerning one from the other is not always easy or pleasant.

The world would have us believe that we achieve true happiness by driving the right car, wearing the right clothes, owning the right home, having a satisfying career, and amusing ourselves with the proper accessories and diversions. Christians value many of these worldly goals. But are they of Caesar or of God?

The followers of Jesus in the days of the early church believed the "world does not know us" and that it "did not know him." Our modern world makes it easy to spend every waking moment concerned with acquiring more possessions. The world promotes the belief that the person who dies with the most toys wins.

Today's lesson plainly states, "Sin is lawlessness." Almost daily we hear another news report, read another newspaper article, or hear about someone in our neighborhood who has fallen victim to those who could not satisfy their worldly desires by lawful means. As Christians who reject sin, we reconcile ourselves to Jesus' plan for us: "He appeared to take away sins....No one who abides in him sins" (RSV). It is so simple that we can hardly comprehend. Through faith in Jesus, through hope in the world yet to come, and through ordering our lives to continue his work, we purify ourselves and co-exist with this world while not being seduced into its sin and desires.

PRAYER: God, help me remember that possessions the world offers may bring temporary comfort but cannot provide the everlasting peace that comes from accepting your gift of salvation. Amen.

SATURDAY, MAY 6 • Read Luke 24:36-44

Throughout Jesus' ministry, many of his actions have a primary purpose and a secondary purpose. While the secondary purpose may provide immediate relief from suffering, Jesus' primary purpose is to demonstrate God's power and authority.

In this passage Jesus appears among the disciples; we suspect that the doors were locked and that his appearance is sudden. Jesus once more raises his now familiar question: Why do you still disbelieve after all we have been through together? Once again, even after victory over death, Jesus must convince the frightened disciples that "it is I myself. Touch me and see." Jesus then asks for food and eats, confirming that he indeed is real, while diverting their attention from fear and doubt. With the post-Resurrection communion of touch and of sharing food, again Jesus demonstrates that these remarkable events are not for his own benefit but for the benefit of the disciples and the people, that they might believe and have faith.

Having once again demonstrated God's power and authority to his friends, Jesus now reminds them of all that was written in Hebrew Scriptures and the necessity of the fulfillment of these things. He brings together in this little room the two great themes of God's covenant relationship: God has authority over all the world and has established a covenant with its people; and God's promise of a Messiah has been fulfilled, not with a warrior king like David but with a human sacrificial Lamb who redeems all the world.

PRAYER: God of open doors, may I experience the Christ in such a way as those disciples; may I hear him say to me, "It is I myself." May I touch and see, thereby recognizing your power and authority over all the earth—even over the power of death. Amen.

SUNDAY, MAY 7 • Read Luke 24:45-48

This week we have considered the issue of authority: God's authority over the world and the world's authority over us. We have observed that what the world wants is not always what God wants. However, just as Jesus always came back down the mountain to minister to people in need, so too must we reconcile our place in God's kingdom with our place in the world. It is not a simple task, but if we order our thinking and put our relationship with God first, then we will be in a position to carry out Jesus' work, even as we carry out the necessary labors to live in the world.

After appearing to his friends in the room where they have gathered, Jesus "opened their minds to understand the scriptures." Prior to the Resurrection, the disciples continued to question Jesus' demonstrations of who he was. Now that the final demonstration of God's authority has taken place and the scriptures have been fulfilled, the power of the Holy Spirit works through Jesus to bring understanding to those minds previously incapable of comprehension.

Jesus speaks a clear message: Now that you understand, you have much work to do. Why did God intervene in the lives of the Hebrew people for so many centuries? Why was the Messiah sacrificed as a Passover Lamb instead of conquering the enemies of the people?

Now the disciples understand the answers to the questions. Jesus' death and resurrection have taken place so that Christ might redeem all the people of the world through the preaching of repentance and forgiveness and through faith in Jesus' name. The disciples lack only one thing: the power of the Holy Spirit. It too will come, enabling them and us to carry out God's work in the world.

PRAYER: Christ, open my mind and heart so that I may understand your work of redemption in the world. Then empower me to carry out that work. Amen.

My Cup Runneth Over

May 8–14, 2000 • *Susan Passi-Klaus**

MONDAY, MAY 8 • **Read John 10:11-13**

Have you ever given serious thought to firing Jesus? No doubt some circumstances have led you to raise questions about Jesus' performance. During one of those periods in my life, someone dear to me challenged—perhaps invited—me to get to know the "real" Jesus. I discovered that I had to revise my version of the Lord's job description.

I've often assigned the Son of God to the task of being the divine fixer-upper; a higher being-of-all-trades; my own personal rescue worker "on call" for breakdowns in faith, heart failures, and leaky souls. In my spiritual searching, I have come to accept that Jesus is not a heavenly handyman, nor is he a public relations executive or a military general.

The writer of John's Gospel describes Jesus as the "good shepherd." Oddly enough, herding sheep scarcely ranks as a fast-track career appropriate for the boss's son. In fact, it's a rather lonely and solitary existence; the pay isn't great; the co-workers are dogs; and stubborn, self-absorbed sheep are always straying.

Yet this humble image symbolizes Jesus' work in human lives. As the good shepherd, Jesus cares and protects, leads to safe choices and peaceful places, and keeps God's herd together. He protects us from enemies and thieves who would rob us of a full and meaningful life. He tends the gate to God's salvation. And he's willing to die for us in the line of duty.

What a job description! No wonder so many others have turned it down.

PRAYER: Good Shepherd, remind me to guide and care for others through whatever work I choose to do. Amen.

---

*Author in process; freelance writer, Franklin, Tennessee.

TUESDAY, MAY 9 • Read John 10:14-18

I'm a lousy follower. Put me at the head of a table, at the center of attention, or at the top of a list, and I'm right at home. But ask me to be a follower instead of leader, to be satisfied with runner-up over first place, or to take a backseat when I'm used to driving, and I'm doomed to confusion. Perhaps that's why I so often feel like a lost sheep.

Sheep are notorious for not watching where they're going. With their noses buried deep in the business of feeding themselves, they're often too engrossed in their own gratification to hear the shepherd's voice. When they finally look up, they're clueless about their whereabouts. With eyes focused downward and not paying attention to directions or dangers along the path, sheep often wander astray.

And when sheep fail to listen for the shepherd's voice, they find themselves at the mercy of their enemies who attempt to scatter them from the flock in order to overpower them. Like some sheep, I'm just plain stubborn—I'm sure I know a better way or a shorter cut to get to where I'm going.

I also forget to look up. Like sheep I'm easily distracted by the details of life and fail to recognize or choose to ignore my Shepherd's voice. The greater my self-involvement the more vulnerable I become to my enemies.

Thank goodness my Shepherd doesn't give up on me. No matter how large the flock, he knows me and calls me by name. I can always trust that he will not abandon me. When he sees trouble coming, he brings me close to him and continues to care for me and watch over me. Thank goodness Jesus forgives my wandering ways and always guides me back to safety and home...beside him.

PRAYER: Lord, when I hear your voice, help me look up! Amen.

WEDNESDAY, MAY 10 • Read Psalm 23

One day with an overdrawn checking account, a depressed husband, and a feeling of "been there, done that" at the ripe old age of forty-four, I sat in a chair across from my minister. Crying my way, a tissue at a time, through a laundry list of Why me's? and What now's?, I needed comfort and advice. My husband's lucrative career had vanished as the result of downsizing. Our retirement savings were disappearing rapidly, and I was battling a lethal combination of laziness, fear, and guilt about returning to work.

Why didn't God give me answers I could understand—immediately? Should we move, hire a lawyer, sell our house? Should we surrender the last of our nest egg, sacrifice my writing career to a "real job," sell out our dreams to the need just to get by? I not only wanted answers; I wanted written instructions in large print—a video would have been ideal. At the very least, an angel with a hand-delivered script, a clearly marked map, or a revealing lightning bolt would suffice.

A short time later God did send an angel—in the form of an opportunity to write meditations for this publication. God also sent a lightning bolt delivered through Psalm 23.

When we allow God, our Shepherd, to guide us along the right paths, God leads us out of the maze of Why me's? and What now's? When we surrender our obsession with knowing when, where, and how, we allow God to redirect our steps and to guide us to safe places.

Though time has provided answers and new directions, I remain financially challenged; my job search is on hold; and I'm another birthday closer to a midlife crisis. However, the panic, fear, and anger that characterized my struggle to lead God rather than to follow is gone. This healing psalm reminds me that God will lead me in God's own time and way, not only to solutions but to spiritual sanity.

PRAYER: Lord, my cup runneth over. Thank you. Amen.

THURSDAY, MAY 11 • Read Read Psalm 23:4

One of my strongest childhood memories is one created by the grandmother I called Dearie. During summer vacations I had the privilege of sleeping beside her in the big bed with blue-flowered sheets.

If I close my eyes I can easily recollect the sight of her in brush rollers and hairnet, lavender pajamas, face "greased" with cold cream. She smelled of Ivory soap, VO5, and the dusting powder I bought her every June birthday from the five and dime. Being so close on those warm summer nights, I was blessed to listen as she knelt beside the bed and whispered her prayers. And though some nights I secretly wished she'd hurry up, I mostly waited patiently for her to finish her talk with God.

Dearie had a family reputation for having very long talks with God. I would struggle to stay awake for as long as she prayed, waiting for the best part—she would finally get around to praying for me. I recognized my turn in Dearie's prayers because I'd hear my name whispered, "Susie," and she'd unfold her hands and reach to hold mine. Then her voice would lower again, keeping the rest of her meditations between her and God. I do know that she began every prayer with the words "The Lord is my shepherd" and ended every prayer with the words "Lord willing."

Today I find no greater comfort than knowing that she had these words to comfort her through her husband's alcoholism and abandonment, her children's illnesses, so-called "family scandals," and, eventually, through her own mental illness.

I am grateful to the psalmist for authoring these beautiful words that offer a gift of strength, reassurance, and guidance in the midst of our journey here on earth. I am particularly grateful that my grandmother Dearie, when in need of comfort and assurance of God's presence, could turn to this psalm in her well-worn Bible and find some peace.

PRAYER: Lord willing. Amen.

FRIDAY, MAY 12 • **Read 1 John 3:16**

Long before the box-office success of the movie *Titanic*, I read stories about that tragic disaster at sea and the unsettling loss of human lives. The most thought-provoking question inspired by my reading was this: Would I have stayed behind on the sinking luxury liner and given someone else my seat on a lifeboat? I've never been at peace with my answer.

Standing on the ship's deck so close to both life and death, what would I have chosen? Could I have left my husband behind? Would I have given up my seat to a stranger? to my own mother? to my best friend? to someone older, weaker, or more frightened than I?

And then comes a deeper question: Am I capable of loving anyone enough to die for him or her? That decision almost paralyzes me. Yet Jesus died for me and you, and this verse suggests that we be willing to die for others in Christ.

Although God taught us this lesson symbolically through the physical death of God's son, I believe that dying for the sake of others occurs in many ways. God asks for our willingness to sacrifice ego, comfort, judgment, and security to help those who are powerless, abandoned, bewildered, or empty.

Each time we serve others with no thought of receiving anything in return, we give up our life to Christ. I also believe that real love is an action, not a feeling. We must be willing to walk the talk and die to live. Whenever we put legs on our prayers, hands to our good intentions, and raise our voices in advocacy of others, we die to ourselves and help others live more fully. The greatest act of love comes in giving oneself for others. Death is no longer an ending; through Jesus Christ, death is just the beginning.

SUGGESTION FOR MEDITATION: **For whom or what would you be willing to die? Consider how you might expand that willingness to include those you currently exclude.**

SATURDAY, MAY 13 • Read 1 John 3:17-24

Not long ago, I took my turn guiding a study group to a richer understanding of the tenth commandment: "Thou shalt not covet" (Exod. 20:17, KJV). Through our discussion, members came to define coveting as a desire to have others' possessions, wanting something so much that we risk getting it at someone else's expense.

At first, some of us hoped our spiritual maturity had settled any accountability issues. After all, most of us had evolved beyond the "acquiring" phase of our lives. We all admitted that we lacked little in terms of possessions, and we claimed to have learned that more is never enough.

But as we began a deeper search into the meaning behind this final commandment, we came to life-changing realizations. We learned that we often covet because we don't believe there's enough to go around. We covet because we haven't fully grasped that we are all one.

Both the tenth commandment and today's scripture convey that it's not enough that we have what we need and don't wish for more. We also must provide for the needs of others. Until we come to understand that we're in this together—we are all one—then we just "don't get it."

We must be willing to go to any length to help others. If the food has to come from our plate, if clothes must come off our back, if more room must be found in our already crowded heart, if more time must be shared in our extraordinarily busy day—so be it. We are called each day to give to the fullest. Only then may we approach God with bold confidence and clear conscience.

SUGGESTION FOR MEDITATION: "Christ has no body now on earth but yours, no hands but yours, no feet but yours. Yours are the eyes through which the compassion of Christ is to look out on a hurting world."—Saint Teresa of Avila

It took great courage to follow Jesus during his life, perhaps even more to stand up for Jesus after his physical death. Consider factors that influenced Jesus' reputation: his bringing dead people to life, giving sight to the blind, forcing demons out of untouchables. Jesus' followers needed bold spirits.

How could the disciples explain accompanying such a controversial character—to be known by the company they kept with a man who turned water into wine, made friends of his enemies, and predicted his own rising from death?

Would you risk your reputation to associate with someone so unwelcome in certain circles, so upsetting to powers-that-be, and someone so likely to get you into trouble as well? Even if you chose to brave the consequences of a relationship with such a questionable character while he lived, could you remain loyal and committed after his death?

Peter and John's allegiance to Jesus beyond the grave humbles me. When I determine to put my feet in their shoes as they stand before the very men who had sentenced Jesus to die, their courage overwhelms me.

Today such loyalty and integrity seem hard to come by. We too easily place our faith in earthly people, places, and things that we can explain, attain, or gain. Spiritual truths and principles are far too intangible in our "we've-got-to-see-it-to-believe-it" world. Yet God continues to call us to remind the world that Jesus is timeless; his teachings remain relevant; and the truth he spoke is eternal.

Just as John and Peter courageously announce to Annas, Caiaphas, and other skeptics that Jesus is alive and well and still at work healing human lives, we too accept the call to continue God's work and to stand up for Jesus!

PRAYER: Jesus, I will stand by you as you have always stood by me. Neither death nor the passage of time can part us. Amen.

No Longer Strangers

May 15–21, 2000 • M. Douglas Meeks*

MONDAY, MAY 15 • Read Acts 8:26-34

The road from Jerusalem to Gaza cuts through the middle of nowhere. The man riding in a chariot on the road is an outsider, an African, and an official of a foreign government. He is powerful and different—and intimidating. Strangely enough, as Philip jogs up to the chariot, this stranger is reading one of Isaiah's Servant Songs, a poem that early Christians associated with Jesus' crucifixion. Politely he asks Philip to tell him about the person the prophet is describing. Suddenly Philip, now beside the stranger in the noonday sun, meets the challenge to share the good news of Jesus with someone from a different culture, race, and religious background.

We don't know what fears Philip has to overcome to go and sit beside this strange man. The angel of the Lord tells Philip to go, and he goes. Philip knows that if you accept Jesus, you must also accept all whom Jesus would befriend. Jesus' friends come from all nations and races; they include pilgrims and wayfarers; they seek to know more about God's love. Jesus welcomes the stranger; when we welcome a stranger in Jesus' name, we see Jesus our friend in the stranger's face.

What strange road is the Holy Spirit asking us to go down? What friend of Jesus is hoping that we will come along for the ride?

PRAYER: God, I want to be among Jesus' friends. Go with me on the road and give me welcoming words to speak when they are needed. In Jesus' name. Amen.

---

*Cal Turner Chancellor Professor of Theology and Wesleyan Studies, The Divinity School, Vanderbilt University, Nashville, Tennessee.

TUESDAY, MAY 16 • Read Acts 8:35-40

The strange man asks Philip a strange question: "What is to prevent me from being baptized?" What could possibly prevent a believer from being baptized? Does the stranger think Philip might refuse because of the color of his skin or because he comes from a different class or because of his politics?

It's almost as if Luke in writing Acts tries to think of every possible excuse that one might give against accepting certain persons as members of the community. Luke then gives an example of how wrong the exclusion of any of God's chosen would be. Samaritans, Saul the persecutor of Christians, a Roman centurion: those once considered enemies now find themselves in God's embrace.

The Ethiopian whom Philip baptizes represents everything that is foreign to Jesus' first followers. But God's plan includes welcoming foreigners. Psalm 68 celebrates the scope of God's reign by referring to this faraway land: "Let Ethiopia hasten to stretch out its hands to God" (v. 31).

Whom does Jesus invite to his table? Those people in the famous Leonardo da Vinci painting will be there but also the people we thought were nothing like us. The Ethiopian pilgrim will be there too, brought in off that hot, dusty road. Jesus will wash his feet and ask him to sit down to eat and drink at the table with all his friends.

PRAYER: God, you have promised that in your reign there will be no more strangers, only friends. Teach me to welcome foreigners and pilgrims, all those who are far from home. In Jesus' name. Amen.

WEDNESDAY, MAY 17 • **Read Psalm 22:25-31**

A favorite movie scene of mine is the final one in the Sally Field movie *Places in the Heart*. A small southern town has been torn apart by racial strife. In church on Sunday the congregation passes the Communion plate. As the bread goes from hand to hand, we see that communing "together" are the bloody adversaries of the town. And as the camera fades for a long shot, we see that present also are those who have died: the black man killed by an angry mob, the police officer who was shot.

The final verses of Psalm 22 picture the time when "all the ends of the earth...all the families of the nations" will worship God together. But God doesn't stop with national and racial boundaries; economic barriers will also fall: "The poor shall eat and be satisfied." Nothing will prevent God from breaking down the walls that separate us.

Remarkably this psalm even looks forward to a time when the last barrier among human beings will be destroyed. Verses 29-31 show generations worshiping God together—and not just grandparents and grandchildren. That would not be so unusual. But the generations that lie buried in the earth will bow down before God with the generations "yet unborn." Even the dead find inclusion in God's celebration of love.

Every Sunday, and especially during Easter, we praise God for Christ's victory over death. An old German hymn echoes Paul's great declaration that nothing separates us from God's love (Rom. 8:38): Jesus lives! Our hearts know well / naught from us his love shall sever; / life, nor death, nor powers of hell / tear us from his keeping ever.*

PRAYER: God, teach me your steadfast love and everlasting kindness that all hunger may cease, all separation end. In Jesus' name. Amen.

Jesu Lebt by C. F. Gellert, 1757; tr. Frances E. Cox, 1841. Found in *Rejoice in the Lord*, Wm. B. Eerdmans (1985).

THURSDAY, MAY 18 • Read 1 John 4:7-12

During the tumultuous days of controversy over President Clinton's testimony before the grand jury, a *Kudzu* cartoon pictured Will B. Dunn pondering the meaning of life. "God is love," he says. And then a few panels later: "Of course, it depends on what your definition of the word *is* is." As is usual with good cartoons, this observation offers more than a rather painful laugh about an incident we'd like to forget. Pastor Will B. Dunn asks us to think about the word *is*, a pivotal word in our verses from First John. The verb *to be* in one form or another is crucial for expressing what we believe about God.

Moses, confronting the burning bush, wants to know God's name, and God replies, "I am who I am" (Exod. 3:14). In John's Gospel, Jesus gives the disciples "I am" statements that connect him to God: "I am the bread of life" (6:35) and "I am the good shepherd" (10:11), for example.

When 1 John 4:8 says, "God is love," we should not overlook the word *is*. The love that *is* God cannot be pictured with hearts and flowers or airbrushed couples in the sunshine. God's love is not static or prettified; God's love is life and is revealed to us this way: God's only Son was sent to die that we might live. Contrary to the rules of grammar, *is* becomes an active verb. "God is love" means living, acting, serving, giving, returning the gift, loving one another. Then God lives in us.

God loves the world so much that the gift of Jesus becomes the ultimate definition of love. How then will we tell the world about this God whom no one has ever seen? "By our love, by our love."

PRAYER: God, I thank you for loving me before I knew how to love. Give me your Spirit and teach me to love others so that strangers may become friends. In Jesus' name. Amen.

FRIDAY, MAY 19 • Read 1 John 4:13-21

No one has ever seen God; but through Jesus, God becomes visible. An ancient Byzantine Rite for Vespers asks, "How shall I tell of this great mystery? He who is without flesh becomes incarnate; the Word puts on a body; the Invisible is seen; He whom no hand can touch is handled; and He who knows no beginning now begins to be. The Son of God becomes the Son of woman: Jesus Christ, the same yesterday and today and forever."

Jesus, the "joy of heaven," comes to earth, in Charles Wesley's words, "to fix in us [his] humble dwelling." Only in our struggle to tell the mystery of Jesus, who became, like us, capable of pain and subject to death, do we begin to appreciate the remarkable promise made here: God abides in us when we abide in love for one another (1 John 4:16).

Sometimes abiding means enduring, becoming a means of grace by "hanging in there," like the preacher who outlasts situations of conflict. Sometimes abiding means speaking out, praying, running the food pantry, baking pies, pushing pencils, chairing meetings year after year when no one else wants the job. Always, though, it means loving: "Those who love God must love their brothers and sisters also."

Abide is an old-fashioned word, but even modern translations keep it because nothing else begins to express the closeness of the community of God and Jesus. We are invited into this community, enabled by the Spirit to live in Christ to the glory of God. This is perfect love, "pure, unbounded love," "all loves excelling," and the reason we have nothing to fear.

PRAYER: God, give me courage to see you in other faces. Free me from my fears by your perfect love. In Jesus' name. Amen.

SATURDAY, MAY 20 • Read John 15:1-4

Most gardeners delight in pruning. Cutting back makes a garden look neat: the faded roses in November, the maple shoots too close to the tree's roots, the leggy chrysanthemum stems that will bloom too soon. But pruning people is another matter. Trimming away our excesses—and sometimes what we consider to be essentials—is not easy. Jesus, however, asks his followers to be ready for a good pruning. Peter left behind a family fishing business (and his impetuousness); Mary Magdalene gave away her wealth (and her psychological disorders); Paul renounced his privileged place (and his persecution of Jesus' followers).

Pruning paradoxically leads to more growth and stronger growth. Everyone knows that if you want an apple tree to bear more apples, you have to prune it. It seems cruel to cut away at a living thing, but the pruning results in more fruit.

The word in John's Gospel for "prune" has the same root in Greek as *catharsis*, a word we associate with tragedy in classical drama. Although we find it painful to watch the tragedy unfolding on the stage, at the end of the play members of the audience feel cleansed or emotionally purged. They go home with renewed energy.

Jesus has talked about the need for this cleansing before. As he prepares to wash the disciples' feet over Peter's strenuous objections, he says, "Unless I wash you, you have no share with me" (13:8). When we experience cleansing, we share in Jesus' presence and thereby receive a model for our own acts of love.

"Wash me thoroughly," says the psalmist. "Purge me with hyssop....Create in me a clean heart, O God, and put a new and right spirit within me....Restore to me the joy of your salvation" (Ps. 51:2, 7, 10, 12).

PRAYER: Give us, O God, the courage to live with less, to love you more, and to serve those in need. In Jesus' name. Amen.

SUNDAY, MAY 21 • Read John 15:5-8

Paul spoke of the church as a human body with Christ as the head. John saw the church through Jesus' eyes as a vine with branches and God as the gardener. Both metaphors reflect thought and use images of living, growing organisms.

Perhaps modern church members have a harder time accepting the vine image, and not just because we have mostly moved off the farm and don't watch the cycle of grafting, watering, feeding, pruning, and harvesting anymore. Our culture so values individualism and independence that it becomes problematic to think of ourselves as intertwining branches, barely distinguishable from one another and totally dependent on the vine. Most folks don't much like the notion that we can't take care of ourselves. We're happy to bear fruit but don't expect us to give credit to the vine, and we'd just as soon that the gardener didn't interfere. We like to pull our own weight, and we don't want to feel obligated to anyone.

But Maya Angelou reminds us that "nobody can make it out here alone." Alone, no branch bears fruit. Being and doing unite in the vine and branches; if we abide, we will bear fruit. The gospel invites us to wholeness and growth by inviting us to live always in Christ's presence. Wholeness resides in the community of love that starts with Jesus' abiding in God and embracing us into that abiding love. Thus we embody God's love of the world.

The church, according to Samuel Stone's hymn "The Church's One Foundation," is made up of "elect from every nation, yet one o'er all the earth; / her charter of salvation, one Lord, one faith, one birth." The last stanza joyfully affirms that the church "on earth has union with God the Three in One." To God be glory.

PRAYER: God, bring us to your household as heirs not strangers, that we may be one people in your love. Amen.

Victory through Love

May 22–28, 2000 • Wayne G. Reece*

John Wesley wrote in his *Directions for Singing*, "Sing lustily and with a good courage. Beware of singing as if you were half dead, or half asleep; but lift up your voice with strength."

So does the psalmist remind the Israelites to sing. Whether the Israelites are celebrating the new year, enthroning a king, lamenting their conditions, or praising God, they are to sing.

The psalmist requests that the Israelites sing a "new song." Why? What's wrong with the old song? We know the old songs. We have sung the old ones during memorable occasions—camps, Sunday school, funerals, weddings, around the piano. Why do we have to sing something new?

The new song acknowledges God's continuous creation of new life, new hope, new love, new promises. Each morning breaks like the first morning; with it comes a new day of challenges and opportunities to be in the new world God has created for us. May God's recreation refresh and renew our hearts and our spirits also.

Psalm 98 reminds us, as it did the early Israelites, that God did not create this world just for them or just for us: "All the ends of the earth have seen the victory of our God." We must remember that God's world and God's Word are for all people.

PRAYER: O Creator God, hear me as I sing praises to you—both silently and lustily—to thank you for all your glory. Amen (so be it)!

---

*Pastor, First United Methodist Church, Mason, Michigan.

TUESDAY, MAY 23 • Read Psalm 98:5-9

The reformer Martin Luther wrote, "Next to theology I give to music the highest place and honour. Music is the art of the prophets, the only art that can calm the agitations of the soul; it is one of the most magnificent and delightful presents God has given us."

Psalm 98 reminds us of the power and the importance of music. As we try to express the various feelings of our emotions, the different depths of our faiths, and the many thoughts that cross our minds, music seems to be the truly "universal language."

Wherever we might be, though we might not understand the words of the songs, the rhythm and beat of the music seem to resound within us. The psalmist encourages us to "burst into jubilant song with music." Then he lists a variety of instruments that can assist in our heavenly noise.

Can we even imagine that the rivers and the sea and the mountains would "resound...clap their hands...sing together for joy"? God's creation comes with a built-in need and desire to "praise God from whom all blessings flow."

However, some people cannot or will not allow music to move them. They sit on their hands. Their mouths have clenched lips. They close their ears to the words and phrases that God's people and God's creation can lift up.

We are to "sing before the Lord, for he comes to judge the earth," not on the basis of our music or our singing but on the strength of our faithfulness.

Our songs and music are only one great way to open up to God and share our faith—to God and to others.

PRAYER: O Creator of nature and Sustainer of joy, help me open my lips in praise to you. Amen.

While still a young boy, I remember driving past a church with a neon sign that read, "Jesus Only," except the first three letters had burned out. Thus the sign read, "Us Only." My father said the sign truly described the members of that church, since they did not welcome outsiders easily.

This passage from Acts relates the powerful story of the Pentecost of the Gentiles. In Acts 2 we read about the coming of God's Holy Spirit upon the people gathered for the Jewish observance of Pentecost. We regard that event as the beginning of the Christian church.

However, many of the early Christians were Jewish men and women who converted to Christianity and who often continued to think in old ways. Many still believed in the need for circumcision before baptism.

Acts 10:9-16 records Simon Peter's vision, in which God convinces Peter that nothing that God makes is unclean or profane—not even Gentiles. Cornelius (a Gentile) also has a vision in which God tells Cornelius to send men to Joppa to enlist the help of Simon Peter. Peter complies with their wish and journeys with them to Joppa.

There, in the presence of six Jewish Christians, God's Holy Spirit pours out "even on the Gentiles," and they speak in tongues and praise God.

This baptism of Cornelius—with water and the Spirit—marks a watershed in the missionary and evangelism movements of the Christian church. No longer can the new Christians believe that the Spirit is only for them; the Spirit is for all God's people.

How many of us exclude people from our churches either by thoughts or traditions that keep us from being open to new people or new movements of God's spirit?

PRAYER: O God of all nations and all peoples, may I open my heart to others, knowing that they are also your creation. Amen.

THURSDAY, MAY 25 • Read John 15:9-11

In this lesson from John's Gospel, we read Jesus' words on love and commandments. In the three New Testament lessons this week, we read the words *commandments* or *commands* at least eight times.

Here, on the eve of Jesus' death, you can almost envision his looking into the faces of the disciples and saying, "As God has loved me, so have I loved you. What more can I say? What more can I give? Just abide in my love."

The *American Heritage Dictionary* defines *abide* with these words: "To wait patiently for. To be in store for. To withstand. To accept the consequences of; rest satisfied with. To continue; to endure." So Jesus tells his disciples to wait for the love that God has given. The disciples can rest satisfied with the love that Jesus has showed them. The disciples can continue and endure because of God-given love.

After all the hard walks and hard talks Jesus has had with them, after all the confusion and questions the disciples have mentioned, after all the healings and teachings and warnings—Jesus encourages disciples of all times to remain open to God's love. Why? "So that my joy may be in you, and that your joy may be complete."

Jesus is not concerned about leaving his disciples money, prestige, success, honor, or a retirement home. He wants them to be full of joy, a joy that is deep and withstanding and full of contentment. Happiness is temporary, but God's joy is complete.

Do you sense that rich, abiding love—that rich, deep joy?

PRAYER: O God of love, lift me from the chaos that surrounds me with anger and anguish, with hatred and harm. Love me as you loved Jesus. Amen.

FRIDAY, MAY 26 • Read John 15:12-17

"You did not choose me but I chose you."

Too often we think that becoming a Christian is simply a personal decision, a choice we make. In this day of "smorgasbord faith," we think we can select from many opinions, all of which may seem to be equal and true.

However, maybe after our wandering and wondering, we have come to a place in our life and faith when we have begun to question the validity of the "smorgasbord faith." Maybe we find ourselves firmly convinced that Jesus' way is the only way. Jesus' statement makes us realize that our Christianity is not our choice; instead, Jesus says, "I have chosen you."

Isn't it great to know that even though the world seems to reject us, tends to ignore us, and doesn't need us that Jesus does, and Jesus has chosen us.

Jesus chooses us to "love one another." Even though we often operate in life, both inside and outside the church, by hating one another, wanting nothing to do with one another, Jesus wants us to show love. We must come to realize that "love" is a verb as well as a noun and assume its active quality in our daily living.

Jesus chooses us as "friends." No longer do we need to feel like servants, doing Jesus' legwork here on earth. Instead, we have the privilege of being friends with him and with those he has befriended. What better family reunion than to come together in a common bond through our friend Jesus!

Jesus chooses us "to bear fruit." Our loving friendships demonstrate the benefits of that love. Love is not just something to keep to ourselves, but we must grow in grace, peace, and power. People must be able to look at us and say, as they did about the early Christians, "Look how they love each other."

PRAYER: **O God of love, strengthen me to love, to bear fruit, and to love those whom you love. Amen.**

SATURDAY, MAY 27 • Read 1 John 5:1-3

When I was in the sixth grade, our Sunday school class would recite a Bible verse for the opening session. One Sunday we said together: "Do unto others as you would have them do unto you." We said it perfectly; haloes seemed to materialize above our heads. But when we sat down, the boy next to me pulled the chair out from under me, and I fell down.

The boy had said the words, but he didn't keep the command. So in John's epistle we read, "This is how we know that we love the children of God: by loving God and carrying out his commands." Many persons do not think about loving as a commandment. They think they operate not "under the law" but "under grace." Yet we are commanded to love both God and neighbor, as well as "the children of God."

The expectation is that we will show care and concern for all persons in need. It is not enough for us to know and say all the good words, like my "friend" did. We must open our hands, our hearts, our churches to those whose lives and faith are "achin' and racked with pain." We must show our love for God by showing love to others.

Someone once wrote, "Some people do good because law requires it. Others do good because love desires it." So in our own ways, as children created by God in love, we must love one another...we must love one another...we must love one another....

John, more than any other biblical writer, emphasizes the command to love. And so we must.

PRAYER: O Parent of your children, help me love your whole family. Amen.

SUNDAY, MAY 28 • **Read 1 John 5:4-6**

The refrain of an old hymn goes, "O victory in Jesus, my Savior forever! He sought me and bought me with his redeeming blood."

We culminate our thinking together by considering the epistle's affirmation: "This is the victory that has overcome the world....the one who came by water and blood—Jesus Christ" (NIV).

In the midst of our competition and cares, in our rush for success and status, in our expression of doubt and despair—today's reading graciously reminds us that we can overcome the world through victory in Christ.

How is this accomplished? God only knows.

Why is this accomplished? God only knows.

For whom is this accomplished? Perhaps we know we can be victorious, if we are "born of God." Just loving does not do it. Just action does not achieve it. Just feeling does not create it. God's grace and love and power through the risen and ascended Christ will bring us the victory.

Remember the moments in sporting events when the cheer goes up, "Victory, victory, that's our cry, V-I-C-T-O-R-Y!" How often do you cheer from the sidelines of life that victory is yours? How often do you believe that you have won the game of life despite overwhelming odds? How often do you act as if you were on God's winning side?

As you ponder these questions on this day set aside for worship in the faith community of your choosing, remember that Christ has chosen you—to love, to believe, to give, to live, to be victorious in a world that seems to be your enemy.

PRAYER: O God of victory, lift me up from the depths of my life and give me new life, new hope, and new courage with the victory that is mine through Jesus. Amen.

Faith with Trust

May 29–June 4, 2000 • Gene P. Richter*

MONDAY, MAY 29 • Read Psalm 1

One recurrent theme in this week's readings is that of faith with trust. While these two terms may appear to be synonymous, when used to describe qualities pertaining to our Christian beliefs and convictions, the nuances of their meaning do not always parallel. To illustrate: Some time ago, one of the Midwest states experienced a severe drought. A local pastor suggested having a special gathering in which those assembled would offer specific prayers for rain. Imagine the surprise of a number of those gathered when they noticed a teenager approaching carrying an umbrella! The faith of this young woman was, indeed, coupled with a complete and total trust.

Surely faith with trust is a major theme in this first psalm. "Happy are those who reject the advice of evil people" (TEV). Confident believers are happy because their faith is adequate to provide them total trust. Verse 3 reads, "They are like trees that grow beside a stream, that bear fruit at the right time (TEV).

Verse 4 offers the contrasting situation: "But evil people are not like this…, they are like straw that the wind blows away" (TEV). Do these two differing views convey something to us about our faith with trust? Indeed they do! When bad things happen to good people, their example of solid faith and unwavering courage strengthens us. Verse 6 concludes, "The righteous are guided and protected by the LORD" (TEV). This assurance sustains our faith with complete and confident trust!

PRAYER: Enrich my spirit within me, O God, that I may remain confident, exemplifying a faith-filled trust, whatever circumstances I face this day. In Christ's name I pray. Amen.

---

*Retired Presbyterian minister; member of the Pittsburgh Presbytery, living in Indianapolis, Indiana.

TUESDAY, MAY 30 • Read Acts 1:15-17, 20*b*

Faith with trust! Today's reading reports Peter's words to the believers assembled in the upper room, the place where the disciples had shared with Jesus his final meal. Peter tells them that the actions of Judas, "a member of our group…[who] had been chosen to have a part in our work" (TEV), have been predicted in the scriptures. Verse 20*b* reads, "May someone else take his place of service" (TEV).

One can well imagine the intensity of emotion among those gathered in the upper room when Peter stands up to speak—disappointment, frustration, and even anger may all be present. However, Peter calmly and confidently states the facts about Judas's actions. Perhaps Jesus' words come to Peter's mind: "Pass no judgment, and you will not be judged" (Matt. 7:1, NEB). Surely Peter's keen awareness of his own need for God's love, mercy, and forgiveness allows him to simply state that the disciples must choose a replacement.

If we take a moment to reflect on past memories, many of us can recall events where we did or said things that we later regretted. At such times we, like the apostles, come to a fuller appreciation of God's mercy and forgiveness in our own lives. In fact, the spirit of God's love in Christ takes on a whole new meaning. Through this realization, we also recognize the need to strive to treat others as we would like to be treated—with a great deal of faith and trust!

SUGGESTION FOR MEDITATION: "The LORD is near to those who are discouraged; he saves those who have lost all hope" (Ps. 34:18, TEV).

WEDNESDAY, MAY 31 • Read Acts 1:21-26

Early on in my first pastoral charge, an active member of the congregation gave me these words of advice: "When you're bogged down in a seemingly impossible controversy, remember those often quoted words of the church: 'We've never done it this way before!'" Any persons involved in making decisions for the church or its people are quite aware of the significance of these seven words.

The practice of drawing lots, as described in today's reading, has a long biblical tradition. A footnote to Joshua 14:2 explains that drawing lots "was usually done by using specially marked stones to determine God's will" (TEV). The key phrase here is *God's will*. Thus we find in Acts 1:24 how those assembled pray, saying, "Lord, you know the thoughts of everyone, so show us which of these two you have chosen" (TEV).

Long-practiced tradition or not, the drawing of lots symbolizes a trusting faith in God. The concern of the ancient faithful does not focus on whom to blame when one's choices fail, as might be the case for a fair number of us today. For these saints of long ago, God has no failures! This perspective truly reflects a trusting faith. Is this not a tradition worthy of our emulation?

SUGGESTION FOR MEDITATION:

> O God, our help in ages past,
> Our hope for years to come;
> Our shelter from the stormy blast,
> And our eternal home!*
> > Isaac Watts (1719)

The United Methodist Hymnal (Nashville, Tenn.: United Methodist Publishing House, 1989), 117.

THURSDAY, JUNE 1 • Read Luke 24:44-53

ASCENSION DAY

The details surrounding the events of Ascension Day nicely demonstrate a prominent theme of this week's readings. Believing Christians have observed and celebrated Ascension Day on the Thursday of the sixth week after Easter since the fourth century. Those first followers of Jesus were "filled with great joy" (TEV). Now they have seen and can believe and trust totally, for Jesus has said, "Because I live, you also will live" (John 14:19, TEV). They bear witness to these events, and now they go and proclaim the good news of God's mercy to all people everywhere (Mark 16:15-16; Acts 1:8).

Today's scripture reading offers a rather detailed account of Jesus' crucifixion and resurrection, as well as the effect these events had on Jesus' disciples and eyewitnesses. When we try to put ourselves into their situation, we can better understand and appreciate their enthusiasm. Perhaps the question we need to think about is this: Do we, as believing Christians living two millennia later, feel or experience this same level of personal elation? Clearly our honest answer would be, "No, not all the time." And that response is true of those living in Jesus' day as well. The subsequent books and letters of the New Testament bear witness to that reality.

So we find ourselves once again offering our humble thanks to God through Christ for God's ongoing mercy and forgiveness. We, like Jesus' first followers, continue to stumble and fall, but we find ourselves buoyed up by honest faith and total trust. Only then may we go forth to help others, so that they may strengthen and encourage those whose lives they touch.

PRAYER: O God, illumine the path I must take this day, that I may guide and comfort all I meet. In Jesus' name. Amen.

FRIDAY, JUNE 2 • Read 1 John 5:9-13

Suspension bridges are not particularly uncommon to many Americans, especially those people living in the vicinity of the coastal regions. Daily commuters cross these engineering marvels with hardly a thought to their many implications. On the other hand, many others, having lived much or most of their lives in the country's interior, might view these marvelous accomplishments somewhat differently.

Consider a tourist from the Midwest, for instance, visiting New York City and crossing the Verrazano Narrows Bridge between Brooklyn and Staten Island for the first time. This individual may not be quite so fearless as the daily commuter. The bridge's splendor, which can be seen for miles, may bolster one's faith that the bridge's expanse reaches from one shore to the other. If the tourist continues to merely look at the bridge without crossing it, faith remains shrouded in fear. But suppose fear is overcome, and the bridge is crossed? As the traveler proceeds onto the bridge, the fuller level of confidence enables faith to become trust. Trust in the structure's ability to support allows the tourist to cross confidently over the one-mile stretch of sea water in lower New York Bay.

Such a crossing illustrates the point made by the writer of 1 John 5:9, "We accept human testimony, but surely divine testimony is stronger,...[it] is indeed that of God himself, the witness he has borne to his Son" (NEB). Just so does our faith—when coupled with honest, sincere, and confident trust—become stronger. Jesus both spoke of and demonstrated this type of trust during the period of his earthly ministry.

SUGGESTION FOR MEDITATION: Consider a situation in your life that generated fear in you. How did you respond to this situation? What experiences have built your trust?

SATURDAY, JUNE 3 • Read John 17:6-12

The seventeenth chapter of John's Gospel contains what some have called Jesus' "priestly prayer." This prayer describes events that immediately precede Jesus' arrest and death. Jesus prays, "I have made you known to those you gave me out of the world" (6, TEV). In verse 12 he continues, "While I was with them, I kept them safe by the power of your name" (TEV). Jesus' thoughts as revealed in this priestly prayer vividly convey his concern for those God has given into his care.

Reflecting on the fuller meaning of these thoughts may bring uneasiness. In deep anguish, Jesus prays in verses 9 and 10, "I do not pray for the world but for those you gave me, for they belong to you. All I have is yours, and all you have is mine; and my glory is shown through them" (TEV).

Let us consider that last thought for a moment. If God's glory in Christ is shown through us, then we must ask ourselves, "Do we honestly reflect God's love in Christ by the things we do and say?" The writer of Hebrews expresses this same idea: "It is a fearful thing to fall into the hands of the living God" (10:31, RSV).

Fearful indeed if we were to try to reflect God's love in Christ alone! Let us remember that we are not alone. In verse 9 Jesus says, "I pray for them....for those you gave me" (TEV). There's the key! God gives the believing faithful to his son's care; Jesus, in turn, prepares these committed ones to help and enable others—not just so they can better handle daily concerns, but so that they may go forth proclaiming God's love, mercy, and forgiveness! Let us then demonstrate our faith, trusting that Jesus Christ does shower the glory of God's love upon each of us, every day of our lives.

SUGGESTION FOR MEDITATION: In what areas of my life do I display Christ's glory? In what areas of my life is the light of that glory diminished?

SUNDAY, JUNE 4 • Read John 17:13-19

Verse 13 of today's reading continues the theme of God's love in Christ, which provides our assurance of faith. Jesus prays, "I say these things in the world so that they might have my joy in their hearts in all its fullness" (TEV). The assurance of these promises is essential to all who strive to be God's faithful emissaries. As our advocate, Jesus continues this plea in verse 15: "I do not ask you to take them out of the world, but I do ask you to keep them safe from the Evil One" (TEV).

Jesus surely intends to communicate these thoughts to God. However, the implications of these prayer thoughts come to rest with those who have been and continue striving to be Jesus' faithful followers. The words of his prayer in verse 16 relate a painful truth: "They are strangers in the world, as am I" (NEB). Here we see the impact of this message on our daily lives. Jesus pulls no punches, and the remaining verses of the text clearly express this truth: The believer's path will not necessarily be easy; the way will be the way of truth!

Jesus realizes the nature of the journey laid out for the faithful followers. Jesus sends them out, but their strength for the arduous journey comes from a source beyond themselves: "I dedicate myself to you, in order that they, too, may be truly dedicated to you" (TEV). The world in which we live as Christians becomes the arena for ministry. Confident of the Lord's presence, we step into this arena faithfully, trusting in the empowerment of the spirit of God's love in Christ. With this kind of assurance, let us "go and do likewise" (Luke 10:37).

SUGGESTION FOR MEDITATION: What keeps you from stepping into the world in confidence? What might bolster your faithful trust in God's ability to empower you for the journey?

Life in the Spirit

June 5–11, 2000 • M. Robert Mulholland Jr.*

MONDAY, JUNE 5 • Read Acts 2:1-4

Life in the Spirit is for others

We often remember Pentecost, the birth of the church, more for the gift of the Holy Spirit than for the purpose of the gift. This common failing of the Christian community existed throughout the ages. We consistently seek the gifts of God for ourselves rather than for God's intended purpose.

The gift of the Holy Spirit offers an ideal example. Persons often view the unbelievable gift of the very presence of God in the believer as a "possession" that sets the recipient apart from others. In some circles a hierarchy of gifts establishes a "pecking order" of different levels of being Christian.

The gifts of God, however, are not personal "prizes" in some kind of spiritual contest. The gifts of God enable us to be God's persons for others, agents of God's grace in a hurting and broken world. The events on the day of Pentecost clearly reflect this purpose. The gift of tongues, such a cause of division within the church, is given so that those of other languages might know God.

Instead of confirming us in our comfort zones, the gifts of God thrust us out beyond our comfort zones. They thrust us out to those who differ from us, to those whose "world" is far removed from ours—not necessarily in geography but in the "languages" of attitudes, perceptions, behaviors, values. We receive God's gifts not for ourselves but for the world.

PRAYER: Gracious and loving God, help me be open to all the gifts you place in my life and responsive to those persons around me for whom you intend the gifts. Amen.

---

*Vice President and Chief Academic Officer of Asbury Theological Seminary, Wilmore, Kentucky.

TUESDAY, JUNE 6 • Read Acts 2:5-13

Life in the Spirit is abandonment to God

New Testament scripture more than once links being filled with the Holy Spirit with being drunk. At Pentecost observers dismiss the disciples' behavior as drunkenness. The writer of Ephesians urges us not to be drunk with wine but to be filled with the Spirit (Eph. 5:18). Why is such an association or contrast made?

Drunken persons are no longer in control of their behavior. They abandon normal values and constraints that usually govern their behavior. They are no longer their own but under the control of an alternate mode of being.

Many of the same dynamics operate in the life of persons filled with the Spirit. Such persons are no longer in control of their life—God is. The "normal" structure of their life—that pervasive, self-oriented structure of being—is abandoned. The structure of a new self, a Christ self, begins to exercise control of their life. The values and perceptions of the false self, which carefully protects and promotes its own agenda, are replaced by the values and perceptions of the Christ self, which increasingly seeks to be God's agent of liberating grace in the life of the world. Persons filled with the Spirit are no longer their own; they are God's persons.

A life lived under the Holy Spirit's guidance may puzzle a world where life is a constant struggle to impose one's control, where manipulation, abuse, self-justification, and self-protection represent the norm. To such a world, life lived in radical abandonment to God is a life that has lost touch with reality. But being inebriated with God is true reality.

PRAYER: Gracious and loving God, fill me so full of your Spirit that my spiritual drunkenness may bring liberation and healing to the world around me. Amen.

Life in the Spirit is life in God's future

As we enter a new millennium, much is spoken and written about "the last days." Some believe that the world will never see the twenty-first century. Some believe that we are still in the "last days" since, technically, the new millennium doesn't begin until January 1, 2001. They anticipate the end of the world at the close of this year.

In his Pentecost address, Peter makes a bold assertion in his rephrasing of the passage from Joel. Joel wrote, "After these things, God declares...."* (Joel 2:28). Peter, however, sets this verse from Joel in a new frame of reference by stating, "In the last days... God declares...." For Peter, the outpouring of the Holy Spirit upon the community of Jesus' followers has inaugurated "the last days." For Peter and his hearers, "the last days" signal the coming of God's kingdom, a time when God's new order of life and wholeness will supplant the old order of death and brokenness.

Peter is only the first of the church to proclaim that, through the gift of the Holy Spirit, God's realm of wholeness and life has broken into the world's realm of brokenness and death. For century after century, the church at its best has not been obsessed with calculating "the last days." However, through the Holy Spirit, the church has consecrated itself to being the incarnation of God's realm of wholeness and life in the midst of ongoing ages.

Rather than focusing on the question, "Are we living in the last days?" a better question might be, "Are we, through the fullness of the Holy Spirit, incarnating the life and wholeness of God's everlasting realm in our days?"

PRAYER: God of all ages, may the power of your Holy Spirit manifest kingdom living in my life today. Amen.

---

*A translation from the Greek Septuagint.

THURSDAY, JUNE 8 • Read Psalm 104:24-34, 35*b*

Life in the Spirit is fullness of creation

Working out of the materialistic perspective of our culture, we often not only take creation for granted but presume it to be the ultimate reality. Human life becomes merely a more complex creation to be understood chemically, genetically, and biologically within creation.

The psalmist gives us a radical alternative. The psalmist attributes all creation to God, a frame of reference that differs greatly from that of our culture. The psalmist's understanding means that creation moves beyond its being something for our use or abuse, something to advance our purposes and fulfill our desires. Creation is part of God's purposes, and the context of human life rests within those purposes.

The psalmist goes a step further and indicates that the spirit of God animates creation, a radical contrast to our cultural belief. The psalmist reveals creation as a spiritual matter, not merely a material matter. For all too long the church has separated the "spiritual" and the "material" segments of life or, at best, held them in an uneasy tension.

The psalmist also indicates that creation is an incarnational reality—the dwelling place of God's spirit. Paul speaks of God as the one who "fills all in all" (Eph. 1:23). It is in the midst of the created order that we know God and walk with God.

Life in the Spirit is more than some kind of personal communion with God in the individuality of our being. Life in the Spirit means knowing God as the animating reality of the entire world in which we live. It entails not only knowing God as the Life of our life but of knowing God through God's creation and serving God as faithful and responsible stewards in creation.

PRAYER: God of all creation, open my eyes to see you through your creation; open my heart to love you through your creation; open my life to serve you in your creation. Amen.

FRIDAY, JUNE 9 • **Read Romans 8:22-27**

Life in the Spirit is yearning for wholeness

Creation groans (8:22), the redeemed groan (8:23), and the Spirit intercedes with sighs (8:26). The Greek term used in all three places denotes a deep, agonized yearning that wells up from the core of one's being.

Earlier Paul has said, "The creation waits with eager longing for the revealing of the children of God" (8:19), and "that the creation itself will be set free from its bondage to decay and will obtain the freedom of the glory of the children of God" (8:21). Paul seems to be saying that something in the depths of creation yearns for our wholeness as God's children.

More than that, something within the depths of our own being hungers and thirsts for that wholeness. Augustine wrote that our hearts are restless until they rest in God. We are created in God's image. Nothing short of the fullness of that image will ever satisfy the profound hunger of our hearts.

We discover the good news of this passage in God's yearning for our wholeness. Perhaps the greatest aspect of the gift of the Holy Spirit is the affirmation of God's presence in the depths of our lives, groaning and yearning and longing for our wholeness in God's own likeness.

Have you ever wanted something so badly that you could "taste" it? Something of such perceived value that you would give up everything to have it? Something of such significance that all else paled to insignificance? Have you ever realized that this longing describes God's feelings about your wholeness in God's own image? The gift of the Holy Spirit, perhaps more than anything else, is the presence of God's love that agonizes for our wholeness.

PRAYER: O God, may I groan for wholeness in your image as much as you desire it for me. Amen.

SATURDAY, JUNE 10 • Read John 16:4b-15

Life in the Spirit is Christlikeness (I)

In these passages Jesus speaks of the role of the Holy Spirit.

First, the Holy Spirit will testify about Jesus. The Spirit does this by manifesting the very nature of Jesus in the lives of believers. As the indwelling presence of Jesus, the Spirit convicts of sin, of righteousness, and of judgment.

Convict of sin—but a new definition of sin: Sin is a failure to believe in Jesus; that is, to refuse to acknowledge that Jesus is the nature of our wholeness. With this definition, sin becomes less a matter of what we do as of how we are. Paul puts it succinctly: "All have sinned and fall short of the glory of God" (Rom 3:23). When we sin we fall short of God's glory, God's nature, in which we were created. The presence of the Holy Spirit within reveals our distance from the image of God.

Convict of righteousness—"because I am going to the Father and you will see me no longer." What a strange way to convict of righteousness! What Jesus seems to say is that while he is with them, they can see what life in the image of God is like. Now the Spirit fills that role in the believer's life.

Convict of judgment—"because the ruler of this world has been condemned." The Holy Spirit constantly reminds us that life lived by the world's values, perspectives, and practices is a "dead" end.

This understanding of the gift of the Spirit differs greatly from those who think the gift of the Spirit is a personal possession that sets them apart from others, provides them with "warm fuzzies," caters to their every whim, and generally serves as their spiritual security blanket. The presence of the Spirit is a call to radical discipleship.

PRAYER: Living God, fill me and fulfill me through the gift of your Spirit. Amen.

SUNDAY, JUNE 11 • Read John 15:26-27

Life in the Spirit is Christlikeness (II)

Testifying may take place in one of two ways. One way describes the details of a matter as an observer. For example, one could testify to the nature of skiing by explaining how a person moves rhythmically and smoothly down a snow-covered slope. The other way manifests in one's own life the reality under consideration—actually skiing down the slope.

The Holy Spirit testifies in the second way. Jesus told his disciples that the Spirit of truth abode with them in his earthly presence and, after his departure, would be in them through the Holy Spirit (John 14:17). Life in the Spirit is far more than some type of ecstatic experience of God. It is the indwelling presence of the risen Lord in the believer's life, a presence so essential to Christian life that Paul says, "Anyone who does not have the Spirit of Christ does not belong to him" (Rom. 8:9).

We too are to testify in the latter manner. While we find it necessary to tell others about the fullness of God's healing and transforming love given to humans in Jesus, our more essential task is to become the presence of God's love for others. Jesus expected his followers to be like him in the world: "Very truly, I tell you, the one who believes in me will also do the works that I do and, in fact, will do greater works than these, because I am going to the Father" (John 14:12). The fruit of the Spirit-filled life, instead of setting one apart from others, is a life that manifests Christlikeness.

PRAYER: Gracious and loving God, fill me with your fullness that I may be all you want me to be in the world. Amen.

The Inner Workings of Grace

June 12–18, 2000 • *Jerry D. Keeney**

MONDAY, JUNE 12 • **Read Romans 8:12-17**

Grace is a divine energy acting within us. It is not merely a juridical decree that God pronounces over us. The Holy Spirit engages our human spirit with grace in a process of stimulus and response.

A phrase in verse 14, "led by the Spirit," is instructive for this engagement. The verb *led* also carries the meaning of "enticed, incited." The Holy Spirit leads, entices, incites the human spirit. The human spirit experiences this impulse, forms an understanding of it, tests this understanding for validity, and decides on an appropriately responsive action. The Holy Spirit teases the heart into acknowledging and responding to its true love, our "Abba."

This passage expresses the progression of this engagement within us. If we make our spirit a debt-slave to the body's random and spontaneous impulses, we are living toward death. But if our body becomes a servant (instrument) of our spirit and if our spirit responds to the Holy Spirit's enticements— that is, grace—we are living toward life. When we respond according to our nature as "image of God," we function as sons and daughters of God, reflecting the character of our "Abba." The Spirit of God does not evoke enslaving fear; it incites familial affirmation out of which our hearts emit the glad and spontaneous cry, "Abba!"

SUGGESTION FOR MEDITATION: Pay attention this week to the inner stirrings in your heart—observe, notice, own with neither self-condemnation nor pride—seeking to identify the enticements of grace and to respond in gratitude.

---

*American Baptist clergy, spiritual director, writer, retreat leader, living in St. Louis, Missouri.

TUESDAY, JUNE 13 • **Read Isaiah 6:1-3**

The defining moment of Isaiah's life crystallizes around loss. With the death of King Uzziah, a void opens in his heart that reflects a void in the nation. The king, highly respected and perhaps a close friend of Isaiah, has died after bringing Judah to its greatest glory since Solomon. The stigma of leprosy had earlier forced him from the throne, though he had continued to ensure stability for eight subsequent years as the power behind his son's throne. Now Uzziah's death jeopardizes the future of Isaiah's beloved community.

Where might one turn in such a disorienting time? Isaiah turns to the Temple with its familiar ritual. He finds more than ritual; he finds God. Maybe Uzziah's death served as the indispensable condition for Isaiah's seeing God. The Hebrew reads, "In the year of the death of King Uzziah, then I saw the Lord." While the Hebrew form makes this statement implicitly temporal, it might suggest in our minds a causal relationship. Had this earthly ruler and friend become a heretofore unsuspected obstacle to Isaiah's seeing the real Ruler and ultimate Friend? Were Isaiah's life and the life of the nation so centered in King Uzziah that they had transferred all their hope and accountability from the real Ruler to this earthly one? Did the disappearance of a temporal object of Isaiah's desire for meaning, purpose, and fulfillment free his heart to see his desire's infinite, ultimate, eternal, and only true object? Perhaps the void that Uzziah's death hollows out in Isaiah's heart is the only uncluttered space available into which grace could make its move.

SUGGESTION FOR MEDITATION: **Has a "king"—some ruling force in your life—died, creating an opportunity to see the real Ruler? Does some ruling pattern in your life need to be dismantled in order to open a space where grace can operate afresh?**

WEDNESDAY, JUNE 14 • Read Isaiah 6:4-8, 13

Picture a majestic oak dominating the landscape. Now picture a stump where the oak stood. This image of Judah cut down expresses the profound foreboding that King Uzziah's death causes in Isaiah. Yet the stump serves as a sign of promise, not doom, at the conclusion of Isaiah's call experience. What happens to transform the stump into a symbol of hope rather than despair? The contrast between God's holiness and Judah's unfaithfulness shocks Isaiah into recognizing and confessing his complicity in Judah's vulnerability. Then, touching a live coal to his "unclean lips," the Lord cleanses Isaiah's troubled soul, saying, "Your guilt is removed and your sin erased" (AP).

Imagine the stunning effect these words have in a soul filled with self-loathing. Isaiah sits for a long moment, awed by the paradox of fresh vitality at the very point where, moments earlier, the live coal had threatened injury and even death. He savors the singing currents of new life, as an Adam awakening into the first, freshest awareness of having just been created in God's image.

No wonder Isaiah's vision concludes with the stump as holy seed (6:13), rather than Judah as dead stump. His experience of the inner birth of new life assures him that "there shall come forth a shoot from the stump of Jesse" (11:1, AP). Isaiah knows this because he is of this stump, and its new life already sprouts in him. Going forth now as God's spokesperson, his message will be more than a theological abstraction; it will be grace embodied—and infused into the community.

SUGGESTION FOR MEDITATION: What part of your body / soul will be cleansed and regenerated when the live coal of God's grace touches it? How can you share your "good-news" life with the community?

A boy helping at a concession stand secretly pockets coins, perceiving this as his only means of buying a coveted pair of cowboy boots. A father repeatedly buys his son out of trouble to protect a college sports career that promises a future in professional sports. An Olympic skater conspires to injure a competitor to improve her own chances of winning gold.

These instances all ascribe glory to the wrong object. Such pursuit distorts priorities, corrupts values, injures character, and erodes justice. When we ascribe to God the glory due God's name, we do more for ourselves than for God. We order our lives aright as we recognize and extol the beauty of God's true nature and character. When we fail to ascribe the glory that is due God, we establish a spiritual disorder in our lives with repercussions in our relationships and society. What should be valued is demeaned, and what should be deemphasized is magnified.

Another form of spiritual disorder stems from attributing to God something other than glory, ascribing to God qualities that are untrue to God's character, such as aloofness, indifference, and distance. To impute these qualities distorts our image of God and limits our ability to know God truly. If we ascribe to God petty anger, graceless judgment, and begrudging acceptance toward human beings, our image of God will dispose us to avoid divine encounter rather than seek it.

Because what we glorify reveals more about the dynamics operating in us than about that which we glorify, "Ascribe to the Lord the glory of his name."

PRAYER: May the glory of your goodness, beauty, and truth, O God, throw its light across all that draws me today, clarifying my choices and bolstering my integrity. Amen.

FRIDAY, JUNE 16 • Read John 3:1-17

Nicodemus, at middle age, has long ago settled into a pattern of religious life. Firmly ensconced in the leadership group (the Sanhedrin) that defines religious correctness, his religious questions are all answered—or so he thinks. Then a young man, Jesus, comes teaching, preaching, healing. He is attractive but disturbing. Nicodemus notes discrepancies between Jesus' teachings and the tradition. A discussion with him could be useful.

Discreetly Nicodemus visits Jesus and broaches the subject of Jesus' mighty works. Jesus gently redirects Nicodemus's attention by suggesting, "Nicodemus, you can't be seeing the kingdom unless you're being born of the Spirit" (AP).

Nicodemus takes this comment personally, replying incredulously, "How can a man be born when he is old?" (RSV) Perhaps he is asking, "Can it be that what I thought was simple curiosity is the very spirit of God stirring in my heart? Is new life in this middle-aged heart really possible?" His mind leaps on to ask, "Can one enter a second time into the mother's womb and be born?" Thus he clumsily breaks through the boundaries of rigid, conformist rationalism; he moves from left-brain to right-brain operations with the emotional disorientation that often accompanies spiritual reorientation.

Notice what Jesus has done. He has deftly refocused Nicodemus's attention, turning it from theological abstractions about outward forms to the operations of grace in his personal experience. Jesus recognizes the ferment of grace in Nicodemus's heart, affirms it, and helps him explore it. Jesus is a master spiritual guide, more concerned to bring the Spirit to birth in the soul than to condemn the soul.

PRAYER: Jesus, lead me into the depths of my soul and expose to me the operations of your love there. Bring your Spirit to birth in me again today. Amen.

SATURDAY, JUNE 17 • Read John 3:16

Anselm of Canterbury (1033–1109 C.E.) said, "I believe so that I may understand, and what is more I believe that unless I do believe, I shall not understand" (*Prayers and Meditations*). Believing means (a) giving mental assent to ideas and (b) exercising trust. John talks about our believing in relation to Jesus in a particular way. The phrase in John 3:16 is literally "believes into him." Embracing Christ with a mind-set of trust positions us in a Christ-centered frame of reference. It places us in a new spiritual atmosphere where we breathe the breath of God, the Holy Spirit. The Breath blows on the coal of the image of God within us, igniting eternal life, life that partakes of God's very nature.

Jesus encourages this movement of mind and will in Nicodemus, and John seeks to stimulate this movement in his reader when he speaks of the pivotal act of "believing into him." "Believing into Christ" reverses a process of "perishing" and begins a process of "gracing." To perish is to waste away, to rot; grace continues forever, ripening us and bearing the fruits of the Spirit within us. "Believing into Christ," then, is not a merely forensic transaction that alters our standing before God. It is a movement of the heart—stimulated by grace—that ignites the growth of Christ-life in us.

Does Nicodemus make this move; does he "believe into Christ"? John 7:50-51 and 19:39-40 offer evidence that he does. Do we continue to make this move in daily response to grace? Where is the evidence?

PRAYER: Brother Jesus, I trust you. Ignite in me this day that which expresses the beauty, goodness, and truth of your Spirit, to the glory of God. Amen.

SUNDAY, JUNE 18 • Read Romans 8:12-17

Abba is an Aramaic word that encompasses the spontaneously intimate, trusting love between a child and a father. Jesus' use of the word in reference to God is truly striking—even shocking—for his use denotes his wholly different footing with God than that of the conventional religious leaders of his time. Religion avoided speaking the name of God (YHWH). A sincere but rigid reverence created cold distance between God and God's people in contrast to Jesus' intimacy with God. Jesus' reverence for God found root in an intimacy that flows from awareness that the Holy One is not at arm's length, let alone light years' length, from us. God is within our heart's embrace.

As a grandfather I have a feel for this kind of intimate relationship. For a time when our grandson was about eighteen months old, he used the word *daddy* to address me as well as his father. When he addressed his father it was "Daddy!" When he addressed me it was "Daddee!" He knew which of us he was calling, and we knew which one should answer. He knew which was his father and which his grandfather, and he valued supremely his daddy's presence. However, his use of the same word to address me and his father, with the only variance being one of inflection, conveys something so special in its effect on me that words only hint of it. Similarly, Jesus' use of *Abba* implies a reaching for a distinctive word to express his intimate experience of God and to evoke in us a response of glad and trusting love toward God.

When we cry to God "Abba!" with the desire, the trust, and the expectancy of a beloved child, that experience bears witness to the grace at work in our heart.

PRAYER: Abba!

Human Weakness and God's Power

June 19–25, 2000 • Ha-Kyung Cho-Kim*

MONDAY, JUNE 19 • Read 1 Samuel 17:32-49

A young David without armor faces a seasoned warrior who comes prepared for battle. When David faces a giant champion named Goliath, he fights as the representative of Israel just as Goliath represents the Philistine army. The armies agree that if David kills Goliath, the Philistines will serve the Israelites. But if Goliath wins, the Israelites will serve the Philistines. From a human perspective, the odds clearly favor Goliath.

David relies on God's strength for this battle. In the past he has experienced God's power when he faced lions and bears victoriously. In each case he cast himself on God, and God rescued and sustained him. David's experiences give him courage to face Goliath; he commits himself to the Lord's cause completely. David knows his own weakness, but he trusts in God's power. This trust enables him to stand before the great giant and win the victory.

In the same manner we can face our "Goliath" in life because we can count on God's strength. We too remember God's rescue and protection of us in the past. And we trust that God will do the same in present situations. We recall that David was a man of prayer. Let us tap into God's power through our spiritual disciplines so that we find the strength to engage in the struggle of freeing others from their "Goliath."

PRAYER: O Lord, give me boldness to overcome giants in my life. I do not want to depend on my own power but on your strength. Empower me to be and do more than I can think and imagine. Amen.

---

*Resource Director for the New England Conference, The United Methodist Church, living in Amesbury, Massachusetts.

TUESDAY, JUNE 20 • Read Psalm 9:9-20

Inspired by God the psalmist records much of his own personal experience, which allows him to affirm, "The Lord is a refuge for the oppressed, / a stronghold in times of trouble. / Those who know your name will trust in you, for you, Lord, have never forsaken those who seek you" (NIV). As I recall the events of my own life, I must confess that God has comforted me and healed my broken spirit when I experienced injustice in the form of sexism, racism, and classism.

I embraced Christianity at the age of sixteen. The gospel of Jesus Christ freed me from the bondage of sin, ignorance, and self-pity. I got excited because the evangelist John said, "But to all who received him, who believed in his name, he gave power to become children of God, who were born, not of blood or of the will of the flesh, but of God" (John 1:12-13). To me the gospel brought the message that all are equal; all have the right to become "blessed" children of God through the work of Christ.

But as I grow older I face the reality that walls and boundaries separate me from others—the walls and boundaries of gender and skin color. These walls and boundaries exist even in the church. As a pastor, I also have to face people's fear of strangers.

God compels us to pursue an active search for blessed and abundant life. God journeys with us in the search, revealing the goal, pointing the way, and encouraging us to go on. God journeys with us in the search for justice and *shalom* (peace). The search is a difficult one because it often seems that we can only have one without the other: peace, at the cost of leaving injustice unchallenged; or justice, at the cost of a broken peace.

PRAYER: Lord, show me how I can overcome injustice and strive for *shalom* without recourse to violence, hatred, and resentment. May I be an instrument of your peace. Amen.

WEDNESDAY, JUNE 21 • Read 2 Corinthians 6:1-10

As servants of Christ, Paul and his coworkers endure a great deal of suffering—"afflictions, hardships, calamities, beatings, imprisonments, riots, labors, sleepless nights, hunger" for God's ministry of reconciliation. Practicing Christian virtues (vv. 6-7) enables them to overcome suffering in Christ. They experience fully the paradox of living "in honor and dishonor, in ill repute and good repute."

Dr. M. Scott Peck, in his book *Further Along the Road Less Traveled*, distinguishes between two kinds of suffering: constructive and unconstructive. "Unconstructive suffering, like headaches, is something you ought to get rid of. Constructive suffering you ought to bear and work through" (21). He stresses our need to learn to bear and work through the constructive suffering, or "existential suffering." In other words, God helps us develop Christian character traits, such as courage, through life's suffering. Dr. Peck defines courage as "the capacity to go ahead in spite of...the pain" (23) to meet life's demands.

I think Paul had that courage and understood the paradox of life in Christ. Indeed, Paul did not paint a rosy picture of the life of discipleship. Most early church leaders were jailed and tortured. Many were killed. Instead of asking why suffering occurs and how a loving God can even allow it to exist, let us ask God for the courage to overcome the suffering in Christ.

PRAYER: Lord Jesus, I have feared the pain and suffering that love brings. Give me courage to risk and to embrace suffering for your name's sake. Amen.

THURSDAY, JUNE 22 • Read 2 Corinthians 6:11-13

No one wants to wear the label of "failure." In fact, Paul prays that God deliver him from his affliction. Three times he asks God about his "thorn in the flesh," and God replies, "My grace is sufficient for you, for power is made perfect in weakness" (2 Cor. 12:9).

I remember when my mother, a faithful minister of the word of God, was struck down by a stroke. Like Paul, she prayed for healing, but she did not get well. Many of her Christian friends unkindly questioned her faith, having been influenced by the teachings of the "Success and Wealth Theology." God used my mother's life in mighty ways, and yet her request for recovery was not granted.

She experienced disgrace, and she cried out like Paul: "Open wide your hearts also." I would think that her friends' abandonment hurt her very deeply. During the last six years of her life, she endured the loneliness of suffering. And God used it to sanctify her, forming her in the image of Jesus Christ. My mother often quoted 1 Corinthians 1:27: "God chose the foolish things of the world to shame the wise; God chose the weak things of the world to shame the strong" (NIV).

Admitting our weakness makes us humble; we learn to lean on God's strength. I suspect that without his weakness, Paul would have trusted his own strength rather than the power of the Holy Spirit working through him.

PRAYER: O God, have mercy on me and do not abandon me as others do when I am in trouble. Hear my cry; come to me; walk with me through "the dark night in order to wean it from sweetness and to purify its sensual desires." Amen. (*Daily Readings with St. John of the Cross*, 24).

FRIDAY, JUNE 23 • Read Mark 4:35-38

This miracle and the one that follows tell of happenings that take place on "the other side," which is Gentile territory. I visited the lake on which this storm occurred, and our lecturer indicated that sudden storms still occur today as they did in biblical times. He explained that the storm is like a "tornado within the sea."

In today's reading, the wind and the waves fill Jesus' disciples with fear. The disciples waken Jesus, saying, "Teacher, don't you care if we drown?" Their fear of death leads to panic.

As a young child I experienced the horror of the Korean War. My mother and I survived the B-29 bombing, but we lost five members of our family. During the war I witnessed human cruelty expressed toward other human beings. These events caused me to take life and human depravity seriously. I learned to look for the really important, rather than for the superficialities. Early on I learned that human existence has limits: We all will die. Then what is the meaning of life between birth and death? I have come to the conclusion that life on earth is like a "boot camp," equipped with many obstacles and screaming sergeants. Our living, loving, and learning in this life determine how we spend eternity.

Shortly after giving birth to a baby girl, I nearly died. My experience of that time was so wonderful and peaceful—I happily found myself in the presence of the risen Lord. But my mother's intercessory prayer to Christ drew me back to life. The experience has convinced me that we need not fear death when we live under God's grace and power.

PRAYER: O risen Lord, help me overcome the fear of death. May your Resurrection power bring joy and boldness and allow them to flow through my life so that I may be your faithful servant. Amen.

SATURDAY, JUNE 24 • Read Mark 4:35-41

We notice Jesus' calm serenity, which strongly contrasts with the disciples' terror. One thing we must note in this miracle is Jesus' example of absolute peace and confidence. The miracle points us beyond the storms and stresses of life to the One who controls nature. And like the disciples, we too raise the question: "Who is this?"

Jesus, awakened by the horrified disciples, "rebuked the wind and said to the waves, 'Quiet! Be still!' Then the wind died down and it was completely calm....[The disciples] were terrified and asked each other, 'Who is this? Even the wind and the waves obey him!'" (NIV). The answer to their question and ours is that this is Christ, the Son of God and the Lord of nature and all of life. We confess that too often in the stresses and storms of life, we panic and begin to question God's ways, which lie beyond our understanding.

Let us not allow the stress and strife of our present situation to overwhelm us. Instead let us seek to understand what we can learn from the situation. We need to remember God's presence with us in the past and affirm God's continued presence with us. Experiences of stress and strife can help us grow in the Spirit, making us more open, genuine, sincere, transparent persons. Faith that expresses courage in the face of life's great storms looks beyond the things that are and encourages us to dream (envision) the things that can be. Let us be quiet and still. Let us trust God who gives us serenity and confidence.

PRAYER: God, grant me the Serenity to accept the things I cannot change, the Courage to change the things I can, and the Wisdom to know the difference. Amen.

SUNDAY, JUNE 25 • **Read 2 Corinthians 6:1-13;
Mark 4:35-41**

God must delight in using weak and imperfect people. King David and Jesus' disciples provide good examples. God answers a polite "no" to Paul's request for removal of his "thorn in the flesh." God's reply is, "My grace is sufficient for you, for my power is made perfect in weakness." God seems to say to Paul, "Trust me, Paul, your disappointments are my appointments." The result is history: Paul planted churches all over the known world.

History shows us that God uses imperfect people despite their weaknesses and failures. John Calvin, a lawyer-theologian, left a wholesome impression upon the life of his day, yet he burned Servetus on the grounds that he was an Anabaptist. John Wesley, the founder of Methodism, failed the Georgia mission and made a disappointing husband. The Puritans of New England contributed greatly to the cause of civil liberty and to the work of education, yet they harried the life out of some of their own women whom they believed to be witches. We too have weaknesses. Accepting our human weaknesses makes us humble and encourages us to seek "a spirit of power, of love and of self-discipline" (2 Tim. 1:7, NIV).

We give our praise and thanksgiving to God, who delights in using weak and imperfect persons like you and me; who encourages us to begin again; who is transforming us to become servants with the Christlike virtues of "purity, understanding, patience and kindness;…sincere love;…truthful speech" (2 Cor. 6:6-7, NIV).

PRAYER: Dear God of constant love and faithfulness, I yield to your transforming power so that my caring and sharing may resemble the pattern of the life of your son, Christ Jesus. Amen.

Generosity and Anguish

June 26–July 2, 2000 • Laurence Hull Stookey*

MONDAY, JUNE 26 • Read 2 Samuel 1:1, 17-27

Generosity and anguish seem inseparable partners. David's agonized lament grows out of a great generosity. There is first David's generosity toward Saul in declining to slay the monarch when the opportunity exists. Stronger still is Jonathan's generosity to David; as the king's eldest son, Jonathan might well expect to inherit the throne. Yet he befriends the outsider who will be given the crown. Indeed when it seems Saul might slay David, Jonathan intervenes to protect his friend from his father's wrath.

Out of all this generosity comes monumental grief, for we weep most bitterly at the deaths of those whose love we have experienced most amply, not at the funerals of strangers. This is one of the laws of life. But another such law is that beyond the tears, generosity begets generosity. Ultimately King David seeks out the sole living heir of Jonathan, Mephibosheth, and takes him into the palace as if he were a son; in the face of the revolt by David's biological son Absalom, Mephibosheth rewards David's generosity with loyalty (see 2 Sam. 9:1-13; 16:1-4; 19:24-30; 21:7).

What is evident in human interactions is writ large in the divine nature. God is both the most fully generous and the most deeply anguished being in the universe. That is why the cross is the central symbol of our faith; there these two forces intersect, and in their intersection we identify the source of the world's salvation.

PRAYER: Bountiful Sufferer, reveal to me and to all people your graciousness and your agony; enable me to use sharing and sorrowing redemptively. Amen.

---

*Hugh Latimer Elderdice Professor of Preaching and Worship, Wesley Theological Seminary, Washington, D.C.

Jairus experiences torment; his little daughter's life hangs in the balance. Even as he appeals to Jesus, members of the leader's household come saying, "Your daughter is dead. Why trouble the teacher any further?" By their counsel, they set generosity and anguish in opposition: "Don't ask Jesus to give precious time to a hopeless cause. Come home quietly, Jairus, and bear your sorrow bravely."

These household members have noble intentions. Being religious people, they know the multiple pressures religious leaders ever confront; they do not wish to wear Jesus out with pointless requests. ("Pastor, we didn't call you to tell you Dad was ill; he was in a terminal coma. You are so busy, and we knew there was nothing you could do for him.")

But people in anguish are rarely in a position to judge what is beyond hope and what is possible for the astounding generosity of God. Knowing this, Jesus ignores the well-intended members of Jairus's household and goes to the bedside. The people are "overcome with amazement" at the result of Jesus' ministry there.

While at times we must refrain from wasting our energies on marginal causes, at other times, like Jesus, we must override those who wish to protect us, for only by so doing may the generosity of God be revealed. The task of knowing when to guard against what is popularly called "burnout" and when to be prodigal with our assistance sometimes calls for the discernment of a Solomon. But the self-giving heart of God always turns to those in distress. Even if we cannot raise the dead, we are emissaries of One whose goodness can cause others to be "overcome with amazement."

SUGGESTION FOR MEDITATION: **Recall times when with great benefit you have ignored the counsel of those who sought to protect you. Pray for wisdom to know in the future when to use your "veto" power.**

WEDNESDAY, JUNE 28 • Read Mark 5:25-34

In the account of the woman who touches Jesus' cloak, Jesus apparently is unwittingly generous. Without his consent, the anguished woman seems literally to have pulled energy out of him, so that he knows "immediately...that power had gone forth from him." Caught in this act, the woman expects a stern rebuke that is not forthcoming. Jesus will not add to her dozen years of suffering by condemning her desperate action; instead he commends her faith.

Is it possible that true faith can involve a bold initiative on the part of the believer, such that power goes forth from God? As a professor of worship in a seminary, I frequently find that direct prayers trouble some students; they fear they will offend God with their forthrightness. Instead of praying, "O God, save us from our confusion," they deem it better to say, "O God, we hope that perhaps you might somehow consider saving us from our confusion."

But in giving us the Lord's Prayer, Jesus taught us boldness. Our having asked initially that God's will be done frees us to be almost outrageously demanding: "Give us. Forgive us. Save us. Deliver us." If we are in true distress (for this is no excuse for frivolous requests), by praying with such directness, we reach out and touch the cloak of the Almighty. And at this God does not take offense but actually commends us for our forthrightness. Such a daring approach to God puts us squarely within what some would call "the chutzpah tradition" of Hebraic piety. When we suffer anguish, we have a claim on the mercy of God—not because we are perfectly pleasing to our creator, but because God is hopelessly generous toward creation.

PRAYER: When I am in distress, O Lord, free me from all timidity; give me the nerve to draw forth power from your ample storehouse. Amen.

THURSDAY, JUNE 29 • **Read 2 Corinthians 8:7-11**

Paul is raising money for the poor in the church at Jerusalem. He appeals to the pocketbooks of the Corinthians by citing "the generous act of our Lord Jesus Christ, that though he was rich, yet for your sakes he became poor." The rationale is not "Do unto others as you would have them do unto you," but "Do unto others as Christ has done unto you."

A beggar accosted a social worker and a client while they walked. The social worker ignored the appeal, while the woman on welfare gave the man a dollar. Aghast, the social worker exclaimed, "You can't afford that!" The woman replied, "You and others have been so generous in aiding me. And shall I turn aside this man who has even less than I have?" This woman responded because of an example. So Paul asks the Corinthians to respond to the character of God: Do unto others as God in Christ has done unto you.

Statistically, those in lower economic categories proportionally give away more than those in upper brackets. Why? Likely because the poor know how much the help of others means, while we the affluent kid ourselves into believing, "I did it on my own. So can you." Those who live on the edge know best the value of generosity. And the Incarnation notifies us of how close we are to the edge and of what we cannot do for ourselves; through that self-emptying, God reveals (often to our discomfort) our deep indebtedness to grace.

Thus Paul calls us to "excel" in generosity. A popular maxim advises us that it is impossible to be too rich or too thin. But that is not the biblical word. The biblical word is this: "It is impossible to be too generous."

PRAYER: O God, you have given me so much. In the midst of that abundance give to me one thing more; grant that I may excel in having a generous heart. Amen.

FRIDAY, JUNE 30 • Read 2 Corinthians 8:12-15

If Paul's argument in verse 14 seems convoluted, his proof-text in verse 15 seems a piece of tortured exegesis. Read wrongly, his citation from Exodus 16:18 can be taken to mean: "Rich as they are, the rich do not have too much; so let them keep it. And poor as they are, those in poverty still have enough; let them be satisfied."

But that is not the meaning; the verse Paul cites is from the story of the manna in the desert. There God provided each of the Israelites with the same amount of this mysterious food, whether they harvested abundantly or sparsely. Thus, of those who gathered more manna and those who gathered less, each was discovered to have the same amount. God graciously provides for all. Everyone will have enough.

So Paul asks the Corinthians to live out God's equality by sharing with those in need. Anguish on the part of some of God's people should call forth generosity from the rest of God's people. Thereby all will have adequate provision, as they did when God gave manna in the desert. To us, the message is this: An interdependence of action edifies all of God's creation.

Too often we prefer to cherish a stubborn sense of independence, but this leads to a destructive social isolation. Perhaps a symptom of such isolation is the deferral of intended action. Paul implies that the Corinthians "last year" eagerly started a fund-raising campaign but never completed it. How often have our intentions to be generous gotten stalled? What have you intended to do and not gotten around to doing that might be taken up and put into action this very day?

PRAYER: Abundant Giver of all that is good, create in me both a generous heart and a zeal to put into practice now all that I have intended to do but have too long deferred. Make this day my occasion for action. Amen.

The beginning of this psalm recapitulates all we have been considering this week. We do not know precisely what plunged the psalmist into the depths; it seems to have been some action deemed sinful, so that the distressed author cries out: "If you, O Lord, should mark iniquities, Lord, who could stand?"

Perhaps Christians in our age have so overreacted to the legacy of a medieval preoccupation with guilt that we hardly think of ourselves as sinners at all. But the psalmist calls us home. Were God to keep tally of our sins, who could be justified in the face of divine righteousness? A realistic answer will engender anguish in anyone.

But a joyful exclamation immediately follows: "There is forgiveness with you, so that you may be revered." And therein is the beginning of our preparation for the celebration of the Lord's Day today. We go to worship tomorrow not out of habit or social convention but out of gratitude for the generosity of God. Reverence springs from astonishment and astonishment from a comparison of our failings to God's faithfulness.

Jesus' resurrection demonstrates that divine faithfulness most convincingly, and the the Lord's Day serves as a perpetual commemoration of that event. Thus we make our preparation for Sunday worship in the conviction the God does not leave us in the depths but hears our plea and sends deliverance. What God does for us God does for all who cry for help.

PRAYER: Helper of the helpless and hope of the forlorn, blessed are you for your goodness. By the grace that saves us, transform me and your whole church, sanctifying your people for service by the power of the Spirit. Amen.

SUNDAY, JULY 2 • Read Psalm 130:5-8

Having contemplated personal anguish and divine generosity, the psalmist concentrates finally on patient waiting and fervent hope as interlocking characteristics of God's people.

If we are unwilling to wait, we are beyond the possibility of hope; we may as well give ourselves over to utter despair. And if there is nothing for which to hope, waiting is pointless; we may as well fall immediately into total hedonism (which may indeed be the same thing as utter despair). Fortunately the very nature of God spares us from this morass.

All across the world this day Christ's people assemble to praise the God of hope, upon whom we wait more than a sentinel watches for dawn. This regular weekly praise is itself a form of testimony—a witness to an often forlorn or jaded world that God is worthy (the root word of our term *worship*) to be served consistently and that the idols will all fail us, despite their seductive glamour and distracting charm.

Today the church cries to the world as the psalmist cried to Israel: "All peoples, hope in the Lord. For with the Lord there is steadfast love." At the same time that we address the world, we address ourselves, for the church is never far from slipping into distraction and idolatry. That is why week after week we are called to worship, to hear anew the word of the Lord in which resides our hope.

We remember then this day all of our sisters and brothers in the faith and bind ourselves to them in prayer and mutual concern. With the faithful people of every age and place, we wait patiently and hope fervently for the salvation of our God.

PRAYER: **Renew your church, O Lord, that the people you have redeemed may rejoice and give faithful witness of your graciousness to an anguished world. Amen.**

God's Life on Earth

July 3–9, 2000 • Patricia Beall Gavigan*

MONDAY, JULY 3 • **Read Mark 6:1-6**

We easily recognize powerful gifts. A powerful speaker with captivating stories provides a dual attraction of entertainment and knowledge! We not only hear; we see. And sight reveals both the astounding event and the one who empowered it. Truly, powerful gifts are difficult to deny.

But we can separate the gifts from the person, which is what the people of Nazareth do when Jesus returns home after weeks of powerful itinerant ministry. Some in Nazareth cannot accept his teaching and wisdom because he doesn't have the right credentials or profession: "Is not this the carpenter?"

Some in Nazareth find Jesus' capabilities unbelievable because they deem him "one of us." He can't be extraordinary: "Look, we know his mother is Mary; we know all his brothers, and here are his sisters." Many find Jesus undesirable because he requires change. He places safe understandings, cherished prejudices, social certainties, religious convictions, secure traditions, and predictable future at risk.

Unacceptable, unbelievable, undesirable. Are you like those in Nazareth? In whom do you recognize powerful gifts yet reject personally? When do you trust the currency of common humanity and deny the uniqueness of the Incarnation? Where do you accept the works of God yet deny the person of God? How does Jesus threaten your future?

PRAYER: Lord, I want you to do mighty works in my life and my surroundings. Help me answer these questions honestly, then work by your Spirit to change me. Amen.

---

*Cofounder and Executive Administrator of South Park Community Trust, a Christian charity in England; writer, teacher, and preacher.

TUESDAY, JULY 4 • Read 2 Samuel 5:1-5, 9-10

These initial words spoken to David have import beyond his own time. They call to mind a primary theme developed in ever-increasing depth throughout the Bible: the mystery between deity and humanity, between spirit and flesh. What, if anything, have they to do with each other? Many societies have perceived God as "other," different, remote, powerful—often sinister. Usually God is not knowable. Then we have people—"us," ourselves, others—whom we know and don't know, whom we love and fear. The perceived gap between people and God has always existed. Gaps between people vary depending on kinship, geography, culture.

This story evidences no gap between people. The tribes greet David with the words, "We are your own flesh and blood" (NIV). From the same nation, they mean these words literally. But Jesus has not always been our own "flesh and blood." Alive with God, Jesus' nature is spirit; but at the set time he is transformed, taking on flesh and coming to dwell among us. Jesus becomes human, physically flesh and blood. Because of this, we who believe in Jesus also experience transformation. Baptism births us anew, and God's spirit infuses our being.

Life takes on new and startling meaning. We exist not only as individuals, but we have a corporate life. As members together, our physical bodies compose the physical body of Christ on earth. Jesus is not tangibly present, humanly present; but we are—filled with God's spirit, living God's life, doing God's work. Christians often recognize one another even if they have not met previously. They know one another; they are one. The Spirit has empowered them to say, "We are your flesh and blood." Jesus has filled the gap between God and people. Jesus' life in us fills the gap between people and people.

PRAYER: Spirit of life, enable me to become more profound and more practical in my membership in Christ's body. Amen.

WEDNESDAY, JULY 5 • Read 2 Samuel 5:1-5, 9-10

At last David takes up his kingship! Herein we discover evocative links with Jesus, the king who is to come. Bethlehem figures significantly in both men's lives, serving as David's home and Jesus' birthplace. A sense of pilgrimage is also present: The prophet Samuel journeys there to find David; Mary and Joseph journey there for the census.

Both David and Jesus wait years to take a public position. While anointed king many years earlier, David is no usurper. He evidences radical faithfulness to the increasingly demented Saul. Many times Saul tries to kill him; nonetheless, David trusts in God, venerating Saul as God's anointed leader. After Saul's death in battle, political machinations to establish David on the throne more quickly lead to the cold-blooded murders of both Abner, Saul's army commander, and Ish-bosheth, Saul's direct heir. In each instance, David repudiates the action and has the perpetrators killed. He will become king only in God's own time. Similarly, Jesus also waits for God's time. He remains silent and hidden well into adulthood before being stirred by the Spirit into a public position.

David's boyhood vocation is that of shepherd. At his anointing Samuel declares God's word: "You…shall be shepherd of my people Israel." Jesus extends this role, declaring, "I am the good shepherd. The good shepherd lays down his life for the sheep" (John 10:11). The first king looks after God's people; the second king dies for them.

"David was thirty years old when he began to reign"; tradition says that Jesus was thirty years old when he began his ministry. And "at Jerusalem [David] reigned over all Israel and Judah thirty-three years"; at Jerusalem Jesus gave up his life for all the world at thirty-three years.

PRAYER: Holy God, may these links of place, patience, and purpose connect me to greater and more passionate service to you and others. Amen.

THURSDAY, JULY 6 • Read Psalm 48

Earth, animals, people, time, space—all creations of God. All created by God, all gifts of life. But all from another dimension, another realm. We call God's habitation "heaven"—but what or where is it? We call God's environment "eternity"—but what do we really comprehend? We perceive and believe God's being as "spirit"—but what can we really express? Very little, for we are creatures of flesh. We dwell in a material world. Yet certain things that may not matter ultimately do matter a great deal now.

One of these is place. An offspring of space, place is of great importance. As creatures of the earth, we find it impossible to experience anything lest it happen in a particular place. Even the most mystical experiences can't occur unless one is located! Throughout the Bible and in this week's scriptures especially, we see that place means a great deal to God.

Micah proclaims Bethlehem, David's city, to be God's chosen place generations before Jesus' birth. Jesus is unable to minister in Nazareth. He has to go elsewhere to do the works of God. David captures and rebuilds Jerusalem, formerly a Jebusite stronghold. It becomes Israel's capital: the focus for worship and center of government. Zion becomes a visible sign of unity in a country devastated by war.

Place has importance for us too. Reflect on your home, your place of work, your places of service. These places bear witness to God's work in your daily living; they are holy; they are your Zion. With others—either many or just a few—do what the psalmist exhorts: "Walk about Zion, go all around it, count its towers, consider well its ramparts; go through its citadels."

Walk, go round, pray, bless. Consecrate again these physical places, where God lives through you on earth today.

PRAYER: Holy Spirit, lead me deeper into the mystery of God's life through the places in my life. Amen.

FRIDAY, JULY 7 • **Read 2 Corinthians 12:2-7**

Love sometimes compels us to do foolish things—things against our better judgment, things that give away too much, things that we regret even as they're happening.

So with Paul. Burdened by his love, compelled by his desire to communicate, quite against his own desire he tells his beloved Corinthians something that he wishes he might keep to himself. He recounts a mystical encounter. He attempts to describe heavenly mysteries experienced on earth. But he's pressed, awkward. He knows he cannot adequately describe them. We experience his frustration. Although fourteen years have passed, he is still unable to fathom what really happened.

Where was Paul in time? Where was he in space? What was happening to his physical body? What words of God or wonders of worship did he hear? What spiritual realities are either so delicate or so explosive that humans may not speak them? Paul writes of Paradise but can make no earthly sense of it. We experience his confusion as he repeats, "Whether in the body or out of the body I do not know; God knows." We will never know many things. Yet many things God would tell us willingly. With love as our motivation, the greater becomes our capacity to receive God's gifts and experience God's mysteries.

Christ's passionate love for God and people empowered his service and led to his suffering. Paul's passionate love for Christ enabled his service and suffering. God gave each all that was necessary—the grace, the spiritual experiences, the physical resources—to live his vocation fully, as difficult as that vocation was.

So with us. Let love be the ground of our being and the source of our life, and God will empower and enable us.

PRAYER: Lord Jesus, pour the wisdom of love's foolishness into my open heart. Amen.

SATURDAY, JULY 8 • Read 2 Corinthians 12:7-10

These are moving, extraordinary verses. They spotlight a person completely captivated by Christ. Initially Jesus' brightness blinds Paul. Subsequently Paul allows Christ to overshadow virtually everything in his life. Paul's abandon is complete, his fidelity flawless. Paul enacts this fidelity in his daily life and service. There is no place Paul won't go, no mission he'll refuse if the Spirit directs. This scripture emphasizes not only his willingness but also his contentment "with weaknesses, insults, hardships, persecutions, and calamities." Paul endures the awful realities of his vocation.

Paul's humility heightens this commitment further. Apparently the perfectionism that tempts many of God's servants does not tempt Paul. He has gone even further: "I will boast all the more gladly of my weaknesses, so that the power of Christ may dwell in me." Paul, liberated by Christ, does not attempt to hide or protect his areas of vulnerability.

In one key area, however, Paul doesn't seem to have an accurate understanding of his own personality or of God's. Read verse 7 again. Certainly he understands the thorn in his flesh to be a messenger of Satan, but perhaps this thorn does not exist, as Paul reasons, "to keep me from being too elated." God loved Paul deeply, trusted him profoundly. God gave Paul the revelations and visions, and God gives freely. God does not ask us to pay a price for God's own giving.

More likely, Paul's "thorn" is part of the terrible cost he pays in his humanity for his deep involvement with God's work on earth. This involvement makes him vulnerable to spiritual dynamics otherwise hidden, and Paul ceaselessly challenges the powers and principalities hostile to love.

PRAYER: Lord of earth and heaven, allow my weaknesses to empower me. May I gladly receive what you have to give. Amen.

SUNDAY, JULY 9 • Read Mark 6:7-13

When God sends us out in obedience, we become vulnerable. The form of vulnerability may vary, but the fact does not. Sometimes steps of faith limit physical provision.

Jesus sends out the twelve with the charge "to take nothing for their journey except a staff; no bread, no bag, no money in their belts." Many in ministry have set out on similar ventures, inspired by God's call yet without visible economic resources. Others have known extreme cultural vulnerability, sojourning in unfamiliar places, perhaps foreign countries or inner cities.

Emotional vulnerability may develop. Responding to God may remove us from supportive families, cherished friends, close-knit communities. Our love makes us vulnerable. God's love changes us; our love for God motivates us; God's love for others moves us. We embrace being sent out, charged with trusting our lives to God's provision and power.

However, in living by love we can develop an inappropriate vulnerability. Motivated by love, we may easily come to expect acceptance. Surely if God sends us in love, and we live in love and communicate love, we will be loved!

Not so, according to Jesus. In some places, people won't welcome us. They won't receive us and hear us. When we have that experience, when it's time to leave, we're to "shake off the dust that is on [our] feet as a testimony against them."

In other words, leave it behind! Don't take your negative experience with you. Don't enter the future caked with the dust of rejection. Shake it off; leave it where it belongs. Acknowledge the truth—and move on. Be clear about God's request of you—and obey. Trust God for the rest.

PRAYER: Holy Spirit, show me those relationships and situations in which I should be vulnerable and those in which it is unwise to be so. Amen.

Our Inheritance in Christ

July 10–16, 2000 • *Beth A. Richardson**

MONDAY, JULY 10 • **Read Ephesians 1:11-14**

"In Christ we have...obtained an inheritance." This phrase from today's reading surprised me—I have never thought of myself as being eligible for an inheritance.

I tend to think of inheritance as money, property, stocks, furniture. Growing up as a preacher's daughter, I knew early on that my inheritance wouldn't be like that. But that didn't concern me. I knew that our family was dedicated to something much more important than making money: We were part of God's work.

As I read this passage I felt excited, as if I had received a phone call from a sweepstakes or a fax from the estate of a recently deceased, distant relative. There's good news! I have an inheritance through my relationship with Christ!

Hearing Christ's word and believing in Christ mark us "with the seal...the pledge of our inheritance." *Seal* and *pledge*—two strong images and legal terms. No one can dispute this inheritance. It's airtight, wrapped up, in the bag.

What is this inheritance? It's not a portfolio of stocks, a fancy car, furs, or jewelry. It has no earthly value, but it is more valuable than gold or diamonds. Our inheritance is that we share Christ's status as a child of God, and we reap both the benefits and the responsibilities of that inheritance.

SUGGESTION FOR MEDITATION: What do you think of when you hear the word *inheritance*? List the things you have inherited from Christ.

---

*Ordained deacon in the Tennessee Conference of The United Methodist Church and the Director of Electronic Publishing for The Upper Room.

TUESDAY, JULY 11 • Read 2 Samuel 6:1-5, 12b-15

Our inheritance in Christ includes a rich relationship with God our loving Father and wise Mother, our Anchor, Rock, and Source of Hope. In 2 Samuel 6 David models that relationship with God as he brings the ark of God back to Jerusalem. (The Philistines had stolen the ark. See 1 Samuel 4.)

David has gathered 30,000 men, not for battle but to escort the ark back to its home. The scene is one of utter praise and joy: "David and all the house of Israel…dancing before the Lord with all their might, with songs and lyres and harps and tambourines and castanets and cymbals." They dance, sing, and play instruments in an act of worship, worshiping God with their voices, their spirits, and their very bodies. When they reach Jerusalem, David makes sacrifices and "offerings of well-being before the Lord" (v. 17). David serves both as king and spiritual leader, modeling for the people a relationship with the God of Israel.

Our relationship with God is central to our inheritance in Christ. Today's story implies that that relationship is a joyful one. Our worship setting, either corporate or private, should include praise and joyful utterances. We worship the God of creation, the God of joy and hope, the life-giving God. Whether we worship with songs or instruments, prayers or dancing, vocally or within our hearts, let our worship reflect the exuberance of David and all the people of Israel dancing before the Lord.

PRAYER: God of joy, let me today praise your holy name through my words, my thoughts, and my actions. Let my prayers dance within me, reflecting the joy of my relationship with you. Let the joy of your name be written on my heart. Amen.

WEDNESDAY, JULY 12 • **Read Ephesians 1:3-10**

Our inheritance in Christ includes our relationship with others. Jesus spent his ministry surrounded by people—the rich, the poor, the comfortable, the outcasts. Jesus said that if we are in relationship with God then we also are in relationship with one another.

Today's scripture tells us that we have received in Christ every spiritual blessing. Not only that, but God has actually adopted us as God's children. What does it mean to be adopted children of God? To me it means that God chooses *each of us*. What a special thing for those of us who can understand it.

But what of those people who have never known what it means to be a loved child of anyone? What of the children who spend their childhood moving from foster home to foster home? What of the children who live on the streets, parented by other children?

In Zimbabwe a whole generation of children have no parents or families. AIDS has left these children orphaned. Nearly fifty percent of the population of Zimbabwe is under the age of fifteen. The bishop of Zimbabwe is encouraging the United Methodist pastors to adopt as many children as they can. The bishop himself has adopted over twenty children.

How can children know what it means to be adopted children of God if they have never experienced a loving, caring relationship? Our inheritance in Christ requires that we reach out to others. We become the hands and arms of Christ in the world today, hugging lonely people, healing wounded hearts, and making homes for homeless children.

SUGGESTION FOR MEDITATION: **What action can I take today to be the arms of Christ in the world? What three things can I do to make a difference in the life of one of God's adopted children?**

THURSDAY, JULY 13 • Read 2 Samuel 6:6-12*a*, 16-19

Our inheritance in Christ includes the responsibility to use our gifts of power and privilege wisely. Whether we lead many or few, we must use our power and our privilege with care.

David returns the ark to Jerusalem. At the beginning of his reign as political and spiritual leader of Israel, David risks his own safety and security for the needs of the people.

The lectionary leaves out one of the more interesting parts of the story: verses 6-12. The procession of the ark has set off. Suddenly the cart holding the ark wobbles and David's friend Uzzah reaches out his hand to keep the ark from falling. When he touches the ark, God strikes him dead, which gives David second thoughts about taking the ark on to Jerusalem. So David leaves the ark at the house of Obed-edom. I can imagine David talking with God: "You want me to take this ark to Jerusalem? What if another disaster happens? It would look very, very bad."

After three months of prosperity for Obed-edom, David assumes the responsibility and the risk on behalf of the people he is to lead. The journey of the ark begins again. After six paces, David makes a sacrifice to the Lord. Then as the ark makes its way, "David dance[s] before the Lord with all his might;...girded with a linen ephod" (v. 14). Once David settles the ark in its place, he serves a meal of bread, meat, and raisins to all the people of Israel. David, the leader, overcomes his personal fears and failures to care for the spiritual and physical needs of his people.

SUGGESTION FOR MEDITATION: **What are my areas of power and privilege? What changes do I need to make in these areas?**

FRIDAY, JULY 14 • Read Mark 6:14-29

Mark's story of the death of John the Baptist is a gory tale, and I struggled with what we might learn from it about our inheritance in Christ. I discovered in the story the contrast between the inheritance from the world and our inheritance in Christ. Our inheritance from the world is one of violence. Bombs and bullets become tools of diplomacy. We use death to teach others not to kill. We do not model Christ's way of peace for our children.

Our inheritance in Christ is nonviolence. While born into a violent culture, Jesus never used violence against another. He lived in an occupied country where armed soldiers were a common sight. As a child he may have learned about his family's flight to Egypt and Herod's murder of the boys his age who were left behind. Herod killed Jesus' "mentor," John the Baptist, at the beginning of Jesus' ministry. Jesus faced threats and ultimately death at the hands of cultural leaders. But Jesus never struck another, never advocated physical resistance or revenge.

In fact, Jesus' message was peace and nonviolence: "Do not resist an evildoer" (Matt. 5:39). "Love your enemies and pray for those who persecute you" (Matt. 5:44).

Our inheritance of nonviolence calls us to model a different way than the culture's. We are called to search for alternatives to bullets, bombs, and killing. We are called to teach our children the way of peace, to see in every person the face of Christ, to love our enemies and pray for our persecutors.

PRAYER: Wise God of peace, teach me new ways to live and relate in the world. Where there is hatred and violence, let me be a maker of peace. In Christ's name. Amen.

SATURDAY, JULY 15 • Read Psalm 24:1-6

Today's reading begins with a celebration of the Creator God: "The earth is the Lord's and all that is in it, / the world, and those who live in it." This psalm reminds us that our inheritance in Christ also connects us to the earth, to creation. We are connected to God, to other people, and to creation.

I have discovered that some of my best prayer time happens when I'm outside—pulling weeds, planting flowers, watching the birds, taking a walk. When I am outside I feel close to God; I know that I am a part of *God's* creation.

I've had a good teacher—my Grandpa, who has showed me how to live out a holy connection to the earth. All my life I've watched him tend his backyard garden—tilling the soil, planting the seeds, harvesting the vegetables, and praising God. He says he plants the seeds, but God sends the sun and the rain and makes the seeds grow.

At ninety-four, Grandpa still works his garden from February to November. He "sells" most of his harvest to local church members, and the proceeds benefit the church's mission fund. Last summer's drought killed most of his garden, the peas, tomatoes, beans, and corn. Since the summer crop was already dead, he went ahead and planted the entire garden in his fall crop. With the new season, Grandpa had a whole garden full of turnips. I am not a great lover of turnips, but they brought in over $1,000 to help with the church's outreach to others. I pray that if I live to be his age, I will still be praising God in the garden.

PRAYER: Creator God, you are the gardener and I am your helper in the fields and orchards. Teach me to walk gently on your earth, caring for and protecting all of your creation—plants, animals, water, air, and land. In your holy name I pray. Amen.

Sunday, July 16 • Read Psalm 24

This week we have looked at our inheritance in Christ as a relationship with God, others, and creation; our responsibility in power and privilege; and our legacy of nonviolence. We have the love and grace of a caring Parent, the blessings of adoption into God's family, and the powerful example of our brother Christ in his ministry to all.

We are beloved and chosen children of God, who invites us to enter God's reign. The psalmist asks, "Who shall ascend the hill of the Lord? / And who shall stand in [God's] holy place?" The answer is this: "Those who have clean hands and pure hearts." As inheritors in Christ, we are invited to enter into God's reign, reaching out to others with the hands of Christ and opening our hearts to God's wisdom, will, and wonder.

May we reach out to others in healing ways, showing wounded children and the child-hearts of wounded adults that they too are adopted children of God. May we use our power and our privilege in responsible ways, in the awareness that we can either build up or break down the lives and spirits of others. May we practice nonviolence in our relationships with others and with the earth, ever learning and teaching the ways of peace.

The psalmist invites us to enter God's dwelling place with songs, instruments, and dances of praise. Praise God today and every day, for we are beloved, adopted, and blessed children of God.

PRAYER: Christ my brother, may I praise God in my dancing and sitting, singing and talking, planting and harvesting, sleeping and waking. May I praise God in the sanctuary...and at school, work, home, or in the car. May I praise God with every action, every heartbeat, and every breath I take. Amen.

God's Dwelling Place

July 17–23, 2000 • *Tom Allen**

MONDAY, JULY 17 • Read 2 Samuel 7:1-7

How quickly we assume we know what God needs; and our intentions, like David's, are good. The king of Israel lives in the finest of dwellings, a house made of the most fragrant wood the land has to offer. Should not the king of the universe and the sacred laws be housed in such surroundings? David thinks so and Nathan agrees, until God waits for a moment of stillness to speak in the dark of the night, "Are you [David] the one to build me a house to live in?" God purposefully calls and lives among a people; tent and tabernacle have sufficed as tangible houses of the Spirit's presence.

No doubt we honor the Creator with our magnificent houses of worship. "Only the best," we say and rightly so. But we forget that the church exists wherever the people of God gather—wherever, whenever, and however they worship. The covenant binds community, and in community we find ourselves strengthened and empowered to become God's people. The faithful who surfaced after the collapse of the former Soviet Union offer living testimony to this truth.

A house does not create a home. Relationships nurtured with patience and kindness, through laughter and tears, make a home. May we find our rest, our hope, our sanctuary, and our home in the One whose spirit calls us to reach beyond our self-imposed walls. May we never forget that we are the Spirit's most magnificent creation and the temple in whom that Spirit chooses to dwell.

SUGGESTION FOR PRAYER: **Remember the people of the world who worship in the midst of persecution.**

---

*Minister of Education and Administration, First Baptist Church, Southern Pines, North Carolina.

TUESDAY, JULY 18 • Read 2 Samuel 7:8-14a

God has a way of using our past to bless us and move us into our future. In today's text God recalls the past to stir the memories of a prophet and a king. From pasture to palace, God has been with David. From Egypt to Sinai, God has been with God's people. The floor of God's temple has been earth, its ceiling sky—such a wilderness has offered sanctuary and rest.

The time came when God's people needed to stop, not just to rest but to settle. Israel needed a home, a country, and all the attendant challenges that come with being a nation. Without those challenges, Israel would be slow to grow both numerically and spiritually. Their guidance and growth would come from God, who would be a parent to them and to future generations.

In the rush of our lives, we need to find within ourselves a home, a place of calm, a center of settled rest. Saint Augustine expressed awareness of this need when he wrote of the "restless heart" that would only find its rest in God. We all know persons who live restless lives. Maybe we are part of that community. We begin to wonder if faith in God really matters.

Yet we need not live ungrounded or static lives. Our challenge is to ground ourselves, to settle ourselves in God—whether in a place of worship, a commuter train, or a noisy, active household. A gracious grasp of the truth that God longs to live with us and among us, so that God can live through us, can be a place of beginning. God grant that we can be still long enough to hear and grasp this word of grace.

PRAYER: Loving God, in the busyness of my life, help me find my rest in you. Quiet my spirit, so I might know you are with me every hour. Amen.

WEDNESDAY, JULY 19 • Read Psalm 89:20-28

The psalmist echoes the writer of 2 Samuel 7 in this hymn by affirming God's work in and through the life of David. God has selected David, anointed him, and supplied him with courage and strength to rule God's people. God promises to do great things through the life of David. Above all, God's faithfulness will prevail, even when numerous enemies confront David and his kingdom. David, though a model of imperfection and a case study in how poor choices affect our lives, is God's anointed servant, the one chosen after God's own heart to lead a people whose special calling is to bring about God's rule and reign of justice and righteousness.

The Davidic monarchy fulfilled a purpose. Many would claim that with the Babylonian conquest and destruction of the holy city, the institution ultimately failed. However, in the midst of the monarchy, with all its opposition, we hear the psalmist affirm that God will never cease to reign. In the midst of sin, rejection, and exile, God's faithfulness and lovingkindness will ultimately prevail.

Christians have affirmed such a truth throughout history. The Resurrection is God's final word, and the church is God's messenger of that word. The church, though an imperfect institution, exists by an act of God's grace. A loving and faithful God continues to bring about the kingdom through the lives of those who make up the church, who have responded to the call of salvation and have committed their lives to establishing God's rule and reign in our world. May we, as imperfect vessels through whom God works, be found faithful to that calling.

SUGGESTION FOR PRAYER: **Pray that the body of Christ, in all its many facets and expressions, may continue to strive for unity.**

THURSDAY, JULY 20 • Read Psalm 89:29-37

In today's text, God, through the psalmist, affirms God's total commitment to the covenant with David and to the generations that will come after the shepherd king. God can be trusted. Can David?

We read the psalm knowing David's story. If the text is post-exilic, the readers also knew the story. They recalled David's fall: David disobeyed. David lied. David committed adultery. David broke God's laws. David sinned. David suffered the consequences.

David's life often mirrors our own, although maybe our sins are not as blatant. We sin, but we sin—as *The Book of Common Prayer* reminds us—"by what we have done and by what we have left undone." And like David, we too must deal with the consequences of sin, even after a loving and faithful God has forgiven us. Covenant is a two-way street. Yet the redemptive story played out in scripture brings a certain sense of peace.

For the believer, peace comes in knowing God does not abandon this temple created for the Spirit's indwelling. We fall, we sin, we face sin's consequences; yet God's promise will always be kept, God's covenant never broken. The family of God, though broken and often dysfunctional, by God's grace remains intact. Our heritage of faith, against all odds, lives on because God lives. *Selah.*

SUGGESTION FOR MEDITATION: **Pray for insight from God about someone you love and to whom you wish to pass on your heritage of faith. Reflect on creative ways in which to do this. Thank God for the heritage of faith that someone passed on to you.**

FRIDAY, JULY 21 • Read Ephesians 2:11-22

When we bought our first home, our quarter-acre lot joined two similar lots in our subdivision. You could tell where one neighbor's yard stopped and another's began, by locating a well-concealed boundary marker. Most of the time we mowed our lawns close to where we thought our neighbor's property line was and watered and fertilized that area. The lushness of our lawns soon became the best way to determine whose line was where.

When we all became parents, we talked from time to time about fences, about establishing physical boundaries for our children's safety and our sanity. But we never got around to it. Something about a fence made us uncomfortable.

Each family was different, holding different religious and political beliefs. We came from all over the country. We had diverse educational and family backgrounds. Still we were neighbors, good neighbors. To this day, those yards remain connected, and the longing for the greenest and lushest lawn continues to stimulate healthy and fun competition.

Today's text reminds us of our oneness in Christ. The writer does so, in part, by speaking of the wall between Jew and Gentile that Christ's redemptive power has brought down (v. 14). When we hear news from Northern Ireland or the Middle East or even in our own denominations, we wonder if that wall is not being built again—and this time even higher. God grant that each of us, in whatever manner we have chosen to express our belief in Christ, can do all we can to hammer away at that wall, one brick at a time.

PRAYER: God of all, help me this day to build a bridge and not a wall between those with whom I may differ. Amen.

SATURDAY, JULY 22 • Read Mark 6:30-34

Several years ago, my wife and I were given the gift of a tour of Israel. We cherish the memories of that pilgrimage, as well as the lessons we learned. One such insight came on Friday night, the eve of Shabbat, the sabbath. I knew the sabbath to be a time of rest but expected an Israeli sabbath to resemble my Sundays—different from the rest of the week but often busy. Imagine my surprise when the nation almost came to a complete standstill. I sensed celebration in the air. The day God rested and, thereby, redeemed for creation continued to be observed, probably as God intended, in that ancient land.

God created our bodies for work and sleep, play and rest, labor and leisure. Sabbaths can provide that on a weekly basis, and we ought to be intentional about making our sabbaths restful. Yet today's text challenges us to remember the importance of finding times of rest between our sabbaths.

The disciples have experienced the gruesome death of John the Baptist. They find themselves part of an entourage that is often detained because someone wants to see or hear or touch Jesus. In this instance, they can't even eat. They need quiet and solitude for rest and recovery.

Perhaps we should consider having brief moments of sabbath between those weekly celebrations of the Resurrection. Perhaps we need God's sabbaths of complete rest more often than fifty-two Sundays each year. God grant that today we might find a place to quiet our busy lives and to experience the gift of sabbath, even before Sunday.

PRAYER: God of rest and quiet, grant me this day just a few moments of sabbath-like solitude. Teach me that I, like all your disciples, need to be still and know that you are God. Amen.

These few verses remind us of the power of Jesus' presence. Word of his healing gifts has spread quickly. Mark's words indicate a frenzied desperation among the people. Whatever it took, whatever the cost, they had to be in Jesus' presence, if only to touch the fringe of his cloak.

Each of us remembers times when we have prayed in moments of crisis for Jesus to be alive and present and with us. Often we bathe our prayers in tears, telling God in our desperation that something has to change, something must happen now.

And then we read the Bible and find we are not alone. In our desperation, we discover persons who, like us, needed Jesus centuries ago. They had his physical presence. We know that presence as resurrected and alive in all believers. With this realization, we discover that we find Jesus in the words and touch of others.

This text should compel us to continue to reach out to God in Christ, but should it not also compel us to consider how we can incarnate the Christ of Gennesaret? People may never rush to us for help or throw themselves at our feet in an act of desperation. But what if our lives so mirrored Jesus that friends or family or neighbors in need would know they could come to us and find a trusted confidant, a compassionate listener, and a praying pilgrim?

May we who journey along this road of faith never hesitate to share our deepest needs with One whose heart can carry those needs. May we also be ready to open our heart to those who need someone with whom they can share.

SUGGESTION FOR MEDITATION: Today trust the deepest needs of your heart to God. Ask God for insight and wisdom to minister to those who, like you, are also in need.

Imagine That

July 24–30, 2000 • *Mary Donovan Turner**

MONDAY, JULY 24 • **Read 2 Samuel 11:1-15**

It is a story embroiled in violation, adultery, misplaced loyalties, arrogance, deception, and murder. It is a stark, understated account of a king who abuses power, whose moral fabric is beginning to unravel. And it is a story about a woman who becomes a victim of the king's abusive power. We know little about her, only her name and that she is beautiful. We do not know what she thinks or feels; she says nothing.

There is another in this story, Uriah the Hittite, the husband of Bathsheba. He is the foil, the sharp contrast to all that dismays us about the great King David. In contrast to David who stays home when he should be with others on the battlefield, Uriah goes out to save his community. He lives out his commitment, fully and wholly, by denying himself nourishment and pleasure, his identification with other soldiers so complete. He is honest, faithful, trusting, courageous. (The king himself depends on one with these values to keep his kingdom and power intact!) But in the end, Uriah's integrity does not guarantee his safety or shield him from danger. He is the one who loses his life. He seems to have been powerless in contrast to the great King David. Or maybe not.

Perhaps this story is God's way of challenging us to imagine that commitment and compassion are not weakness and that the ability to command and oppress is not strength.

PRAYER: God of true strength and wisdom, lend me your vulnerability and compassion. Amen.

*Carl Patton Associate Professor of Preaching at Pacific School of Religion, Berkeley, California; ordained minister in the Christian Church (Disciples of Christ).

TUESDAY, JULY 25 • **Read Psalm 14**

Psalm 14 is not, as are many psalms, a prayer; the psalmist does not speak to God but for God. These are words of lament and distress about the world's condition; the psalmist imagines the world as God sees it and as we frequently experience it.

God is looking for the wise ones, for those who seek God. God finds none. "No, not one" who knows and lives as if there is a God. The matter of intellectual assent to the idea of God is less important here than how we alter our lives because of it. We betray or honor God by how we choose to live.

When the foolish one says there is no God, the vacancy in that one is filled with self. The person becomes ultimate wisdom. The thinking of the foolish one cannot detect self-deception, making that one vulnerable to error and self-righteousness. Self-deception cannot see beyond its own limits and needs. It is stifled. It suffocates. It is limited. It lives in a closed circle of certainty—a denial of community.

We can easily distinguish between wisdom and folly when we read Psalm 14 but find them difficult to discern in our own lives. When are we misguided? When do our self-sufficiencies blind us to the needs and desires of those in the world around us? When are we living as if we do not believe in God? What does God really require?

If this psalm (and Psalm 53, which is virtually identical to it) is not a prayer, how did the Israelites use it in worship? Perhaps it functioned as a call to confession for the Israelites just as it does to us. It calls us to confess the many ways in which we deny God's presence. And to repent. So that when God looks upon the world in search of wise ones, God will not be disappointed.

PRAYER: Dear God, open our eyes, our ears, our hearts, our hands to the world around us. Amen.

WEDNESDAY, JULY 26 • Read Psalm 14

The Hebrew Scriptures repeatedly call the community to a care and concern for those less fortunate and less powerful and more vulnerable than themselves. When one gathers wheat from the field, she is to leave grain for the alien, the widow, and the orphan who have none. And when gathering grapes off the vine, one is to leave fruit for those who have none. How one shows concern is a part, a crucial part, of living up to one's covenantal commitment with Yahweh.

In Psalm 14, how the foolish deal with the poor graphically demonstrates the stark contrast between the foolish and the wise ones. Those who do not seek God, who have gone astray, who are perverse, who do not do good, are those who devour the poor just as casually as they eat a loaf of bread.

These are the same ones who would "confound the plans" of the poor, making life even more difficult in a world that already oppresses, ignores, alienates, and denies them. The foolish ones imagine that the poor are defenseless in the world because no God stands with them.

Those who seek after God know that to oppress another child of God is the most egregious offense to Yahweh. How can we honor a parent by destroying the child? To be wise we must take account in our religious practice and in our politics of the most vulnerable ones among us. Dare we imagine a world where the spiritual, physical, and emotional needs of these are filled?

PRAYER: Dear God, help me imagine myself with unlimited compassion and concern for others. Amen.

THURSDAY, JULY 27 • Read Ephesians 3:14-21

While appearing in the middle of the book of Ephesians, this text has the quality of benediction and blessing about it. These intercessions are filled with gratitude. The author bends his knees, not in submission or defeat but in awe of this God who gives every family its name. Every family, then, is part of a great web of being, each related to the other.

The prayer asks that those in the community be strengthened, rooted, grounded in love, empowered, and filled with all the fullness of God, becoming a tapestry of unimagined beauty. The language of the prayer, while abstract, is strong; it is powerful. Its greatness, its loftiness, only serves to reinforce what the writer of the prayer has known. The community needs to be wrested from its small understandings, its reduced expectations, its diminished theologies to understand the breadth, the length, the width, and the depth of God's mystery and power.

The prayer does not tell us how this wresting comes about, but it does fill our imaginations with the sights and sounds, thoughts and feelings of God's wonder stirring in our lives. When have we known the strength of God's power within us? How do we remain rooted and grounded in the love of God so amazing we cannot possibly understand it? How do we empower others, the community, for faithful service. When will all be filled with the fullness of God?

The prayer stirs within us a great longing that this "benediction" written for others some 2,000 years ago might fall gently upon us to renew and restore and to stir our dormant imaginations.

PRAYER: Dear God, what does it mean to live in your fullness? I long to know. Amen.

FRIDAY, JULY 28 • **Read Ephesians 3:20**

Somewhere along the way, as lessons from life take their toll, we lose it. We lose the ability we had as children to be playful, to rearrange the world according to our imaginations, to make believe. We lose our capacity to travel to distant places, solve problems, create alternative worlds, and think our way into new ways of being.

The Old Testament prophets tried to call people to newness. They called people to imagine an alternative way to live—a way grounded in justice and righteousness: a stretching of horizon, a widening of peripheral vision, an expansion of compassion that would both see and include those on the margins.

According to Luke, the Magnificat of Mary imagines a world where structures, paradigms, oppressions as we know them are no longer with us. Jesus helps us imagine such a world when he tells simple parables. He helps the disciples and all who hover about him to imagine a different way of seeing life.

Imagination becomes our "bridge." It shows us how to span the gap, the empty space between the actual and the ideal, the yet and the not yet, between being and becoming. And so the writer of Ephesians prays that somehow the community of the faithful will begin to imagine what God can imagine.

PRAYER: Stir my imagination, God, to see the world as you would have me see it. Unsettle me. Amen.

SATURDAY, JULY 29 • Read John 6:1-15

The time of year is the Passover, a springtime festival that commemorates God's great intervention and protection of the Israelite people in Egypt. Year after year the story of deliverance is told so that the generations can remember how God was present with their earliest ancestors as they began their journey from slavery to freedom.

As John 6 begins, the Passover is approaching. Jesus will spend this festival day in Galilee. The crowds gather around him, aware that there is something extraordinary about his power. He heals, touches, teaches. He comforts. They press in around him from all sides to see, to touch, to hear.

Those in the crowds become hungry. The disciples cannot begin to imagine how the people will be fed, but Jesus knows that he will perform another "sign," another miracle for them. With only the lunch of a small boy, the pressing crowd of 5,000 is fed. The people become even more convinced that Jesus should be king; and in an effort to avoid them, Jesus withdraws to the mountain.

It is a strange story. Jesus performs a "sign" but doesn't want the crowds to be impressed by it. Somehow he wants them to see beyond, to see something different, something more important, something longer lasting. The crowds are easily impressed with bread. But Jesus wants them to know he is Bread, the Bread of Life. And they, as we, have a difficult time understanding this one who is more than we can imagine.

PRAYER: Help us understand, God, this Jesus who was so strong, so weak, so unlike us and so like us. Amen.

Sunday, July 30 • Read John 6:16-21

In the stories of the Exodus, God demonstrates God's remarkable sustaining presence by parting and calming the Red Sea so the Israelites can safely cross over. God also provides food in the wilderness—manna and bread—to sustain the people in their long and grueling wilderness adventures.

The Gospels of Matthew, Mark, and John remember these manifestations of God's presence by pairing the stories of the miraculous feeding of the 5,000 with the calming of the storm-tossed sea. After Jesus withdraws from the multitudes, the disciples, their stomachs filled with fish and bread, board a boat to cross the Sea of Galilee. Jesus has left them, and they are fearful, for it is night. They panic because the storm renders them unsafe on the wave-ridden waters.

Then out of the chaos and on the horizon of their fear, Jesus appears as a sign of hope. He comes to them, walking upon the water. And he says to them, "Do not be afraid."

Do not be afraid. From the mouths of the prophets and angels these words constitute the constant refrain from God to God's people: *Do not be afraid. I am with you.*

The words pale oft times when we hear them in light of the excruciating, painful, fear-driven circumstances within which many people of the world must live. *Do not be afraid.* How do the world's people know that God is there? Perhaps they know through our constant care and attention to their need. Perhaps our vocation, our mission, is to wade into the waters of the world and stand by those who may be swept away. We take their hands and, by our very presence, help them imagine a God who has not forsaken them.

Prayer: God, give me the courage to wade into the deep waters. Amen.

God's Forgiveness and Our Response

July 31–August 6, 2000 • *David M. Easterling**
Laura Easterling**

MONDAY, JULY 31 • **Read 2 Samuel 11:26–12:6**

Sometimes we sin and don't see it. We find it easier to point fingers at another person's sin and disregard our own. Perhaps we think our sin is so well hidden that we don't have to deal with it.

Scripture often describes King David as a man after God's own heart. Yet he sins. Does he think that the law doesn't apply to him? Does he think that God doesn't see what he has done? Is he so focused on his own desires that he forgets about what God desires? Whatever his reason or justification, David's sin separates him from God (Isa. 59:2).

Although David does not seek God's forgiveness in this matter, God reaches out to him through a messenger. The prophet Nathan tells a parable to confront David with his sin. David says that the rich man who stole his poor neighbor's beloved lamb deserves to die. David easily judges another person's sin, but what of his own?

David's secret sin, like our own, is not hidden from God. God continues to love David while being displeased by the sin. God's love does not depend on our goodness. While we were still sinners, God showed his love to us through the passion of Christ (Romans 5:8).

PRAYER: "Have mercy on me, O God, according to your unfailing love; according to your great compassion blot out my transgressions. Wash away all my iniquity and cleanse me from my sin." Amen. (Ps. 51:1-2, NIV)

---

*Author, songwriter, event speaker, and president of Christian Music Connection (CMC).

**Office director of a technology corporation.

TUESDAY, AUGUST 1 • Read 2 Samuel 12:7-13

Like a well-meaning parent, God loves David enough to confront him about his sin, to bring him back into a right relationship. And God does. After Nathan's confrontation, David confesses and receives forgiveness. Yet the sin still carries consequences. The Lord has given David the kingship of Israel and Judah and would have given him even more. "Why did you despise the word of the Lord by doing what is evil in his eyes?" (NIV). This is the age-old question. If we know what is good and if God has given us what we need, why do we desire what is forbidden? Since sin entered the world, people have struggled to avoid it.

What is the result of sin? Sin separates us from God. Separation from God equals death. Therefore, the result (or wages of sin) is death. King David deserves to die for his sin. All who sin deserve to die. However, God does not leave us to our own devices. "The wages of sin is death, but the free gift of God is eternal life in Christ Jesus our Lord" (Rom. 6:23). David confesses his sin to the Lord, and Nathan proclaims his forgiveness: "The Lord has taken away your sin. You are not going to die."

Is that it? Is it that simple? The answer is both yes and no. God forgives the sin. The relationship between God and David is restored. But everybody doesn't always get to live happily ever after in real life. God does not reverse the results of David's sinful action or make everything the way it was before the sin occurred. Uriah the Hittite is still dead. Bathsheba is still David's wife. Their son, the offspring of their adultery, dies. Sin still brings consequences, even when the debt has been paid. "Now, therefore, the sword will never depart from your house" (NIV).

PRAYER: "Cleanse me with hyssop, and I will be clean....Create in me a pure heart, O God, and renew a steadfast spirit within me." Amen. (Ps. 51:7, 10, NIV)

WEDNESDAY, AUGUST 2 • **Read Psalm 51:1-12**

Although the verses in 2 Samuel 12 tell of King David's repentance and forgiveness, they do not convey the depth of remorse that David expresses in Psalm 51. Presumably David writes the psalm after Nathan confronts him about his sin.

Initially David may have hoped to keep his sin secret. When Nathan confronts him, David makes no excuses. He does not seek to use his kingship as a shield from justice, nor does he conspire to develop an elaborate cover-up.

In the depth of his despair, David does not run or hide his face from God. He turns to God and passionately confesses his sin and admits his failure. David agonizes over his actions and cries out for the restoration of his relationship to God.

But why cry out to God? Isn't it Uriah and Bathsheba whom he has truly harmed? Yes, they indeed are victims. But David has broken God's law, despised God's word. "You shall not murder. Neither shall you commit adultery" (Deut. 5:17-18). God holds the power to punish or forgive.

Being human and living in the company of other humans means that we live in the environment of temptation. When God takes second place to our own desires, we will inevitably sin against God and against people as well. When we love God with all our being, then all of our activities and relationships will be right (Matt. 22:37-40).

So David the man turns to God the Creator to reestablish a pure heart, a right relationship, and the joy of salvation. He again places God first in his life. David confesses his sin and trusts in God's unfailing love and great compassion. And David's sin is forgiven.

PRAYER: "Do not cast me from your presence or take your Holy Spirit from me. Restore to me the joy of your salvation and grant me a willing spirit, to sustain me." Amen. (Ps. 51:11-12, NIV)

THURSDAY, AUGUST 3 • Read John 6:24-27

Jesus sends his disciples across the lake to Capernaum, dismisses the crowd, and withdraws into the hills to be alone (Matt. 14:22). Nevertheless, the people want to follow this man who has fed them. Perhaps some people still desire national independence; others may want another free meal; perhaps others hunger to satisfy the longing in their souls.

The crowds go to Capernaum looking for Jesus. Surprised to find Jesus already there and knowing that he has not gone by boat before them, they ask, "When did you come here?"—wrong question. Instead, Jesus asks them to identify their motives for seeking him.

Jesus never sought to become an earthly ruler of this world. He sought to bring people into the spiritual kingdom. He clearly states his identity and purpose to Pilate when he declares, "My kingdom is not of this world...but...is from another place....For this reason I was born, and for this I came into the world, to testify to the truth" (John 18:36-37, NIV).

Because of this mission, Jesus tells the people not to work for the temporary bread that spoils (like manna in the wilderness) but to work for the food that endures for eternal life. He urges them to seek first the kingdom of God and God's righteousness; then all the other more temporary things will be given to them as well.

People still seek Christ for many different reasons. How often do you seek after the food that spoils? Do you worry about earthly matters that are merely temporary? For what do you work? Why do you seek him?

PRAYER: "Surely you desire truth in the inner parts, you teach me wisdom in the inmost place." Amen. (Ps. 51:6, NIV)

Then the people ask the right question, "What must we do to do the works God requires?" (NIV). But are the people ready for the answer? Do they think they will get a simple checklist of dos and don'ts? They already have that. The formula for right behavior was written on tablets of stone and delivered to the Hebrew people about 1,400 years before Christ appeared in human form. So what does Jesus answer? "The work of God is this: to believe in the one he has sent" (NIV).

Jesus' answer seems simple enough, yet the people seem unready to commit their faith so easily. They trust in the Ten Commandments because their ancestors witnessed the miraculous works of God through Moses. So the people call for more signs and wonders. They want more bread. They bargain with Jesus, saying in effect, "Give us what we want; then we'll believe in you." How often do we want to have things our own way? How often do we bargain with God saying, "Prove yourself, then I'll follow"?

John 6 focuses on Jesus' identity. Jesus performs miracles that should clearly proclaim and prove his identity to even the most skeptical person. Jesus explains his relationship to the Father. He even tells the people who he is and why he has come. "The true bread...comes down from heaven and gives life to the world" (NIV).

The bread of life still stands before us, just as he stood before those questioning people 2,000 years ago. "I am the bread of life. Whoever comes to me will never be hungry, and whoever believes in me will never be thirsty." Yet belief is never abstract to Jesus. Belief initiates commitment, love, action, and obedience. How do we do the work of the Lord?

PRAYER: "Save me from bloodguilt, O God, the God who saves me, and my tongue will sing of your righteousness. O Lord, open my lips, and my mouth will declare your praise." Amen. (Ps. 51:14-15, NIV)

So we have heard the gospel story declared and have received forgiveness of sin. A right relationship between God and God's people has been restored. The life, sacrifice, and resurrection of our Lord Jesus Christ have brought this reconciliation about. Now what?

God expects a response. God has called us into relationship, and our Creator asks us to live a life worthy of that calling (Eph. 4:1). But how do we do that?

Within our right relationship to God, we have a further calling into right relationship with neighbor. Jesus commissioned us to "love one another as I have loved you" (John 15:12). But how do we do that?

The writer of Ephesians appeals to the Christian community to lead a worthy or virtuous life. The Christian community expresses its love through the practice of humility, gentleness, and patience. The practice of these virtues will invite peace and unity into the Christian community.

By showing Christlike love, we will develop a right relationship among us. Love forms the bond of peace, uniting us in Christ. We are all part of one body, the church, with Christ as the head. The one Spirit directs our lives. We are called to one hope (or goal): redeeming the world in Christ. We may differ in some beliefs and practices, but we stand united by the essential Christian belief in "one Lord, one faith, one baptism; one God and Father of all" (NIV).

Consider the church of today. How do its members seek unity? In what ways do we focus on the hope of salvation for the world? How do we show love, humility, gentleness, and patience to one another? When do we express Christ's love outside our church walls?

PRAYER: Lord, let me live in peace with your people. Unite our hearts so that we put our hope in you—one God over all, through all, and in all. Amen.

Although we find ourselves united in one body, one Lord, one hope, one Spirit, one faith, and one baptism, it is not God's intention that we be carbon copies of one ideal Christian prototype: "To each one of us grace has been given as Christ apportioned it" (NIV).

Ephesians 4:2-3 mentions characteristics of the Christian life. Today's passage lists several roles that emerge as the result of our Christ-apportioned gifts: apostles, prophets, evangelists, pastors, and teachers. These persons provide the leadership "to prepare God's people for works of service."

Imagine for a moment an athlete who was never coached, a musician who never practiced, or a rescue worker who was never trained. How effective could they be? Talent and instinct might take them part of the way through their tasks, but could they finish well? It is not likely. The same is true of the church. The body of Christ must be coached, trained, and encouraged to practice in order to complete the work of God. Paul recognized that the church must grow and mature to be effective. Without such training and discipline, the church would be destined to be tossed back and forth by "every wind of doctrine, by people's trickery, by their craftiness in deceitful scheming" (Eph. 4:14).

Unity in the faith and in the knowledge of the Son of God is the key for building up the church. The probability of being led astray by deception is diminished when the body of believers knows and recognizes the whole measure of the fullness of Christ. Therefore, focus on Christ, grow and build up the church in love, and seek first his kingdom.

Prayer: "Now to him who is able to do immeasurably more than all we ask or imagine, according to his power that is at work within us, to him be glory in the church and in Christ Jesus throughout all generations, for ever and ever!" Amen. (Eph. 3:19, NIV).

Facing God in Terrible Times

August 7–13, 2000 • Betsy Schwarzentraub*

MONDAY, AUGUST 7 • Read 2 Samuel 18:31-33

Decide

Poor, tortured David. Yes, he is Israel's king, but he is also a father. How had he forgotten that? He clutches his heart in anguish for his son Absalom, whose personal army battles outside the gates at this moment, within a hairsbreadth of taking over the throne.

David shakes his head. *If only I had acted like a father before now, remembering my family as much as the affairs of state!* Absalom's half-brother has done the unspeakable—he has raped his sister Tamar. Absalom has waited for David to assert justice in the family. He continues to wait, languishing in Jerusalem for years, waiting for his father to act in some way to right this terrible wrong.

But David can't bring himself to face the awful truth. He can't decide how to vindicate his daughter or even how to comfort her or what to say to his sons. The entire royal household is unraveling before his weary eyes. So David does nothing. Abdicating fatherhood, he hides behind his kingship.

How do we choose when we must face terrible truths and forsake one role to fulfill another? Often not choosing is the worst decision of all. In those times, God waits for us to ask for guidance. But we remain silent, still trying to handle our dilemmas—or to deny them—on our own.

SUGGESTION FOR MEDITATION: Think about the different roles in your personal life. When have those roles conflicted with one another, and what was at stake? How did you decide what you needed to do? Where was God in the midst of the situation?

---

*Pastor, church consultant, and editor; clergy member of California-Nevada Conference, The United Methodist Church, Davis, California.

TUESDAY, AUGUST 8 • Read 2 Samuel 18:5-9, 15

Act

Joab has no problem making decisions. As the king's commander in chief, he knows how to work events to his favor. "King David has lost his grip," he mutters to himself, as he fingers his sword. Granted, Joab knows of David's order not to kill the rebel leader Absalom. But something has to be done, and David is never going to do it. *Why not feather my own nest by getting rid of the most ambitious heir to the throne?*

Low, overhanging limbs lay Absalom open to the enemy's fatal strokes. Now if Joab's soldier kills the traitorous son, so much the better. Joab can execute his man for disobeying the king and be done with the enemy of the state as well—all without tipping his own hand. *Here's the opportunity!* thinks Joab, when he hears of Absalom's defenseless position. Joab acts swiftly. He snatches three spears from his armor bearers and thrusts them into Absalom's heart. And before that tortured heart can stop beating, Joab's soldiers surround the writhing Absalom and finish the job.

Action and cunning are the marks of Joab's work. Or does Joab kill Absalom because he loves his country more than its misguided, vacillating king? Does the commander's single-minded patriotism save Israel from falling apart in King David's ineffectual hands?

Our daily lives require timely action also. But what guides our action—hunger for power, desire for success, loyalty to country or to a particular relationship? Or is it our love of God? Would Joab have killed Absalom if he had asked God's opinion first?

PRAYER: Dear God, please forgive me for acting in my vested interest regardless of your will and destroying others in the process. I depend upon your grace. Amen.

WEDNESDAY, AUGUST 9 • Read Psalm 130:1-4

Cry out

How can we face God when everything has gone terribly wrong? After our public protests of innocence have died down, and we have spent ourselves on pretense, finally we admit the truth to the One who has known it all along. "Out of the depths I cry to you, O Lord," we whisper. "Lord, hear my voice!"

As our sense of God's mercy deepens, our awareness of God's holiness deepens too. We consciously acknowledge the chasm between God's faithfulness to covenant with us and our indifference to that covenant.

Old Testament scholar Walter Brueggemann says this psalm shows "inordinate boldness," since the poet tries to forge a link between the Ruler of reality and a human in an extreme situation of need. This is the paradox of the God who truly exists. God listens particularly for those who seem utterly cut off, who are beyond redemption by human standards.

"Deep calls to deep" (Ps. 42:7). In the depths of our vulnerability and distress, we cry out to the heights of God's holiness, and God hears us. But a deeper truth exists: God's heart cries out to us first, even before we know enough to ask for help. John Wesley called this mystery "prevenient grace," grace with a terrifying edge. The One who listens for us is still the One who would transform us from the inside out.

Here's the awesome core of the matter—there is forgiveness with God! God's forgiveness is the seed of our new life. It is also our only solid ground when life has driven us to our knees. The purpose of forgiveness is that we will "fear" God. Our fear may move from reverence to awe, from deep dejection to knowing ourselves embraced in the arms of God.

SUGGESTION FOR MEDITATION: When have you been in "the depths" and cried out to God? What happened to change you or your situation? What is God's deep heart saying to you now?

THURSDAY, AUGUST 10 • Read Ephesians 4:25–5:2

Live

If God's forgiveness is the seed of our new life, then how do we grow from there? What signals our Christian growth in everyday situations?

Speak the truth to your neighbors, says the writer of Ephesians, because we are members of one another. We are interdependent; half-truths and evasions catch us all.

Go ahead and get angry but limit your anger in two ways. First, don't let your anger extend past sundown. Second, in your anger don't leave a big enough space for the devil to work. The term *devil* implies whatever or whoever might prompt a person to oppose God.

Ephesians begins where people are. For example, if you have been stealing (or even subtly skimming any personal benefits off the top), change your behavior. Work honestly with your own hands. Why? Because honest work gives you something to share with the needy, and that's a top priority.

The practical advice continues. Words resemble deeds: They change people's lives. So let your words weigh in on the side of grace. Likewise, don't grieve God's Holy Spirit.

Our most terrible times can come in daily settings, when we encase ourselves in the hard shell of negative attitudes and actions. Cultivate positive behaviors instead, says the writer, including kindness toward one another, a tenderhearted perspective on other people's shortcomings, and forgiveness of one another.

We set our daily decisions and actions in this context: the overwhelming degree to which God, in Christ, has forgiven us. Next to that unsurpassable amount of forgiveness, how does our everyday living measure up?

PRAYER: Creator and gardener God, please help me grow from seedling to stalk to fruitful plant, rooted in your great love. This I pray in Jesus' name. Amen.

FRIDAY, AUGUST 11 • **Read Psalm 130:5-8**

Hope

In the inky time of night before trees and buildings become darker silhouettes against a grainy gray sky, four penniless students huddled together among the boulders on the beach of a foreign land. Too cold to sleep and fearful of strangers, we awaited the dawn. *Morning will come*, I reminded myself for the twentieth time. Just wait. Wait.

The psalmist must have known that kind of waiting because he uses a word that implies exactly what we felt that long night: bunched-up muscles tense with expectation, eager yearning for what will surely come but never seems to arrive. Waiting: a mixture of strength, longing, and hope that catches our breath while our eyes search wearily for the first light. "My soul [life] waits for the Lord more than those who watch for the morning, more than those who watch for the morning."

Many experiences can give rise to a long night of tense waiting—hunger, homelessness, hospital test results, a call from the police, loved ones in trouble, guilt that won't go away, painful disease, multiplying regrets, or actions that cannot be undone. We seem to put our life on hold while we wait for that promised new beginning. Can we trust God? Will the morning come?

"O Israel, hope in the Lord!" cries the psalmist. "For with the Lord there is steadfast love." Some older Bible translations refer to God's steadfast love as "lovingkindness" or "faithfulness." But whatever causes our long nights of waiting and whenever we're unsure of ourselves and others, we can count on God's faithfulness—and God's faithfulness is enough.

The morning will come. We have God's word on that.

PRAYER: Dear God, I thank you for being with me through the long hours of my night, as well as in the light of my morning. Help me trust you no matter what brought me to this situation, no matter what I may go through. Amen.

SATURDAY, AUGUST 12 • Read John 6:35, 41-44, 46

See

The Israelites believed that no one could see God's face and live because of the Creator's overwhelming majesty. Nevertheless, a few Israelite leaders caught significant glimpses of God. When Moses met with Yahweh upon Mount Sinai (Exod. 34:33), his face shone with "glory"; and Moses wore a veil when he came down the mountain so he wouldn't scare the people with the radiant light from his face.

When a person lives close to God in prayer, even secularly oriented people notice something different—something authentic, truthful, whole. Jesus states that no one has seen God except the one who comes from God, referring to himself as God's "sent one," whose presence signals God's visible rule on earth. As such, Jesus is the only one in human history who has seen the fullness of God.

Imagine the shock among his hometown neighbors when Jesus says he has seen God! They remember him as the kid next door, Joseph and Mary's son. So how can he breeze back into town now with such audacity and say he has come down from heaven, sent by God?

The fact that Jesus has seen God's fullness still comes as a shock to us, even given what we know now through his striking ministry, his self-giving death, and his life-giving Resurrection.

We are the body of Christ, the corporate body of Jesus on earth in this time and place. Has God also sent us to do Christ's works? (See John 14:12.) If so, God has given us, like Moses before us, the eyes to see our own small vision of God's living presence and work in this world.

SUGGESTION FOR MEDITATION: **Where do you see God in your life right now? What vision is God showing you? Read as a prayer the words to the hymn "Open My Eyes, That I May See."**

SUNDAY, AUGUST 13 • **Read John 6:43-45, 47-51**

Come

If seeing God through the boy next door shocked Jesus' hometown neighbors, then they must have found his next statement incomprehensible: "Do not complain among yourselves," he said. "No one can come to me unless drawn by the [One] who sent me."

Ah, there's the rub. How can we move closer to Jesus, when we cannot take a step toward God on our own, much less understand God's fullness? Only God can bridge the gap between us; God doesn't ask us to supply the power or the understanding; we need only desire the relationship and open ourselves to God.

The scriptures of Jesus' own heritage speak of the primacy of knowing God—not a secondhand knowledge about God but rather a personal relationship with God, a relationship that goes beyond any human relationship. Only God knows us fully in our uniqueness and still loves us entirely.

So here in John, we find we don't need to understand everything about God. We only need to open ourselves to God who can draw us toward Jesus. We reflect the quality of trust in God that Jesus showed by accepting God's transforming work in our lives, moment by moment.

What does it mean to come to Jesus? It means bending our thinking and action to become more like him in justice and compassion. It means gathering up the courage to face God in the terrible times, not just the joyous ones. Even in our strongest moments, we can't do this on our own. Jesus says that those who come near to him have been "drawn," nudged by none other than God. We come of our own free will, but the power to come closer to Jesus comes from grace.

PRAYER: Thank you, God, that you let me see you through Jesus and give me the power to come to him by your grace. Amen.

True Wisdom

August 14–20, 2000 • *Kyungsig Samuel Lee**

MONDAY, AUGUST 14 • **Read Psalm 111:10**

True wisdom lies in *practicing* God's will. How fundamental this truth is to Christian life! Yet we all struggle in practicing God's will. Having true wisdom has nothing to do with one's level of education nor does it have much to do with how comfortably we live. Practicing God's will requires more than a feeling of commitment and more than simply having good feelings toward God. Being aware of God, knowing the Bible, or having good intentions may help us move toward practicing God's will, but they do not necessarily produce the life of true wisdom.

True wisdom indeed begins from the fear of the Lord. We must keenly sense God's unhappiness with us if we go against God's will. Ultimately, however, only the love of God can help us maintain the life of true wisdom. We must be convinced of the God who constantly pursues us in all good intentions. We must have experiential knowledge of the God who loves us even when we disobey. The life and ministry of Jesus Christ communicate this love most definitively.

Many Christians often have difficulty in knowing God's will. However, to persons with true wisdom, the question is not so much what we do not know about God's will as what we do know. Our understanding of what we do know may lead us to true wisdom.

PRAYER: Grant me wisdom, O God, to discern your will and to know your love. Guide me to live the life of true wisdom. Amen.

---

*Assistant Professor of Pastoral Care and Counseling, Wesley Theological Seminary, Washington, D.C.; clergy member of the California-Pacific Conference of The United Methodist Church.

TUESDAY, AUGUST 15 • Read Psalm 111:1-9

Hebrew Scriptures regard the life of praise and sacrifice as the highest value for the wise. Therefore, the wise find themselves in holy worship where praise and sacrifice take place. The wise recognize the great works of the Lord and offer thanksgiving. The Lord's mighty works reveal God's grace, mercy, power, faithfulness, justice, and holiness. More personally, the Lord provides daily food. The Lord exhibits goodwill toward God's people. The psalmist's thanksgiving flows out of true wisdom, as he recognizes his humble position in the scheme of God's creation.

Ideas such as praise and sacrifice are not common to us who live in the social atmosphere of competitive production. Our society values more what we produce or buy than who we are. We derive our value as human beings from devoting time and energy to the production of goods and services.

An increasing number of persons in the United States and other countries are intentionally reducing their working hours. Opting for a simpler lifestyle, they give up a full-time career to move into a career that demands less time commitment. This shift of priorities allows them to spend more time with their families, to enjoy leisure, and to appreciate the "space" in which they can contemplate or live the life of service. Persons who have made this shift report that they find their lives more fulfilled.

Making such a major adjustment requires great courage and wisdom. Knowing what is good for us is important, but living out the life that is good for us is supremely important. Do we really believe that the life of praise and sacrifice is important? If so, what adjustments will we make today to live the life of wisdom?

PRAYER: Grant me wisdom, O God, to live the fulfilled life rather than a fully filled one. May I communicate your presence today in my driven things-to-do and persons-to-meet agenda. Amen.

WEDNESDAY, AUGUST 16 • Read 1 Kings 2:10-12

These three verses briefly summarize the reign of King David. David, as the most revered king in all of Israel's history, is buried within the walls of his city. He has reigned for forty long years. Despite the bloodbath struggle with his sons, he finally and successfully passes his throne to his son Solomon. His kingdom and dynasty continue as God has promised. But now David is gone.

While many of us often wonder whether our lives would change if we knew about our death, I must reluctantly admit that I *do know* my death. I still remember my father's happiness when he told me about his purchase of two cemetery lots—one for himself and one for my mother. Soon after that summer, my parents came to visit me in Los Angeles for a week. The night before their return to Hawaii, they asked me to take photographs of them. They had everything ready and in order for their funeral service except the photographs. I was to be their photographer.

I vividly remember the view through my camera viewfinder. It was "a view from the end." As I focused on current reality, I experienced the event of their deaths through that view-finder. Then I realized that our faith is "a view from the end." We have creation in Genesis, a view from the beginning. Revelation depicts a creation in Christ of the new heaven and earth, a view from the end.

When you know your life's end, and you can take that into your living, everything changes. A view from the end affirms God's grace, which already operates in our lives. A view from the end is a confession that the end time has been breaking into our present time already. I learned this wisdom from my parents.

PRAYER: Grant me wisdom, O Lord, to count the days of my life. Amen.

THURSDAY, AUGUST 17 • Read 1 Kings 3:3-14

How often does God appear to us and say, "Ask what I should give you"? "Wisdom" would be pretty low on my priority list as I find myself vainly keeping the Publisher's Clearinghouse Sweepstakes numbers in my dresser drawer. In my wishful thinking, my mind wanders through the capitalist zone, often thinking about money, pleasure, comfort, freedom, and independence.

That explains precisely why I need wisdom. I need to know what is good for me and to practice it accordingly. Like Solomon, I too "am only a little child" in need of "an understanding mind." As a little child, I do not pursue things that are good for my soul; instead, I am inclined to do what pleases only my eyes.

Here true wisdom involves an understanding mind of good and evil. It begins with humility, knowing that I am only a little child who does not even "know how to go out or come in." Solomon's discerning mind wants to know God's will for all people. True wisdom becomes even more imperative when one is in a leadership position.

Clearly God gave Solomon more than what he asked of the Lord. "Riches and honor" are not bad in themselves. God welcomes both the rich and the poor. However, if our priority does not include walking in God's ways, our possessions can easily get in the way of keeping God's statutes and commandments. We learn again and again that we must seek first the kingdom of God and all other things in life will be added unto us (Matt. 6:33). This is true wisdom by which we can live.

PRAYER: Give me an understanding mind, O God, to know what is most important in my life; then give me courage to order my life accordingly. Amen.

FRIDAY, AUGUST 18 • Read John 6:51-58

The key to understanding the Gospels has to do with one's perception of who Jesus is. The Jews in today's text lack insightful understanding, so they ask how Jesus can be "the living bread." The Jews cannot imagine how the flesh of Jesus—his sacrifice of body and blood—can become the living bread.

Jesus reminds them of God's feeding of their ancestors with manna in the wilderness. The manna nourished the Israelites, not only sustaining their physical being but also sustaining their spiritual needs by helping them realize their total dependency on God. Yet despite their eating of the manna, the ultimate end was death.

The love God extended to the helpless Israelites in the wilderness comes to fruition in Jesus' life and death. As the Israelites could not survive in the wilderness without manna, Christians believe that without eating the flesh of the Son of Man and drinking his blood we cannot have life. Jesus' giving of his body and blood represents the goodwill of God for God's people.

When we truly understand that without Christ's saving grace we cannot live, move, and have our being—our spiritual awakening to our dependent relationship in our Creator—we then inherit eternal life. Our feasting on "the living bread that came from heaven" brings life not death.

God's plan includes the work of resurrection. As we break the bread and drink the cup of Jesus, we no longer thirst or hunger. Through God, Jesus overcame death; now being with God, he offers himself to us, which leads to eternal life. We only need to accept this great work of God.

PRAYER: Nourish me today, O God, with manna that comes from you, the living bread of Jesus Christ. Amen.

SATURDAY, AUGUST 19 • Read Ephesians 5:15-17

The writer addresses these words to the whole congregation at Ephesus. We as a community of followers of Jesus Christ must strive to live the life of true wisdom.

As members of a community of true wisdom, we must first discern the times. Indeed, our "days are evil." Thinking about our time as one of moral crisis has become a cliché. The world continues to turn even when national leaders fall into the trap of deception and corruption. Even affluence can become a catalyst for corruption.

Some may say in apathy that the church is always there despite its inability to influence what happens outside of it. Others may have trouble sensing the church's importance in the global community. However, our current condition resembles that of the church at Ephesus, and we also would do well to heed the writer's advice to live as wise people.

The community of true wisdom also must discern the will of God. This is not an easy task when we consider the diversity of opinion, if not belief, that coexists side by side within the church. However, our different understandings about the will of God may be less dangerous than either our apathy toward or our "boxing in" of the will of God. We must discern the will of God with open-mindedness and with humility, understanding that no human ideas can limit the will of God. Then we would do better to start from the points of agreement about the will of God rather than the points of contention. If, in our community wisdom, the church lives out the will of God to the best of its ability, transformation will come both within and without the church.

PRAYER: Grant discernment of the time, O Lord, as well as your will for the church. Amen.

SUNDAY, AUGUST 20 • Read Ephesians 5:15-20

Discernment of our time and God's will can best be practiced when we consider them in specific and concrete terms. For the church at Ephesus, even sharing a meal can turn into an embarrassing occasion, especially when some members indulge themselves with too much wine. The writer contrasts the two states: inebriation and its degrading consequences as opposed to true fulfillment in the life of the Spirit.

The point of the text here is not so much about drinking as an evil behavior but about the church's loss of identity. The church gathers, seeking the life "filled with the Spirit." Like the church at Ephesus, today's churches, when they fail to discern the time and the will of God, may fall into the same trap of forgetting why the church gathers.

The church is not some organizational machine to maintain in a perpetual existence. The church is not the land or building that a group of people owns and maintains. The church is a group of believers that recognizes the need to celebrate what God is doing among God's people. Therefore, they "sing psalms and hymns and spiritual songs."

Many churches are clueless about God's activities among them. By discerning where God is and what God is doing, these churches may join in the work of the true church. They may discover the life "filled with the Spirit" and join in the singing of spiritual songs, "giving thanks to God...for everything." May your worship today reflect your life filled with the Spirit.

PRAYER: Lead and guide your church, O God. Fill your church with your Spirit. Amen.

Be Strong in the Lord

August 21–27, 2000 • Walter H. McKelvey*

MONDAY, AUGUST 21 • Read 1 Kings 8:1

Then Solomon summoned [all the religious leaders] to bring up the ark of the covenant.

This verse shares both the glamour and power of the kings in the Bible. Clearly King Solomon is in charge. And clearly civic life in Jerusalem intertwines with religious life—the secular and the sacred are inseparable. To be a citizen is to be religious. The Ark of the Lord's covenant has not adorned the Temple in Jerusalem. So the king directs the leadership to bring the religious foundation of the nation's faith and being to the Temple. The Ark represents the one sovereign God. It houses the commandments and depicts the fundamental principles of the faith.

We live in a different world. This kind of decree or summons would hardly survive in any religious or governmental arena. A decree or summons of this nature would turn people off and probably generate apathy toward the faith.

Yet in our Christian faith and practice, wouldn't it be great if we believed that the God we meet on Sunday in church will meet us in the government hall, work hall, school hall, and on the streets? Common understandings between religious and civic circles elude us. Today our challenge focuses on the need for a new oneness, a kind of solidarity that will direct us back to basics and affirm the value of our Christian faith understandings in all areas of life.

PRAYER: Dear God, just as Solomon summoned the leadership at Jerusalem, today this remembrance challenges and summons me. Help me to be obedient to the challenge. Amen.

---

*President-Dean, Gammon Theological Seminary, Atlanta, Georgia.

Then the priests brought the ark of the covenant of the Lord to its place, in the inner sanctuary of the house.

When I was a little boy, I remember that my mother and several other communion stewardesses (only women at that time) in this rural two-point Methodist Church charge were summoned by church ritual and elected by the quarterly conference to prepare the table for celebration of the Lord's Supper. They took pride and extreme care in preparing the altar and the elements for this holy meal. The cross, brass cup, tray, and candleholders were polished spotless. The women filled each Communion cup carefully and checked the uniformity of each tray of bread, which they then covered with white cloths. Their behavior and demeanor conveyed the sacredness and necessity of the task.

The orders of worship elevate the celebration of the Holy Eucharist. The altar table becomes the inner sanctuary. The congregation focuses on the symbols of God's son, his body and blood, as central.

At the time of the setting of this scripture, biblical history and chronology had not yet seen God through Jesus, but the people revered God's presence as revealed in the Ark and through the Commandments. The priests were set apart to perform this special and sacred duty of placing the Ark in the most holy place of the sanctuary. The very act called and challenged all the people to acknowledge the adorning of the Temple with a higher glory. The task was not a business-as-usual activity but demanded special attention.

To what sacred tasks do we find ourselves called? How do our approach and demeanor convey the special nature of this task to others?

PRAYER: Dear God, help me know that you are foremost and special in and to life. May my praise of you and my service to you be seen as special, this day and every day. Amen.

WEDNESDAY, AUGUST 23 • Read 1 Kings 8:10-11

The glory of the Lord filled the house of the Lord.

In most religious and denominational circles, we find ceremonies, rituals, and sacraments for all occasions. Denominational resource centers provide rituals, hymns, devotional guides, prayers, and other orders for use on almost any occasion at any time.

Our exposure to many of these resources has rendered much of our Christian behavior routine and less experiential. For example, the routine church and routine worshiper hold an order for the Sunday service of praise that is largely methodical and habitual. Without looking at the worship bulletin, we expect a prelude, a hymn of praise, an invocation, a responsive reading, an affirmation of faith, a pastoral prayer, an offering, a hymn of preparation, a sermon, a hymn of invitation, a benediction, and a postlude. At some points the order of service may vary, but we know that basically these elements comprise our order of worship; and it takes us about an hour, give or take a few minutes, to complete it.

In addition to the routine church service and worship order, we have in our possession guides for daily living and daily prayer. These routines often become perfunctory, providing little or no meaning. Doing them gives us a sense simply of satisfying that daily Christian task. There is little room apart from the fulfillment of this routine task to experience, see, and hear what God is saying.

Sometimes we must withdraw from our holy places and let the Lord of life set the agenda. When the glory of God fills our temples, the routine work of the faith becomes secondary. We experience anew God's blessings in different and unusual ways.

PRAYER: Dear God, help me see the value of the routine, while opening my eyes to the possibility of new experiences inside and outside my temple. Amen.

THURSDAY, AUGUST 24 • Read 1 Kings 8:22-30

"Hear the plea of your servant and of your people Israel when they pray toward this place."

Solomon has built the Temple, and the Ark has come to rest in the holy of holies. Israel has come into the Promised Land, established a central sanctuary, and now "rests" from its labors. Solomon, in his prayer, praises God for God's faithfulness to the people and expresses the hope that the Temple will be a meeting place for the people and God.

A prayer of dedication is appropriate in various and sundry circles. We dedicate our lives; we dedicate our properties; we dedicate our children; we dedicate ourselves in marriage; we dedicate our churches. The act of dedication is a special time, usually an awesome and memorable moment. To dedicate means to sanctify and set aside. Through this process an anointing ensues. A dedication signals the higher order of a particular act: It knows no bounds in the context of relationships. It is not limited in response. It is final and complete.

Solomon's prayer of dedication signifies the conclusion of a task. Our scripture notes that the Ark now resides in the Temple. Solomon, in so many words, says to the Lord that the placing of this symbol in the Temple is the result of his dedication to God. "I want the world to know that I am not ashamed of my relationship with you. God, I want you to know that I commit myself to you and you alone. I stand before the whole assembly of Israel and display this act of dedication and devotion and pray that you will always hear our prayers and respond accordingly."

When we dedicate our lives to God, we act in total trust. We filter all of our marching orders before proceeding. Dedication is confessional. It is redemptive.

PRAYER: Almighty God, God of Israel, God of Solomon, God forever, loving and holy God, through your anointing my commitment to you is realized. Thank you. Amen.

FRIDAY, AUGUST 25 • Read Psalm 84

How lovely is your dwelling place, O Lord.

Psalm 84 is a prayer of praise and thanksgiving. It acknowledges the safety, security and blessedness of those who dwell in God's house. The prayer gives honor to the blessings of a journey with God. When we dwell in God's presence, we experience that presence in our lives. In the venues of life we experience fulfillment when we walk with God.

As we approach a new millennium, we sense a plague of insecurity and a lack of hope. Anxiousness and fear linger on every street and lurk around every corner. We have doubts about the present and the future. Our living seems haunted by anxiety.

Our society has tended to deal with all of life's struggles through technological, political, and social structures. We are the keepers of creation with dominion over the works of the Creator, but we seem to forget that our humanity is subservient to the Creator. God is still in charge, still in control. We run into trouble when we neglect or fail to yearn and faint for the courts of our God.

The call from the psalmist challenges us to a new life in God. When we walk with God, we find beauty, joy, happiness, singing, strength, comfort, safety, security, favor, and honor. God's peace encompasses all, making room even for the sparrow and swallow. For those of us who venture to enter the Temple, the place of God's abode, we receive blessings beyond measure.

PRAYER: Dear God, I too would rather be a doorkeeper in your house than dwell in the tents of the wicked. My home is with you. Thank you for your care of me. Amen.

SATURDAY, AUGUST 26 • Read Ephesians 6:10-20

Finally, be strong in the Lord and in the strength of his power. Put on the whole armor of God, so that you may be able to stand.

Health therapists and physicians describe and prescribe methods that will increase our physical strength. They encourage the routines of proper diet, rest, and exercise. We are challenged to learn relaxation, to avoid stress, and to laugh a lot. The list goes on and on. For the sake of our physical strength and well-being, physical behavioral rubrics are the rule rather than the exception. We desire to live above the valleys of physical disease and weakness, so we try to discipline ourselves in response to proven methods.

The approach to spiritual strength and fulfillment in life takes a somewhat different twist in this letter to the Ephesians. The writer challenges us to put on the whole armor of God to strengthen ourselves.

When we become disciplined bearers of God's armor, we see and experience life on a different level. With God's armor we understand that being strong is more than a contention with the physical. God's armor protects, directs, guides, and enables us to stand even when we find ourselves in physical bondage.

If the fruits of physical strength and freedom elude us, we can still stand in strength. We stand in strength because we fasten on the belt of truth, and righteousness is our breastplate. Our shoes are the gospel of peace; faith is our shield; salvation is a helmet; the word of God is our sword; and prayer is an unending discipline.

PRAYER: Dear God, I am truly strong because I am strong through you. No nights are too dark, no days too long, no mountains too high, no valleys too deep because your armor prevails and protects. Amen.

SUNDAY, AUGUST 27 • **Read John 6:56-69**

So Jesus asked the twelve, "Do you also wish to go away?" Simon Peter answered him, "Lord, to whom can we go? You have the words of eternal life."

The challenge for humankind is to keep the faith. The journey is sometimes hard and long. When we receive the ground rules, we sometimes tend to resist paying the price. We want the resulting benefits of the struggle, but we don't want to engage in it.

Our goal is to be in "the number." To be numbered among the recipients of eternal life, we must live as Jesus lived and taught. We find ourselves tempted to review and contemplate easy options. However, Jesus challenges us to yield not to temptation.

Peter and the other disciples' decision to stay with Jesus is not an easy or popular one. The option-oriented, easy seekers leave. When faced with the challenge to live as Jesus lived and taught, they are out the door.

Peter and the others know that no other elective courses are available. They know that the ultimate source of support rests in Christ. Electives and options skew the process. They cloud the issue. They make it easy now with limited access at the end. The disciples' experience and understanding of Jesus have led them to believe that no other way is valid. That is why Peter states, " Lord, to whom can we go? You have the words of eternal life. We have come to believe and know that you are the Holy One of God."

Jesus has the words of eternal life—eternal life now, tomorrow, and forever.

PRAYER: Dear God, thank you for your Son, our Savior, and for the life-giving words that sustain me now, tomorrow, and forever. Amen.

Love's Many Facets

August 28–September 3, 2000 • *F. Dean Lueking**

MONDAY, AUGUST 28 • **Read Song of Solomon 2:8-13**

Arise, my love, my fair one, and come away....

The Song of Solomon has a firm place in the Bible as a reminder that the love of men and women for each other is nothing second-rate. When God created humans, the Creator wove into us warm and powerful currents of mutual attraction. Our bodies reflect God's design and gift, a source of pleasure and delight toward each other.

Sin entered in and infected love with lust. But a greater love has come to us—the love of Christ Jesus that reclaims us for God and restores romantic love as a sign of Christ and his bride, the church.

The eight chapters of this lesser-known book of the Bible celebrate that love found both in human attraction of the sexes and in the divine love that draws us to God. We need to recover that kind of love. In our world, too jaded by romantic love that does not last, the deep, exciting, enduring love that resonates through this ancient book needs the embodiment of modern people.

*Arise, my love, my fair one, and come away....*If it has been too long since you have spoken such beautiful words or recalled the memory of them, this is a time to renew and remember. This facet of love should season, not wither. How? By establishing romantic love on God, who blesses and deepens it. After all, why should the description of romantic love be left to the *National Enquirer*?

PRAYER: Season our human love, O God, with your eternal love. Amen.

---

*Senior Pastor, Grace Lutheran Church, River Forest, Illinois.

TUESDAY, AUGUST 29 • Read Song of Solomon 2:11-12

*Now the winter is past...the time of singing has come, and
the voice of the turtledove is heard in our land.*

A wisdom and hope underlie this beautiful image of a springtime freshness following on winter doldrums.

The wisdom is that human love, fragile and vulnerable,
can have its wintry season. Passions subside, and intimacies
slacken. Divorce is a bleak time, as all who go through it
know. But the winter of the heart may take the form of slow
erosion in marriage, in family, or in friendship ties because
one takes the other for granted. So people end up having all
they can do to get up in the morning, let alone find the energy
to nurture, care, give, communicate, grow.

The hope this passage offers is that winter passes. It does
so because a spiritual strength well anchored in the grace of
God in Jesus Christ has been like winter borne, continually
flowing down under the icy bleakness. It brings back a springtime freshness and thaws frozen hearts. Thawing happens
when the community of worship lifts us from our isolation;
when truth is spoken in love, and we come upon those surprises of grace that open a door where before a dead end
seemed final.

Not long ago I spoke this text to a bride and groom. She is
eighty-six; he is eighty-eight. They were high school sweet-
hearts and went to the senior prom together. Their paths
parted. Marriage and widowhood followed for both. Then they
resumed correspondence, sensed a fresh breeze of love, and
chose to marry.

Each time a I hear a turtledove singing, I think of them.

**PRAYER: Gracious God, bring the springtime freshness of your
grace back to wintry hearts. Amen.**

WEDNESDAY, AUGUST 30 • Read Psalm 45:1-2, 6-9

My heart overflows with a goodly theme....
You are the most handsome of men;
grace is poured upon your lips;
therefore God has blessed you forever.

What's going on here?

It's a royal wedding. The psalm writer is present and effusive in his approval of the young king about to take a bride. We who can remember (sadly now) the splendor of British royal weddings have a link to the grand moment Psalm 45 captures.

But a hint of something deeper and grander by far appears as the psalm continues, "Your throne, O God, endures forever .... / Your royal scepter is a scepter of equity; / you love righteousness and hate wickedness."

Take a leap down through the centuries to great David's greater Son, the Messiah, the Christ, whose realm does indeed endure forever. And keep the spirit of the psalm writer as you transfer this lavish praise to the Son of God who loved us and gave himself for us. Then this psalm invites us to do something we do not do often enough—pour out the best of the heart to the Savior. Being made in God's image and restored to that image by Jesus who came to his kingdom by a cross for us, we respond from the deepest part of us, the soul.

The American television producer/genius Norman Lear once asked the preeminent American theologian/historian Martin Marty what was the essence of worship. "Gratitude," Marty answered, "...outpoured from the heart." And the souls of two very different men found common ground where there is room for all, where the heart overflows in grateful praise to the God who has first lavished regal love upon us.

PRAYER: God of grace, fill me to overflowing with your love, that I may give it back to you in loving service. Amen.

THURSDAY, AUGUST 31 • Read James 1:17-21

He gave us birth by the word of truth.

What can a word do? Plenty. A word can crush or inspire, kill or give life. Such a word connects inseparably to events, deed and word needing each other to be powerful, even life-changing.

The New Testament Letter of James was written to counteract an old tendency of talking but not walking the truth of God. "What good is it, my brothers and sisters, if you say you have faith but do not have works?" (2:14) was the problem, and still is. James meets that dilemma by focusing on God, who fulfills promises and gives us birth by the word of truth!

God has packed the power to redeem and renew us into a word, the holy gospel that bears to us the good news of Jesus who loved us and gave himself for us. Not just any news, not just any religious talk. This gospel is life-giving because it is inseparable from the risen Lord who comes among us through the word that points to him. In Christ we find ourselves on speaking terms with God and are called to speak the truth in love to one another.

In a world pelted daily with words beyond number—dumb talk, phony speech, angry words, pointless yakking—God takes an amazing risk. God entrusts the gospel word to the lips of God's people to speak the truth in love, to upbuild one another in faith, to speak good news where there is none. Think of it: We hang on the word of life as we speak Christ to others again today, which makes us midwives in that wondrous mystery that quickens souls and equips lives to be abundant in works of love.

PRAYER: Speak to me, blessed God, that I may speak life to others. Amen.

FRIDAY, SEPTEMBER 1 • Read James 1:22-27

Be doers of the word, not merely hearers.

James may have been a relative of Jesus who became a leader of the early believers in Jerusalem, a group greatly beset with needs of body and soul alike. No wonder then that this letter is a steady call for deeds as a sure sign of living faith. Hearing but not doing the truth is unthinkable in the new creation Christ Jesus has brought.

I think of my own spiritual journey and consider what puts distance between hearing and doing the word. Procrastination is a common roadblock. I know what needs to be done but postpone it. Distraction also puts distance between hearing and doing—again not willful rejection of the concrete action of faith but giving in to the magnetic pull of busyness or some other excuse. Lethargy, a more serious spiritual malady of inner listlessness, leads to a shrug of indifference rather than arousal to serve.

To all of these excuses and more, the call of God is to be doers of the word. Let the spirit of God do the sanctifying work of carrying the good news of Christ from the ear to the heart—and then to the hands and arms and legs and feet in deeds of loving God and neighbor with all our being.

James calls for specific action, caring for orphans, widows, and all persons in distress. Faithful doing of the word comes from seeing, really seeing, in others with needs of every kind none other than Jesus himself. Jesus told a great story about such seeing (Matt. 25:31-46). Doing because of seeing is blessed beyond words!

PRAYER: Move me, blessed God, to see and do today the deeds that honor you and serve others; and make me glad to do my part. Amen.

SATURDAY, SEPTEMBER 2 • Read Mark 7:1-8

*They noticed that some of his disciples were eating
with defiled hands, that is, without washing them.*

Winston Churchill told the story of the man who leaped into
a river to save a drowning child only to have the mother, when
she held her rescued child in her arms, exclaim, "But you
didn't recover his cap!"

That story tests credibility. Could anybody, especially a
mother whose child was snatched from death, really be that
blind to what counts? Yet I trust Churchill's story because our
fallen humanity has an astonishing capacity for blind, stubborn ingratitude that is deeply embedded.

The moment in Jesus' ministry recorded by Mark touches
upon what makes one clean before God. Jesus has just fed the
five thousand, stilled the storm, and healed the multitudes of
the sick and suffering who rush at him as he comes ashore at
Capernaum—all signs of the kingdom, signs that cleanse us
before God.

Mark carefully notes that some Pharisees and scribes have
come all the way from Jerusalem, a ninety-mile journey, to
confront Jesus with sharp accusations of undermining everything holy *because his disciples ate without washing their
hands*. Yes, to the Pharisees hand washing moves beyond
manners or hygiene; it symbolizes being clean before God.
But that's the point; rightness with God does not come by
scrupulous keeping of human regulations. Cleansing comes by
loving God who first loved us and by translating that received
love into the practiced love of neighbor and self. This is the
cleansing that counts.

Seeing the forest, not just the individual trees, is an old
but relevant principle for this day.

**PRAYER: God of grace, help me love others in the fullness of your
greatheartedness. Amen.**

SUNDAY, SEPTEMBER 3 • Read Mark 7:14-15, 21-23

"There is nothing outside a person that by going in can defile, but the things that come out are what defile."

Is our behavior the product of nature or nurture? That debate goes on endlessly, and it is well that it does because the subject is mighty important.

In this brief passage, set in the context of ceremonial cleanness, Jesus speaks a strong word about nature rather than nurture as the key to behavior. Evil of every sort originates deep down within the soul where all our woes begin.

Despite our fallen humanity, we may not adopt the slogan, "The devil made me do it," and evade our own responsibility. Fallen nature is also redeemed nature. We have a Savior who went to the cross to accomplish that for us. All the religious rules in the world will not turn us Godward, which is the context in which Jesus spoke this truth.

Claim that redeeming love again today, and then instead of getting stuck in the nature / nurture debate, be an influence of genuine goodness toward others. Of course nurture counts tremendously, especially when it springs from a heart where Christ dwells and the fruits of the Spirit are abundant.

PRAYER: Renew me from the heart, redeemer God, and let it show in my words and deeds again this day. Amen.

Justice and Generosity

September 4–10, 2000 • Roberta Hestenes*

MONDAY, SEPTEMBER 4 • Read Proverbs 22:1-2, 8-9

The rich and the poor have this in common: the Lord is the maker of them all.

Scripture often mentions the rich and the poor as common human categories of difference. Yet persons' economic status should not be the controlling basis of our interactions with them. Sometimes we today in our middle-class culture see ourselves as neither rich nor poor. So we feel free to envy or emulate the rich in their comforts, pleasures, and power and to pity or exploit the poor in their powerlessness and vulnerability. We may even ignore the most destitute and oppressed because we feel poor ourselves in our culture of endless consumption.

This proverb reminds us that human worth or dignity is never a matter of money. Human identity is rooted in the creative act of God. The human family displays a profound unity; all people are more alike than different. We all share the same Maker who values and cherishes creation.

When the rich share bread generously with the poor, that action nourishes both. To act with generosity reflects and honors the generosity of God who has given all of us life itself. To act unjustly assaults God's creative unity and yields disastrous consequences. Generosity is one way we break down the barriers between people that injustice builds up.

PRAYER: Generous and gracious God, thank you for the gift of life that I share with all other people. Keep me from a selfish and grasping spirit, and give me your spirit of generosity for all. Amen.

---

*Senior pastor, Solana Beach Presbyterian Church near San Diego, California; formerly president of Eastern College in Pennsylvania.

TUESDAY, SEPTEMBER 5 • Read Proverbs 22:22-23

Do not rob the poor because they are poor, or crush the afflicted at the gate; for the Lord pleads their cause and despoils of life those who despoil them.

Because something *can* be done does not mean that it *should* be done. Because the poor have no power and little access to community resources, it is tempting to take advantage of them for our own gain. The poor are often landless, deep in debt, and vulnerable. They have few defenders in a "bottom-line world."

Vicky is a young woman who six months ago was living in an old car with her six-year-old son and her few possessions. When she could finally rent a run-down room in the poorest part of town, the landlord waited only a short time before raising the rent exorbitantly while refusing to do any needed repairs to make the space safe and livable.

The grocery store in Vicky's neighborhood charges more for food than the ones in the prosperous suburb nearby, and her employer pays her less than minimum wage. "Business is business," we say, yet such actions crush the poor in this country and throughout the world, grinding them even deeper into debt and misery.

Generosity toward the poor is not enough. Justice must accompany generosity. In a picture drawn from the law court, the Lord pleads the case of the poor. God defends them. But God not only serves as the defender of the weak and vulnerable, God also serves as the judge who decides with fairness and equity *for* the poor and *against* the despoiler. How we treat the poor matters to God; therefore, it must matter to us.

PRAYER: Lord, help me join you in pleading the cause of the poor in an indifferent world. Keep me from using other people for my own benefit. Amen.

WEDNESDAY, SEPTEMBER 6 • Read Psalm 125

Those who trust in the Lord are like Mount Zion, which cannot be shaken but stands fast for ever (NEB).

We can easily tire or grow discouraged on the journey of faith. So much distracts and disturbs us as we seek to move closer to God. We end up struggling for survival rather than singing the songs of joy and faith. This Song of Ascents draws us into ancient Israel's journey of faith. Pilgrims would climb the hills on their way to Mount Zion to worship God.

Traveling in this company and joining this song of the faithful may encourage us. We too can assert our confidence in God's help, God's power over evil, and our trust in God's immovable strength. The very hills and the mountain remind Israel of God's protective presence. The psalm expresses an unshakable trust in the dependability of the Lord.

After praising God, the psalm turns to lament and prayer. The land is not yet at peace. Injustice tempts even the faithful. Suffering and evil are still present in the land, just as they are present all over the earth today. But we pray that wickedness will not be "at home" here, as if it belonged here permanently.

Even though we live in a world where wrongdoing and injustice exist, we do not want to be seduced or drawn into participation. When we pray that God will do good to the good and bring destruction on those who destroy, we confess our own belief in moral accountability and our need for God's mercy and grace. Peace will come with righteousness.

PRAYER: Lord of heaven and earth, who brought into being everything that is, including the mountains, the stars, and the sea, help me trust today in your power and in your love; protect me and your people from temptation and evil; give me joy on the journey to peace. Amen.

THURSDAY, SEPTEMBER 7 • Read James 2:1-13

*My brothers and sisters, do you with your acts of favoritism
really believe in our glorious Lord Jesus Christ?*

It has long been said that 11:00 on Sunday morning, when
churches meet for worship, is the most segregated hour in
America. Not only are whites and blacks, Asians and Latinos
largely separated during worship, but class and culture further
divide congregations and denominations in patterns clearly
identified by sociologists. The habits of discrimination have
become so entrenched in the church that most of us take them
for granted.

James denounces discrimination in the strongest possible
terms. Showing favoritism based on external characteristics is
sin. True followers of Jesus Christ live out the values that
Jesus modeled and taught. This text in James challenges every
profession of faith in "our glorious Lord Jesus Christ" that is
not accompanied by a change in behavior related to the practice of discrimination.

Using one example, James supplies multiple reasons not to
show favoritism within the fellowship. Christ told us not to
judge. Honoring the wealthy above the poor dishonors the poor
and disobeys Christ. God has chosen the poor, and who are we
to reject those whom God has chosen? Next, the early Christians' own experience with the rich should have warned them
of the foolishness of their bias. Most importantly, favoritism
represents a failure of love—the command of Jesus that we
love one another. Strong words, these—requiring a strong
response. Living out our faith demands action not words.

SUGGESTION FOR MEDITATION: **We discriminate against the poor
more subtly than in James's illustration. Consider, Do the poor
feel fully welcome in our fellowship? Does our faith community
include the homeless, those with handicapping conditions, the
needy? If not, what needs to change?**

FRIDAY, SEPTEMBER 8 • Read James 2:14-17

What good is it, my brothers and sisters, if you say you have faith but do not have works? Can faith save you?

The world is full of hungry people. Each day about 35,000 children in the world die from malnutrition and preventable diseases. This is a horrible truth. While many affluent people struggle with ways to lose weight, millions lack the barest necessities of life. Empty words, no matter how well-intended, provide no warmth and fill no hungry stomachs.

This overwhelming reality need not paralyze us. Bob Pearce, the founder of World Vision, a Christian humanitarian agency devoted to serving the poor, used to ask, "How do you feed a hungry world?" His answer: "One person at a time." We cannot do everything, but we can do something. A living faith is dynamic and productive. Of a merely verbal faith, James asks, "What good is that?" For the poor, these are merely worthless words. Nothing changes. This omission does not fulfill Christ's law of love. Such faith does no good for anyone, not even for the one professing it.

The surest evidence of a genuine faith is not the ease with which the language of belief is spoken but in the results that emerge as the consequence of a transformational confidence in Christ. Such a faith expresses itself in concrete acts of love to real people who are in need. In Romans Paul speaks of "the obedience of faith." James does not pit faith against works here. He warns of the dangers of a dead faith, a barren faith that has only the form but not the power of conviction or the passion of a godly purpose. Real faith produces real results.

PRAYER: Gracious Lord Jesus, who came not to be served but to serve, give me your heart that I may serve the needy around me in practical ways this day. Forgive me all the times I have used words as a substitute for loving action. Restore in me a living faith, I pray. Amen.

SATURDAY, SEPTEMBER 9 • Read Mark 7:24-30

The woman was a Gentile, of Syrophoenician origin. She begged [Jesus] to cast the demon out of her daughter.

He only wants to get away from the pressures and the crowds. She has an urgent need. He is on retreat. She has heard of him, and she comes seeking help, not for herself but for her daughter who is suffering terribly. He is Jewish; she is a hellenized Phoenician from the province of Syria, an outsider to the faith of Israel. His mission is to the Jews; her mission is to get help for her daughter from this man whom she believes can help her. They seem at an impasse.

The woman humbles herself at his feet while boldly and persistently imploring Jesus for help. He promises her nothing and speaks ironic words that could discourage her. He finds her interruption of his mission to the children of Israel inappropriate; the children's food should not be given to the pet dogs under the table. For now, Israel is his priority, not the Gentiles. But she challenges him. She doesn't reject his comparison but extends it! "Even the dogs get the crumbs under the table." Her overwhelming confidence in Jesus leads her to assure him that even the "leftovers" are enough for her need.

The woman's faith in him surpasses the unbelief and dullness of the Pharisees and scribes who should have welcomed him as one of their own. Jesus responds to her daring faith with approval and delight and sends her home with her request answered: Her daughter receives healing. Jesus responds to the woman's faith in the same way he responds to every demonstration of faith—with justice and generosity. He commends her and grants her request. Another barrier has been broken down.

PRAYER: Lord, give me the boldness and faith of this outsider, this courageous woman, so that I may seek your love and power for the lives of those around me. Amen.

SUNDAY, SEPTEMBER 10 • Read Mark 7:31-37

[Jesus] sighed and said,... "Be opened." And immediately [the deaf man's] ears were opened...and he spoke plainly ....They were astounded beyond measure, saying, "He has done everything well."

This week we have focused on the justice and generosity of God in overcoming every human barrier and obstacle to divine love. In Mark 7 while Jesus is still in a primarily Gentile region, a man who is deaf and who suffers from a debilitating speech defect is brought to Jesus. Probably the man has experienced ridicule and rejection from other people because of his "difference."

Children and adults can treat those with physical disabilities with cruelty, regarding them as less than fully human or not worthy of respect. In some places in the world today, deaf children are locked away, and the disabled are left to die. They are not seen as deserving of love and attention.

Lacking both hearing and speech, the man is both isolated and needy when the crowds beg Jesus to touch him. Jesus, with sublime sensitivity, takes the man aside. He gives him his full attention and deals with him privately—away from the stares and curiosity of the onlookers. The intimacy of this interaction, Jesus' touch and sigh, signals his compassion and care for this one man. The silenced man now speaks plainly. His isolation is broken by the power of Christ coming into his life, just as our isolation and loneliness end when Jesus Christ enters our life. No one is outside the circle of his love. Truly he does everything well.

PRAYER: O Lord who heals, I bring you all my brokenness—the brokenness within and the brokenness in human relationships around me. Thank you for your tenderness and patience. Touch me that I may know and share your love with someone who needs you today. Amen.

Where Wisdom Is Found

September 11–17, 2000 • Rod Barnett*

MONDAY, SEPTEMBER 11 • Read Proverbs 1:20-33

King Solomon prayed for wisdom, a commodity considered more valuable than wealth. In today's passage, the Book of Proverbs personifies wisdom for the first time. Wisdom is a distinctive being; it is the mind of God disclosed. Wisdom plays the role of the prophet with an imperative message. God does not take pleasure in our demise or folly. On the contrary, God desires the close and intimate relationship for which we were created. Without exception, God is always trying to get our attention. Wisdom comes in discovering God's grace and living in the reality of God's presence daily.

However, even with God's wisdom present, pride is our worst enemy. Thinking we know better than God, we allow our pride to create self-sufficiency, distorted intelligence, and false wisdom. Without God we become "fools." Eating "the fruit of their way" describes the consequences of foolishness and pride.

Jesus told a parable about two builders to illustrate the hard truth of consequences. Hearing the words of Jesus and obeying them is the best form of wisdom. Present discomfort in obedience is nothing compared to greater consequences of disobedience in the future.

Wisdom is not the abundance of knowledge or the ability to manipulate situations and circumstances. Wisdom is listening to God and obeying. As we do, God provides true wisdom in daily living.

PRAYER: Dear God, even at my best I am foolish. I desire to be wise. I want to hear your word and obey. Help me make that decision in my life today. Amen.

---

*General evangelist of The United Methodist Church, living in Winfield, West Virginia.

TUESDAY, SEPTEMBER 12 • Read Psalm 19:1-6

God is a God of revelation—wanting both to know each of us completely and to be completely known. God wants to be known, not simply known about. Creation is an explicit part of God's being. Creation tells the story of God. The Bible does not strive to authenticate God's existence through the existence of the universe. Today's passage indicates that the universe evidences the wisdom, power, and majesty of God.

This psalm identifies the Creator as El, God of might and power. The heavens tell forth in the emphatic present tense, denoting a continuous process. The heavens have declared, presently declare, and will forever proclaim the majesty of their source. Though physically silent, creation eloquently witnesses to God's splendor.

The voice of creation cries out. In humanity's best attempts, words fail to describe adequately the brilliance of the heavens. The world points to God with a million fingers. God, whom the heavens cannot contain, appears in every flower and every living thing. God's power displayed in creation reveals our finiteness and affirms the belief that we exist for a purpose: to live in right relationship with the creator Father.

Another wonderful aspect of creation involves our gazing at the heavens or marveling at the expansive spectacle of the earth and acknowledging a sense of peace. Faced with the struggles of life, we contemplate the phenomenon of creation and realize that the God who created all can handle any problem we have. Nothing lies beyond God's power and ability. Again, we become wise by discovering God's creative power at work in our lives.

PRAYER: Dear God, I marvel at your creation. I join with creation to declare your power and majesty. Today, God, I want to trust you, because as I gaze at your creation, I realize there is nothing in my life you cannot handle. Amen.

WEDNESDAY, SEPTEMBER 13 • Read Psalm 19:7-14

While creation declares the power, majesty and wisdom of God, the law of the Lord is greater still. One cannot simply rely on creation to know God and God's plan. Paul mentions that everyone knows about God because nature proclaims God's existence (Rom. 1:19-20). However, revealed spiritual truth must fortify natural religion, and God's self-revelation through scripture discloses God's holiness as well as humanity's sinfulness.

Verses 7-14 focus our attention on the law of the Lord. The law, or *torah*, is not merely commandment or legislation; it refers to the total teaching of the revealed will of God exclusively and completely in scripture. The law or teaching of God reaches perfection in every respect; it restores the soul. We are born again through "the living and enduring word of God" (1 Pet. 1:23).

Often we perceive the concept of law as one of confining structure or burdensome ritualistic rules that prevent us from finding joy or happiness. This perception may result in our viewing God as a mean, nasty, and hateful being. This psalm declares the opposite to be true: While God is holy and just and intolerant of sin, God is gracious and merciful; so God gives the law. The law revives the soul and gives joy to the heart. The law makes us wise and lights our eyes. God's laws warn as well as reward, enlightening and directing our journey of faith.

We learn about forgiveness and God's salvation as we experience the reality of God's law in our daily living. We lay bare before God and God's law every part of our lives, allowing God's love to direct every thought and word.

PRAYER: Dear God, I desire what only your word can provide. I submit to your rule; examine all my words and thoughts. Amen.

THURSDAY, SEPTEMBER 14 • Read Mark 8:27-38

The setting of this passage is Caesarea Philippi, a pagan city known for its worship of Greek gods and for its temples erected to the god Pan. The city serves as a significantly fitting place for Jesus to question his disciples with regard to his identity.

Jesus initially begins his questioning based on public opinion and popular belief: "Who do people say that I am?" At this point none of the disciples declares Jesus to be the Christ. The truth of Jesus' deity, dignity, and function remains veiled from the populace. Individually and corporately the responses provide inadequate answers. Then Jesus turns the question toward the disciples: "But who do you say that I am?" Jesus desires their personal opinion concerning his identity because he wants his disciples to know with certainty his identity and to realize the cost of following him.

Persons often ask for personal opinion concerning numerous situations, items, and personalities. Persons ask for our opinions concerning politics, world issues, and current affairs. Our opinion is sometimes sought with regard to a movie or even a good restaurant. Our opinion concerning religion and faith, because it is essential to our character and way of life, commands specific and unveiled attention.

Day after day we can go through life giving our opinions about matters that range from the trivial to the profound. We engage in discussions about church, the Bible, worship services and styles. However, at some time each of us has to face his or her personal opinion concerning Jesus. Who is he? Who is he to you? It is not that our opinion about other things does not matter, but what matters most is, "Who do you say that I am?"

PRAYER: Dear God, I want to know Jesus in all his fullness. I do not want simply to know about him; I want to know him. Then empower me to let others know who Jesus is to me. Amen.

FRIDAY, SEPTEMBER 15 • **Read Mark 8:29**

There Peter stands, having heard the most searching question any person can hear. Jesus asks, "Who do you say that I am?" In a flash of revelation, Peter replies, "You are the Christ" (NIV). Peter makes a simple and direct confession.

Peter has listened to Jesus preach. He has witnessed Jesus' miracles. Hour after hour Peter has listened to Jesus as they have walked the road or have sat and broken bread around the table. Peter knows that Jesus differs from everyone else, though he cannot quite describe the difference. Now in this critical moment, Jesus confronts Peter with this searching question, and Peter receives a divine insight.

We can recall other instances of divine insight: Hundreds of years earlier, Abram stood on a hillside. God had asked him to look up and see the stars. God had given Abram a promise. So now Abram looked at the stars, and the Bible says he believed—not that Abram had not believed God before, but now he saw the stars and believed. Believed as he had never believed before, in a fresh new way.

And Peter has this same experience. It was not that Peter had not decided to follow Jesus earlier, but now Peter receives a divine insight as to who Jesus really is. We may have a similar experience when we find ourselves in the presence of God. The insight may come through a worship service, a sermon, an anthem, serving food at a soup kitchen, or teaching Sunday school. It may come as we witness simple ways in which God works in our lives. And we believe. It is not that we have not believed before, but God speaks to our soul and provides a divine insight; and we believe more than we have ever believed before. Today may be the time when God wants to provide that moment for you.

PRAYER: O God, thank you for the penetrating questions. May I too acknowledge that Jesus is the Christ, the Lord of my life. May I believe that more than ever before. Amen.

SATURDAY, SEPTEMBER 16 • Read James 3:1-12

James addresses the practical aspect of Christian behavior throughout his letter, couching much of what he says in the concept of wisdom. The wisdom God provides is not to be theoretical; it is meant to be practical. Actually every part of the Christian faith requires practical application in daily living. What an awesome thought that this sovereign God desires to display and manifest that sovereignty in each of our lives every day. God's participation in our daily living makes our lives distinctive; therefore, making a difference in our world.

Wisdom comes in part in determining how God wants to use our lives—where each of us fits into the whole body of Christ. James identifies with his readers, letting them know he understands their struggles. The admonition, "Not many of you should become teachers," is not to stifle one from trying to discover his or her place in the body. Rather it serves as a warning for those who only desire the position for the recognition it may bring. Even Jesus had trouble with disciples who jockeyed for position in places of prominence.

The words of this letter also remind us of our responsibilities, rather than dissuade us from our duties. When we consider ourselves to be something we are not, we open the door for the deadly sting of pride. The Bible often instructs us not to worry about what God is doing in someone else's life.

Knowing that we all stumble and make mistakes, James warns that if we seek the places of prestige and prominence without being called to them, we will amplify our mistakes. Be wise! Discover your part of the body. Then trust that God will supply the wisdom to accomplish that for which you've been called.

PRAYER: Dear God, I want to fulfill my place within the body of Christ—no more, no less! Thank you for providing the wisdom to know where I belong. Develop my awareness of your activity in my life today so I can make a difference. Amen.

SUNDAY, SEPTEMBER 17 • Read James 3:1-12

We began this week with the search for wisdom, and thus we shall end. The depth of a person's character can evidence true wisdom. A person's behavior and actions determine character. James informs us that such behavior includes one's speech. Our wisdom becomes evident in our knowing what to say and what not to say. The proper speech for a Christian comes in saying the right thing at the right time and also controlling the desire to say things better left unsaid.

Remember the exhortation from Psalm 19:14 that the words of our mouths and the meditations of our hearts be acceptable to God. Wise Christians filter their speech first by determining whether the words are true, necessary, and kind.

The writer compares the damage the tongue can do to the destructive forces of fire. The enemy of the soul uses uncontrolled speech to divide and destroy. Words spoken in anger can demolish relationships that took years to build.

Control provides the key. However, we cannot control the damage of the tongue on our own. God, through the power of the Holy Spirit, gives us increasing power to monitor and constrain our speech.

Our speech is also often contradictory. One minute we praise God; the next minute the same tongue utters violent and destructive words. Compare this with Paul's dilemma in Romans 7, where he states confusion over his inability to do what he should rather than what he should not. Again submission to God's spirit is the only remedy. The Spirit purifies the heart and gives the wisdom of self-control so that every part of our behavior, our being, is acceptable to God—even our words.

SUGGESTION FOR MEDITATION: Do you think before you speak? Do you filter your speech with these questions: Is what I want to say true? Is it necessary? Is it kind? How can I temper the hurtfulness of words that must be said?

The Fruits of a God-Centered Life

September 18–24, 2000 • Barbara Wendland*

MONDAY, SEPTEMBER 18 • Read Psalm 1

Psalm 1 tells us that people who pay close attention to God's instructions will be happier than those who don't. Their efforts will be more fruitful too. The psalmist warns us not to follow wicked people's advice or to use them as our models. The results of their behavior, the psalm assures us, have no lasting value. They are mere fluff.

However, Psalm 1 also reminds us that sitting in the seat of scoffers doesn't bring happiness and fruitfulness either. That advice may surprise us, because it's dangerously easy to be a scoffer. It's tempting to make fun of people who act overly pious or who go around wearing rose-colored glasses or burying their heads in the sand all the time. We may discover a smug satisfaction in saying, "That plan won't work," whenever someone proposes a new project or a change in the church. It's tempting to gloat and say, "I told you so," when an effort that we expected to fail fails. It's tempting to scoff at pastors or church members who aren't doing what we think needs doing in the church, especially if we wanted the opportunity to do it ourselves.

By scoffing we try to make ourselves look good and feel good by making others look bad. It's rarely fruitful. In the long run, happiness comes from focusing on what God wants.

PRAYER: **Loving God, help me focus on doing your will myself, rather than telling other people what to do or criticizing their efforts. Amen.**

---

*United Methodist laywoman in Temple, Texas; author and publisher of *Connections*, a monthly letter about the need for individual and corporate renewal in mainline churches.

TUESDAY, SEPTEMBER 19 • Read Jeremiah 11:18-20

Jeremiah has delivered God's message, but the recipients don't like it. In fact, God has told Jeremiah they're planning to kill him. And in the verse that follows today's reading, we learn that the people plotting to kill him are citizens of his hometown—the people he probably thought were least likely to harm him.

Understandably, Jeremiah resents their treatment. He has committed himself to God, and he feels he's doing what God wants him to do, yet he's suffering for it. He's afraid God won't rescue him. He says he feels like a gentle, innocent lamb being led to the slaughter, so he lets God know how he feels: "You got me into this mess, God, so the least you can do is back me up. Do something to get revenge on these evil people for the way they're treating me."

I don't recall ever having to deliver a message that would make people want to kill me, but I've received criticism and been denied church leadership roles for trying to do what I believe God wants me to do. Maybe you've also received criticism for doing what you thought God wanted. It hurts.

Like Jeremiah, we need to express our real feelings to God at such times. Remembering God's past help, we can appeal to the "Lord of hosts, who judge[s] righteously."

We also need to reexamine continually our understanding of what God calls us to do. Then if we still believe we're obeying God, we need to keep on, despite our suffering.

PRAYER: Gracious God, if I am not doing your will, please let me know. If I am, reassure me and help me keep going even if I will suffer for doing so. Help me resist the urge for revenge. Amen.

WEDNESDAY, SEPTEMBER 20 • Read Proverbs 31:10-28

Today's scripture depicts the original "superwoman." She takes responsibility for the care of her children, the house-keeping duties, and various religious and civic jobs. She's also a career woman who works outside her home. The list of her activities is overwhelming. No wonder "her lamp does not go out at night"! She'd have little time for sleep if she did all that this scripture passage describes.

How do you define a capable woman? How do you define a "woman of worth"? What makes a woman more "precious than jewels"? Is it her nonstop activity? her business ability? her care for the needy? her skill in preparing her family's food and clothing? her kindness? her generosity to the poor? her wisdom? According to today's scripture, the woman of worth has all these traits and more. It's not surprising that her children call her happy, and her husband praises her.

These verses describe a woman that many of us may admire. However, this description will mislead us if we see it as a demand for every woman to work outside the home, while maintaining responsibility for all the housekeeping and childcare too. It will also mislead us if we see it as saying that a woman's worth comes only from serving others or from constant busyness.

What do you consider valid evidence of a person's worth? Is it praise that comes from children or spouse? Is it how well known the spouse is "in the city gates"? Is it fine clothing or profitability of marketed merchandise? How much weight do you give to traits such as these?

PRAYER: Dear God, help me remember that being a superwoman or a superman isn't what you require. Amen.

THURSDAY, SEPTEMBER 21 • Read Proverbs 31:29-31

Today's passage describes the "woman of worth" in terms of her relationship to God rather than her busyness, her skills, or her willingness to meet other people's expectations. These verses also warn us that surface qualities like charm and beauty, which society often declares important, aren't what count. "Charm is deceitful," today's scripture asserts, and "beauty is vain."

What really matters, this scripture reminds us, is fear of God, giving God top priority in our lives. Today's passage also assures us that a woman's duty isn't just to provide for others. "Give her a share in the fruit of her hands," the passage instructs us. Helping her husband maintain the high regard of those in the world outside the home shouldn't be her main concern either. Her calling as a woman isn't to be a trophy wife. "Let her works praise her in the city gates," these verses urge.

Some of Jesus' words and actions can clarify this picture. For Jesus, a woman's value did not come only from her role as wife and mother (Luke 11:27-28). Jesus praised both men and women for knowing God's will and doing it, not for meeting society's expectations or for having impressive material products to show for their labors.

Like Jesus, the author of today's scripture gives fear of God top priority. Obeying God is what counts for both women and men. Obeying God, this passage assures us, will make our lives fruitful and will bring God's blessing.

PRAYER: Gracious God, help me remember that knowing and doing your will is what gives me worth. Help me appreciate and praise both men and women for their faithfulness to you and for their works that grow out of that faithfulness. Amen.

FRIDAY, SEPTEMBER 22 • Read James 3:13–4:3

Conflicts and disputes within the church tend to surprise us. Where do they come from? The author of this scripture raises this question, expressing the bafflement many of us feel. And for this author, the answer is clear: They come from cravings that are warring within us. We want things and don't get them. We ask for things and aren't satisfied with what we get.

Why? This scripture suggests several reasons. First, we don't ask for what we want. We just get mad because we don't have it. We see other people getting what they want, and we envy them. We may even attack them in an effort to take it away from them. The second reason for our dissatisfaction is that we ask for the wrong things. We ask only for what will please us, not for what will enable us to do God's will. The scripture assures us that these two mistakes in asking are unwise and result in disputes and conflicts.

In contrast, when directed by God's wisdom we find ourselves willing to yield. We acknowledge that we may be wrong and that the people who disagree with us may be right. When we're wise, we don't pounce on others' mistakes; we're merciful instead. And when we act wisely, we aren't hypocritical. We don't hide our real beliefs or act one way while talking another. Allowing God's wisdom to direct us brings peace and gentleness.

However, covering up disagreements to keep things looking peaceful isn't real peace, and encouraging others to continue in sinful behavior isn't real mercy. The wisdom of God is based on truth; its result is true righteousness, not just the appearance of peace.

PRAYER: Dear God, help me see the difference between the wisdom based on your truth and unwise behavior based on envy, selfishness, or the desire to keep things looking peaceful on the surface. Amen.

SATURDAY, SEPTEMBER 23 • Read James 4:7-8a

Scholars believe a teacher whose job in the church was to teach newly converted Christians probably wrote this letter. The author presents what he or she considers the ABCs of Christian living:

A — Draw near to God.

B — Oppose evil.

C — Act in ways that come from having a pure heart.

How can we practice these ABCs in our everyday lives?

We draw near to God and find God's will in many ways. We draw near by participating in worship with others. We draw near by praying, sometimes alone and sometimes with other people. We read the Bible, reflect on it, and ask God to show us its meaning. We may also come near by reading and reflecting on the writings of other Christians. Some of us come near in silence, maybe by writing. Others come near through groups, by talking and by hearing others' views. Many of us find that music helps us draw near to God. Many see God most clearly in nature's beauty.

When we draw near, we often find God offering guidance. We need to respond to this guidance in two ways. First, we're to resist evil and do whatever we can to oppose it. That often means taking steps to eliminate injustice and to promote justice in the church and in the world. Second, we're to show love to particular people in specific ways that God reveals to us. Making these responses helps purify our hearts.

When we draw near, God shows us where we've been wrong. God shows us where change is needed. And God shows us new directions in which to go.

PRAYER: Gracious God, show me what is keeping me from you. Help me draw near. Then give me the strength and the willingness to do what I find you calling me to do. Amen.

SUNDAY, SEPTEMBER 24 • **Read Mark 9:30-37**

Even though we want to follow Jesus, we often miss the point of his teachings. Jesus' earliest followers evidently had that problem too. Today's scripture describes Jesus' revealing some of the most important information about what God has sent him to do and what God wants; yet the disciples aren't getting the message. They not only don't understand what he means, they're afraid to ask him to explain it.

I feel that way sometimes. When someone makes a statement that is completely foreign to me or that seems hopelessly confusing, I don't even know what to ask in order to end my confusion. That seems to be how the disciples felt. "I'm going to be killed, but three days later I will rise," Jesus says. Undoubtedly that information doesn't fit with anything in the disciples' experience. I can imagine the stunned silence that gives way to a scratching of heads and furtive sideways glances. Dropping the subject is all they know to do. From their example we learn that understanding comes by asking questions.

Next the disciples argue about which one of them is the greatest. They're evidently embarrassed to have Jesus catch them at it. We may think Jesus should have berated their pettiness and their failure to understand what he's been trying to teach them, but he doesn't. He remains patient with them, and evidently with us. He simply reminds them that being first by human standards isn't what counts. "Whoever wants to be first must be last," he explains, reversing the world's values. Then, embracing a child, Jesus reminds us that in welcoming the world's least prominent people, we welcome him; and in welcoming him, we welcome God.

PRAYER: Dear God, keep reminding me that what the world values isn't always what God values. Encourage me to keep asking the questions that will help me find your will. Amen.

The Ironic Ways of God

September 25–October 1, 2000 • Jim McWhinnie*

MONDAY, SEPTEMBER 25 • Read Esther 7:1-10; 9:20-22

Irony…when things turn out to be something far different than what one would expect. The story of Esther is filled with irony. We see it in the episode we have read today. Who would have expected that life would turn out this way? Yet life often doesn't turn out the way one would expect. For that matter, neither do the ways of God.

It was Saturday part-time work. About five in the morning, I slipped on jeans, a work shirt, and steel-toe shoes. I finished changing just in time to answer the honking of my friend's '68 Chevelle. The day turned out to be a shirt-wringer with ten long hours of mopping steaming roof tar. On our way to pick up our pay, my friend stated that his hard-earned money was going to buy a new stereo. I boasted, "Two more Saturdays and I've got wheels again!"

The old-timer walking with us just smiled and said, "I'm gonna buy some cold lemonade." We snickered. Then we thought for a moment and looked at each other with a confirming nod. On the way home, we bought the best lemonade that had ever been made. I think it was the best money I ever spent.

The best way to appreciate great lemonade, my friends, is to work all day in the blazing sun, mopping hot, steaming tar. So it often is with the good things in life. You have to get mighty thirsty for the lemonade to taste mighty good. And sometimes so it is with faith; it tastes best when the need is the greatest. Herein rests the irony of faith.

SUGGESTION FOR MEDITATION: How has your life been tasting lately?

---

*Pastor, Saint Paul's United Methodist Church, Tallahassee, Florida.

TUESDAY, SEPTEMBER 26 • Read Psalm 124

Irony...when things turn out to be something far different than what one would expect. The psalmist sums up hazardous events using words to this effect: "The enemies attacked, the floods came, yet we survived. Surely God was with us!"

Many people enduring such difficult times might cry out, "Lord, why are you doing this to me?" or perhaps, "Lord, where are you when I need you?" But the writer of this song proclaims, "Our help is in the name of the Lord."

Is the good life a bed of roses? According to scripture, no! Is the good life a sheltering from circumstances difficult and tragic? Again, no! Rather the good life is a life that is deep and wide, meaningful and purposeful, thoroughly human and wonderfully divine.

My dad grew up during the Great Depression. Times were hard for dad and his family. Mended clothes and patched-up shoes, soup-bone soup and navy beans, night jobs and taking in ironing—these were the hungry demands that made up those days. Yet, strangely, my dad remembered those days with satisfaction. Somehow the family members had survived. And they had survived with honor. Those demanding times brought about an awareness of the unacknowledged resources of strength, courage, and peace. The difficult demands of the Depression had forced my dad to tap into the great, divine potential within his human soul.

Many people might argue that God wants to indulge God's children with all things good. And this I believe as well. But all things good do not always come easily, wrapped in silver paper and topped with golden bows. Sometimes they are the gifts that come by way of enduring hard times. Ironically, sometimes the good comes by way of the struggle.

SUGGESTION FOR MEDITATION: Consider what moments in your life have been the most meaningful. Why?

WEDNESDAY, SEPTEMBER 27 • Read James 5:13-20

Irony...when things turn out to be something far different than what one would expect. When you're hurting, pray! When you're feeling good, sing! When someone's under the weather, ask for prayers! Remember, prayer has the power to heal the body and soul!

James seems to have muddled his thoughts. Listen carefully to his words: "The prayer of faith will save the sick, and the Lord will raise them up; and anyone who has committed sins will be forgiven. Therefore confess your sins to one another, and pray for one another, so that you may be healed." Doesn't it seem that James has jumbled the concepts of forgiveness and healing? Maybe not.

A few years back, I went to the doctor. I had been experiencing chest pains. I endured the stress test and took the EKG. I had X-rays and blood tests. After all had been done, the good doctor sat me down and said, "Sir, I believe there is nothing physically wrong with your heart. But have you been under stress lately?" Then somehow, in some way, my medical examination became a pastoral conversation.

For centuries, we have separated body and soul. Only in recent years have we come to rediscover the connection between the two. Healing and forgiveness do go together in certain mysterious ways.

Sometimes an illness appears to be based only on medical circumstances, and sometimes forgiveness does not work a miraculous cure. But oftentimes healing of the soul does bring relief from pain. There is always a spiritual dimension to suffering. Pain can demoralize the spirit. The debilitation can discourage the will. Suffering can splinter the heart. Therefore, perhaps we should pray for healing from inside out and from the outside in.

SUGGESTION FOR MEDITATION: How do you respond to pain and suffering in your life? in the life of others?

284

THURSDAY, SEPTEMBER 28 • **Read Mark 9:42-50**

Irony...when things turn out to be something far different than what one would expect. Sometimes Jesus' words can shock: "If your hand causes you to stumble, cut it off." Surely he doesn't mean that literally. Of course not! But Jesus does manage to communicate his feelings about our getting serious about disposing of those things within us that trip us up. "I really mean it!" Occasionally Jesus must use dramatic means to catch our attention.

There is in human life a spiritual inertia that, once set in motion, is reluctant to change direction. We would like to think that a little turn here and a small adjustment there will guide us on to our destiny. But often our lives are directed by the dramatic moments of crisis—a broken relationship, a career change, a sudden illness, an unforeseen tragedy. These moments demand change of us. We must adapt to survive. We can no longer ignore the issue. Like it or not, we need to change course.

I must have crossed Highway 1 a thousand times on my walk to school, following the same routine each and every day. The light turned red...the WALK light flashed on and off and on again...a subconscious glance to check for traffic. Every day before that fateful day, I had crossed that street with oblivious boldness. But on that day, before my foot touched down and following a big-voiced holler, a powerful hand on my collar jerked me to the sidewalk. All I could see was the chrome of a city truck whistling by my face. The huge man towering over me had torn my collar, twisted my back, and hurt my pride; but he had also saved my life. After that I never forgot to look good and long in both directions again. I remembered that shocking moment! Yes, sometimes Jesus is shocking, and sometimes we *must* change.

SUGGESTION FOR MEDITATION: Where do you see spiritual inertia in your life? How do you overcome it?

FRIDAY, SEPTEMBER 29 • **Read Mark 9:38-41**

Irony...when things turn out to be something far different than what one would expect.

"Whoever is not against us is for us."

"Whoever is not with me is against me" (Matt. 12:30).

Look and listen carefully to these two statements of Jesus. They seem to contradict each other.

The first quotation is Jesus' response to those who do the work of the Lord without being followers of Christ. Jesus follows these words with the tender image, "Whoever gives you a cup of water to drink because you bear the name of Christ will by no means lose the reward." The goodness of God's work is good no matter who performs the work. Do not discourage those who seek to do good. Encourage the doing of good. This is, to me, what Jesus seems to say to his (possibly jealous) disciples: Let us not be divided among ourselves. If the goodness of God is being done by others, rejoice!

The second quotation is Jesus' response to the accusation by some in the religious community that Jesus must be of the evil one if he is in the business of ridding people of demons. Jesus here speaks of the same concept as in the first quotation, but he approaches it from the other side in words to this effect: "Do not call the good, evil. Why would evil wage war on itself? Do not speak ill of those who do the good work of God!" And that's what Jesus is teaching us today.

Tragically the community of God evidences so much conflict and division! Too often we seem to be at war with ourselves. Let God's work of goodness be done, no matter who the servant of God might be.

SUGGESTION FOR MEDITATION: What good work is God doing through your life? What good work is God doing through the lives of other persons you know?

SATURDAY, SEPTEMBER 30 • Read James 5:19-20

Irony...when things turn out to be something far different than what one would expect. James expresses great concern about those who wander from the truth. Even in the early days of the Christian community, one could easily become lost in a world of so many different perspectives. I remember the saying, "Better to run deep than to run wide." Seemingly we usually must make this choice. Do I run deep and focus on the fullness that comes with immersion in a certain way of life? Or do I run wide and try to take it all in?

As a river widens, it tends to become noisier, chattering over every rock, meandering as it seeks the path of least resistance. In times of drought, it becomes a dry riverbed. As a river deepens, it tends to become quieter, flowing over the rocks, cutting its own path into the earth. In times of drought, the river weakens but keeps flowing.

Shall I run wide or run deep? Can hearing everything at once, like trying to hear a thousand conversations in a crowded marketplace, ever make any sense? Here and there, the loudest voice can catch our attention for a moment of two. But another quickly replaces it. Can listening in a quiet moment slowly lead us to a deeper layer of conversation that awaits in the soul? Shall I run deep, or shall I run wide?

My wife and I struggle over the television remote control. I feel the impulsive urge to channel surf through 110 possibilities. To be honest, I am searching for something more. I'm never sure what I hope to find; I only know I am searching. From time to time, my wife rescues me from this restless searching and forces me to explore the depths of one—and only one—movie. And that focus is better. Yes, sometimes the many things become clearer through the irony of focusing on the one thing instead.

SUGGESTION FOR MEDITATION: Which will you choose? Run wide or run deep?

SUNDAY, OCTOBER 1 • **Read Matthew 13:10-17**

Irony…when things turn out to be something far different than what one would expect.

"To you it has been given to know the mysteries of the kingdom of heaven."

The ways of the Lord are mysterious indeed. Sometimes they do not even seem to make sense. They often go counter to what would seem to be the reasonable and logical course of action. Yet, I suppose, if God's ways were all that clear, then we would all be doing better in this venture called life.

Many a time following my own limited logic has led me down the wrong path. Like the time my car developed this sputter every time it climbed a hill. With my limited knowledge of automotive mechanics, I logically deduced that I must be having fuel pump problems. I took the car to the garage and told the mechanic, "I think I've got a problem with the fuel pump." Later that day I received a phone call from the mechanic. "Preacher, I have checked that fuel pump over and over again. I can't find anything wrong with it. I did notice, however, that you have a real hesitation problem when you drive up a hill. While I have the car here, would you like me to replace the bad spark plug wire that is causing that?"

I laughed at myself. I thought I had figured it out. But it turned out to be something I would have never expected. My own rational logic had once again underestimated the wisdom of experience.

So much of wisdom comes through obeying with trust the ways of God. They often don't seem to make sense—that is, until you have experienced the exercise of doing them in real life. Be faithful to the ways of God. Dare to trust them. And be ready to be surprised!

SUGGESTION FOR MEDITATION: **Which teachings of Christ, in your way of thinking, seem to defy logic?**

The Integrity of God's Will

October 2-8, 2000 • Barbara Miller*

MONDAY, OCTOBER 2 • Read Mark 10:2-16

God's will

In this passage from Mark's Gospel, Jesus responds to a question about divorce by reminding us of God's original intention and desire for humankind, what we call "God's will." As disciples we seek to know and to follow God's will. With Job we ask if God wills that we and those we love suffer. We seek God's will in specific life choices: Should we stay single or marry? Go to college? Get a job? What kind? How should we deal with difficult relationships or money problems?

God has the answer; we just need to listen. But God's will does not lie in the answers, predetermined and waiting; God's will comes in our listening. God's will resides not in our choices but in our manner of choosing.

A dear friend recently asked me how to reconcile feelings of jealousy with being a Christian. I told her that her perception of jealousy as problematic evidences the presence of the Holy Spirit in her life. God wills that we continually examine our feelings and actions, allowing them to bother and agitate us. The Holy Spirit works in our lives, not only in guilt and agitation, but in refusing to allow negative feelings or actions to consume us.

We enter the kingdom of heaven when we reclaim the innocent trust of the child in God's original intentions. We live in God's will when our process for making choices becomes an honest and ongoing search for joy.

PRAYER: Help me, loving God, to seek your will in all things. Amen.

---

*Voice-over artist; United Methodist laywoman living in Hockessin, Delaware.

TUESDAY, OCTOBER 3 • Read Job 1:1, Psalm 26

The nature of integrity

Honest people are said to "have" integrity. Those who do what they say they will do "act with" integrity. Job's wife asks if he is going to persist in "holding on to" his integrity. The psalmist claims to "walk in" integrity. Integrity seems to be something separate from ourselves that we engage. But this word has deeper significance.

From metallurgy we know that integrity is that aspect of being that describes how a material retains or holds on to its identity and unique character. Seen through this lens, the honesty and trustworthiness of people of integrity are the strands of refined gold that permeate people's being and influence all their decisions. They honor a confidence and see a task through. When mistakes or misunderstandings occur, they accept appropriate responsibility and do whatever is necessary to make things right. We trust such people's motives.

We often sense another's integrity more than we see it. Think about well-meaning people you know who continually strive to become better people. What about them causes you to intuitively sense integrity?

When we view integrity as the aspect of being that defines our identity and unique character, we see that it points to wholeness of the self; "integration" of body, mind, spirit, and relationships. When our whole self is working together in harmony, each choice we make for ourselves and others—large and small, day to day—is guarded and guided by our integrity.

PRAYER: **Lord of love, today may I grow in integrity as I seek to grow in love. Amen.**

WEDNESDAY, OCTOBER 4 • Read Mark 10:2-16

On divorce

Mark's version of this teaching is a hard word to hear for those of us who have experienced the pain of divorce. What are we to understand about our own lives when Jesus says, both publicly and privately, that anyone who divorces and remarries commits adultery?

The grace of this passage comes in the context in which Jesus places marriage and in the passage that follows. Jesus restates God's intentions for marriage from the familiar Genesis story—"God made them male and female...and the two shall become one flesh." The Gospel writer then immediately relates the story of Jesus' rebuking the disciples for keeping children from approaching him. "Whoever does not receive the kingdom of God as a little child will never enter it." Jesus links righteousness with the purity of God's original hope for humanity and the innocence of children, and the characteristics of both declare God's best intention for humanity.

Children question everything, eager to learn. Their trusting, open natures can lead to some painfully honest observations. Children live in integrity, believing in the eternity of today.

While the Pharisees ground their question in Jewish tradition (only husbands could divorce wives), Jesus' response reflects the current cultural practice in which either partner could ask for a divorce. Persons lacking in integrity might seek divorce in order to marry another. A father might encourage a daughter's divorce in order to further a political alliance through remarriage.

When we reclaim God's original purpose and desire in creation and find again the innocence and trust of childhood, we will live again in God's will.

PRAYER: Send your reassuring love, gracious God, to all who struggle in relationships. Amen.

THURSDAY, OCTOBER 5 • Read Job 2:7-10

Our question

God praises Job for living a life of integrity. Blameless, upright, and God-fearing, Job lives in God's will. Through Satan's efforts to prove the faithlessness of human beings, Job has been attacked in body, mind and spirit. First he suffered the loss of his children, then his worldly goods. Now Satan afflicts his entire body with sores. How much suffering can one person endure? That concern lies at the heart of the question from Job's wife: "Do you still persist in your integrity? Curse God, and die." We can identify with her desire to put an end to the pain and suffering.

Job's suffering reflects the undeserved trials we all experience at some time in our lives. Fairness and merit have nothing to do with hardship, pain, and loss. Does this injustice mean that God doesn't care enough to protect us? Does it mean that we are really alone in the world—doomed to work out our own destiny? Or worse, are we simply puppets, subject to the experimental whims of a capricious God?

Job's claim of integrity, his faith in the ultimate love of God despite absolute ruin, can teach us a powerful lesson. Later in the story, Job questions God's motives in allowing such undeserved pain, but Job never questions God's existence. Job does not understand, but he knows an answer exists. The answer comes as an impassioned declaration of God's radical freedom to do as God chooses. What is the message for us?

PRAYER: Thank you for your presence, Lord, in the midst of my trials and suffering. Amen.

FRIDAY, OCTOBER 6 • Read Job 2:1-6

The radical freedom of God

The story of Job invites us to examine the radical nature of God's freedom. We have trouble accepting that God can do as God chooses. But consider how many citizens take for granted our right to freedom. How can we deny to God that which we claim for ourselves?

Still, the Book of Job raises many difficult issues. What does an all-knowing God learn from the suffering of a righteous man? How do we reconcile a God of love with a God who allows torment?

If we think of Job as a literal figure, reconciliation is impossible. But when we consider Job as a symbolic figure, he provides an avenue to explore our own suffering in relationship to God.

We find the grace of Job's story in the deeper implications of God's freedom. That freedom encompasses so much more than the potential for harm. It includes a depth and breadth of love beyond our ability to comprehend. It is the freedom to love with such abandon that the sacrifice of God's only child is not too high a cost.

And though we may not fully understand it, that same freedom is available to us. Job exercises that freedom in his decision to continue loving God through loss, pain, and torment. And that experience serves as the basis of Job's integrity—his willingness to exercise the freedom to love in the face of deep suffering, to hold on to his right to choose his understanding of God when everyone calls him to abandon his beliefs. We join Job in true freedom when we are willing to pay the cost of discipleship and accept the call to follow Christ.

PRAYER: I offer praise and thanksgiving, Giver of life, that you choose to love. Amen.

SATURDAY, OCTOBER 7 • Read Hebrews 1:1-4; 2:5-12

Jesus, living in God's will

The author of Hebrews quotes Psalm 8 to remind us that God made humankind a little lower than the angels, crowned us with glory and honor, and subjected all things under our feet. The author lifts Jesus up as the fitting and ultimate example of this creation, and he refers to us as Jesus' brothers and sisters, children all. It is good to keep in mind the call to become as children as we read this passage. Our "adult" notions of power, glory, and dominion may fill us with too much arrogance for us to be useful guides.

What example does Jesus provide? To be crowned in glory, Jesus suffered death on the cross. He washed the feet of those who were subject to him. By becoming a little lower than the angels, Jesus welcomed all, loved all, gave the gift of his teaching and healing to all who would receive it. This is a lordship of servanthood, humility, deep compassion, and joyful welcome.

Where Jesus saw deep need, he called on his own deep passion to fill it. He lived a life of wholeness, innocence, and integrity, even unto death. Jesus lived in God's will.

God in Christ calls us to just such a life of wholeness and integrity. God calls us to use all of our talents, abilities, and the gifts of the Spirit revealed within us to fill the deep needs of our world in ways that suit our unique abilities. As I travel the country leading people to discover their spiritual gifts, the most prevalent response I hear is liberation. They experience great joy and relief in discovering that God calls and empowers us to live in the ways that bring us the deepest satisfaction and provide the most good.

PRAYER: Giver of all good gifts, help me live by your example. Amen.

SUNDAY, OCTOBER 8 • **Read Job 2:1-6; Psalm 26; Hebrews 2:5-8**

Living in integrity

Satan, the accuser, joins the heavenly court to challenge God's claims about Job. This is only the second reference to a being named Satan in scripture. The first occurs in 1 Chronicles 21, where Satan represents God's anger against Israel. In contrast to the New Testament figure, the Satan in Job is not the embodiment of evil. This figure is a member of the heavenly court, where debate and challenge naturally occur.

If we accept the story as allegory, Satan represents that aspect of creation, within and beyond us, that tempts us to doubt, challenge, and question our faith. Just as debate finds acceptance in God's court, so it is within us. When questions and doubts arise, we do not have to fear or suppress them. We can listen and examine them for what they have to teach.

From Job we learn not that God is capricious but that Satan's assumptions are wrong. Satan begins with an assumption of guilt, of weakness. In the figure of Job, humankind rises to the occasion and maintains integrity through unbelievable suffering. Job offers hope that we can pay the cost of discipleship and still maintain our integrity. Following Jesus' example, we can retain our childlike innocence and humility even while being crowned with glory and honor, with all things subject under our feet.

We are not angels. We are complex and sometimes clumsy, and often wrong. But created in the image of God, with Christ as our head and the Holy Spirit as our guide, we will embrace and learn from misfortune, doubt, and accusations. We will witness to the power of God's love as we grow in faithful stewardship of our gifts, our relationships, and our world.

PRAYER: God of Job, help me continue to grow in grace, even as I embrace my humanity. Amen.

Abandonment and Restoration

October 9–15, 2000 • Odis Fentry*

MONDAY, OCTOBER 9 • Read Job 23:1-9

Oh, that I knew where I might find him.

As we prepare to enter the twenty-first century, the disease that haunts us is loneliness. For many people loneliness and abandonment are very real issues. As I write this, people from entire countries in Central America are finding themselves displaced. Many families in developed countries live on the streets or in shelters. Women and children continue to be homeless, abused, and abandoned.

We still hold to the old tradition of Job and his friends, the tradition that says, Whatever we get we deserve because of our sins. Job and his friends grew up in the tradition that says bad things happen to you because of your sins. Illness and misfortunes in your life clearly signal God's displeasure with you. Today we would say, "It is God's will."

Job's friends insist, as our friends sometimes do, that Job simply accept his punishment: God has decided and mortals cannot change God's mind. Job, though conscious of that tradition, also acknowledges another tradition that says God does not will destruction but restoration and wholeness for God's people. Job chooses to hold on to that tradition and insists that God will hear his cry, "Oh, that I knew where I might find him." When God hears our cry, God will give heed to us. Job's friends choose abandonment and miss their blessings. Job chooses restoration and receives God's blessing.

SUGGESTION FOR MEDITATION: Seek God's restoration through daily prayer.

---

*Superintendent, Los Angeles District, The United Methodist Church; retreat leader on prayer and spiritual formation.

TUESDAY, OCTOBER 10 • Read Job 23:16-17

If only I could vanish in darkness.

Restoration and healing are the primary tasks for the church in the twenty-first century. The age of enlightenment and rationalism have created advancements far beyond what we could have imagined fifty years ago. Advances in medicine have given us more years and better quality of life. Public schools provide education for the masses. Technology has made work easier for many people and life more comfortable. Yet these advances do not close the gap on broken relationships and wounded people. Barriers still exist among races, genders, classes, and nations.

Restoration and healing will require stripping away layers of hatred, animosity, deceit, falsity, and many other emotions and facades that get in the way of giving our lives to God. As we contemplate stripping away those layers, it scares us; doing so can cause pain.

Job's possible encounter with God terrifies him. Job would rather "vanish in darkness" or die than to face the stripping that an encounter with God might demand. Often we hear the phrase, "I would rather die than..." face certain situations. Some people say this in a serious manner; others do not.

Facing up to situations sometimes requires change. Five years ago I received a diagnosis of prostate cancer. It frightened me to death when the doctor told me. But I faced up to it and asked, "What do I do now to live?" After I had surgery the doctor told me, "If you watch your diet, get plenty of exercise, and live the life of faith you are living now, you will be fine." Five years later the cancer remains in my body, but I am still alive. I have found restoration and healing.

SUGGESTION FOR MEDITATION: What situations in your life would you rather "vanish in darkness" than face? Turn them over to God in prayer.

WEDNESDAY, OCTOBER 11 • Read Psalm 22:1-10

My God, my God, why have you forsaken me?

Recently at a national conference I attended, a pastor from Ghana shared with us his experience of the loss of community in Ghana. He lamented the fact that Ghana in recent years has been guided by the dictum: "I think, therefore I am," having lost the African dictum: "I belong, therefore I am." The cry for community and for belonging sounds across our world.

The opening cry reveals the psalmist's deep physical, emotional, and psychological suffering. It bears witness to the psalmist's keen sense of loneliness and isolation, his feeling that he no longer belongs to the tradition of his ancestors who trusted God and experienced deliverance. The psalmist also recalls that God took him from his mother's womb and kept him safe and nurtured him.

The cry reflects both misery and mystery. Why? Why do I feel cut off from my ancestors and my God? Why have I lost my way on the journey? The psalmist begins to discover the solution when he recalls The Story. Forgetting The Story cuts one off from life. Remembering The Story brings restoration to life. Yearning for spirituality, which has emerged over the last decade, is a cry of many people to be restored to life. They cry for help to recall The Story, to be on the spiritual journey that leads to God. The mocking of those who regard illness as proof of God's rejection aggravates the psalmist's misery.

In Mark's Gospel (15:34) Jesus shouts the same cry from the cross. Jesus experienced the same taunting as the psalmist. Jesus withstood the mockers for the salvation of the world. A servant of God in the world today also will experience taunting and mocking.

PRAYER: Lord, help me endure whatever comes that I may serve the present age. Amen.

THURSDAY, OCTOBER 12 • Read Psalm 22:11-15

Trouble is near.

For a long time we have heard that we live in a post-Christian era. Generally this statement means that much of society no longer considers Christianity relevant. Some people believe it means that God is no longer relevant for our time. Reaction to the above declaration falls basically into three categories.

There are those who never believed who will say, "Thank God" or "I told you so." They have never put their hope in God, who is invisible—only in those things that are visible.

There are those still struggling with the confusion between science and religion. They see and experience all the miracles that science has produced, but their experience of religion has no connection with science. Therefore, because of the split between religion and science, they live a life without meaning and hope.

Then there are the believers, the faithful who fear that events occurring around them trigger an experience of distance from God. The psalmist uses the imagery of his day to describe the dismantling of his world and his person. The cry of the psalmist and the imagery he uses to describe his situation are not intended to indicate he has given up hope. His cry and descriptive language are meant to motivate God to take action, to restore God's people to life. At times we must awaken God to our sense of the life-threatening situation, which will move God to take life-restoring action.

Some who live in the world today say, "There is no God." Some people want to believe but have lost hope because of confusion. And some persons who live in the world declare, "When trouble is near, God is present." Where are you?

PRAYER: O God, I thank you for your restorative power. Amen.

FRIDAY, OCTOBER 13 • Read Mark 10:17-31

For God all things are possible.

"How is it with your soul?" is the question that cuts to the heart of what Jesus tries to encourage the rich young ruler to discover. Evidently the rich young ruler has led a blessed life. Opposite the tradition that says illness and other adverse situations signal God's rejection stands the tradition that says wealth and well-being signal God's blessing and approval.

The rich young ruler approaches Jesus with great confidence that everything is fine. He just wants Jesus to confirm his life. So he poses a rhetorical question to Jesus: "What must I do to inherit eternal life?" Other phrases we might hear today include the following synonyms for "eternal life": "the kingdom of God," "to be saved," or "to save my soul." Jesus immediately dispels the notion that the rich man's present lifestyle is enough.

Jesus shocks the rich young ruler and perplexes his own disciples with his answer, which says in effect, "You need to sell your possessions and come follow me." Jesus goes on to declare how hard it will be for rich people to enter the kingdom. The disciples conclude that no one can be saved if people with riches can't be saved, and they ask, "Then who can be saved?"

The possessions we have and the rules we keep do not secure our soul. "Eternal life" or "being saved" do not hinge on what we have or don't have but on what we are willing to set aside in order to follow Jesus, the one who can nourish and secure our souls.

Are you yearning to secure your soul? Don't hang your head and walk away sorrowfully; turn to Jesus and seek help. While realizing you can't save your soul on your own, remember that with God all things are possible.

PRAYER: Lord, help me follow you. Amen.

SATURDAY, OCTOBER 14 • Read Hebrews 4:12-13

Indeed, the word of God is living and active, sharper than any two-edged sword.

Most of us living in twentieth-century America might characterize the majority of this century as the era of certitude. We knew what we believed and clearly affirmed that God was on our side regardless of events in the rest of the world. Our sense of certainty began to dissolve during the last third of the century under the pressure of unprecedented change in all areas of life. The shifting sands of our lives today move us into the twenty-first century filled with anxiety. We have lost our compass, and the future appears uncertain.

The writer of Hebrews attempts to restore hope and confidence among the faithful that the word of God is living and active. Preachers and teachers of the word of God need to proclaim this message with power and conviction. In the midst of the rapid changes taking place in our world, God's word remains alive and active—able to heal and restore the brokenness of life. Life seems so random, chaotic, and violent. The image of Jesus seated on the throne of grace, offering mercy and grace in our time of need, is a reassuring one.

What keeps us on the right path on the spiritual journey? God's sharp word can pierce the uncertainties of the future and discern what is worthy of our faithfulness and what is not.

In the future, the importance of the gift of discernment will come to the fore. Seeking God's will by asking the question, Is this God's will for us? and having the patience to listen for God's answer as we live on the shifting sands of our times become equally important in the days ahead. The piercing word of God can discern far better than our minds can imagine or conceive.

PRAYER: O God, give me the courage to ask questions of you and the patience to listen for an answer. Amen.

SUNDAY, OCTOBER 15 • **Read Hebrews 4:14-16**

Approach the throne of grace with boldness.

A survivor of a Nazi slave-labor camp revisited the place where he had worked. As he stood on the spot where he had watched many people die, he paraphrased Psalm 23 in the following manner: "Though I walk through the valley of the shadow of death, I fear evil for you have abandoned us to the evil of those who torture us." The church of the future will have to consider seriously how we minister to persons who feel abandoned by God because of their experience of violence, torture, and the trauma that still remains.

If we believe that Jesus is sitting on the throne at the right hand of God waiting to hear our cry/prayer, then we approach the throne boldly. The lives of many persons who feel that sense of abandonment might depend on the boldness of God's people in future years.

If we believe God is a God of restoration and healing, then we should willingly storm the gates of heaven with courage and approach the throne of grace with boldness. We know of God's ability and readiness to restore to wholeness broken lives and relationships.

The writer of Hebrews actually encourages us to develop a more vital prayer life—to dispose of our fearful, tidy, and more formal prayers and to become more daring and audacious in our prayer requests. We are called to move from fear to boldness. If we boldly cry to God even now, God will hear our cry and do what God will do.

PRAYER: O God, hear my bold cries to you for those in need of your saving grace. Amen.

In Our Place

October 16–22, 2000 • J. Michael Ripski*

MONDAY, OCTOBER 16 • Read Job 38:1

Job wants to know why he's lost everything. He's a good man. Why is he being punished so? God's job description entails enforcing justice. God makes sure we get what we deserve and protects us from what we don't. It seems to Job that God is falling down on the job.

Job wants to know why God isn't being God. If there is no justice, does that mean there is no God? Job joins Jesus and six million Jews in the cry, "My God, my God, why have you forsaken me/us?"

If bad things happen to good people, then is there no order in the universe we can count on? We'll go to great lengths to keep such a thought at bay. We'll defend God's power and obligation to enforce justice. Job's three friends insist the problem resides with Job. He needs to confess what he's done to warrant his suffering. Job insists the problem rests with God. God is in error. If only God will give Job an audience, Job will make his case and prove God wrong.

Neither Job nor his friends allow for the possibility of God's existence and care despite the experience of injustice. The innocent do suffer. But we need not conclude that God is either dead or impotent. God answers Job from the whirlwind to prove it.

SUGGESTION FOR MEDITATION: **Recall a personal experience of injustice: Someone else got the promotion you deserved. You lost a loved one when you still needed him or her. You were slandered. Meditate on how it threatened your faith in God. Have you found peace?**

---

*Senior Pastor, First United Methodist Church, Hendersonville, Tennessee.

TUESDAY, OCTOBER 17 • Read Job 38:1-7, 34-41

Job's patience gives way to his insistence that God answer why. The Lord gives Job the audience he has demanded. But before Job questions God, God first wants some answers from Job. The Lord begins with this challenge to Job: "Gird up your loins like a man." What follows reminds Job that he is a mortal and not God.

"Where were you when I laid the foundation of the earth?" God asks Job. "Tell me, if you have understanding." The point, of course, is that Job does not have understanding, particularly about life's being fair.

God walks Job around creation, querying Job at each stop about his role in the making of it. Is Job responsible for the size of the earth? Does he cause the clouds to pour out their rain? Does he send the lightning strikes? Has Job provided the lion and raven the means to satisfy their hunger? Is Job the source of the intricate miracle that is the universe?

Of course not, Job must admit. There is so much he does not understand—injustice being only one item on a very long list. But Job comes to realize that his lack of understanding reflects upon his humanity, not upon God's holiness. Job confesses, "Therefore I have uttered what I did not understand, things too wonderful for me, which I did not know" (42:3*b*).

God is God. Job is not. Job repents of his presumptuousness. God has put him in his place, which is our place too—the place where we live by faith, not explanation.

PRAYER: Creator God, forgive me for substituting my flimsy explanations for faith in you. Amen.

WEDNESDAY, OCTOBER 18 • Read Psalm 104:1-9, 24-35c

I did not catch the author's name. What caught my attention was her reference to a five-month retreat. This aspect obviously intrigued the public radio interviewer as well. "Do you feel like you missed out on a lot during those five months of solitude?" the interviewer asked. The author replied, "I have had enough experience to last me the rest of my life. What I am lacking is not experience but an appreciation of the experience I've already had. I want to know what it all means."

The composer of today's psalm is one who looks in awe at creation and cannot keep from singing, "Bless the Lord, O my soul....Praise the Lord!" The psalmist looks at creation and sees the Creator. "O Lord, how manifold are your works! / In wisdom you have made them all; / the earth is full of your creatures."

We do not lack experience; we lack appreciation of our experience.When was the last time we lay on our backs on a clear night and permitted the stars to put us in our place in the cosmos? When was the last time we felt wonder and awe?

The trees are now wearing their glorious autumn wardrobe. Have we noticed? Have we smelled the fallen leaves? Have we heard their crackle? Have we glimpsed a harvest moon on the rise above them? I suspect we are too intent on getting to our next experience to experience what made the psalmist's soul sing the Creator's praise.

SUGGESTION FOR MEDITATION: Give yourself fifteen minutes of solitude today. Place yourself in the presence of creation's beauty. Don't examine it; just soak it in. Just receive the gift. See what happens.

THURSDAY, OCTOBER 19 • Read Hebrews 5:1-6

On the one hand, the author of Hebrews seeks to make a case for Jesus' high priesthood, declaring Jesus to be of the order of Melchizedek, the Canaanite priest-king of Jerusalem during the time of Abram. Regardless of the historical facts, people came to view Melchizedek as a messianic figure who rescued righteous people.

On the other hand, the author of Hebrews wants to attribute to Jesus the virtues of a "regular" high priest. "He is able to deal gently with the ignorant and wayward, since he himself is subject to weakness." This verse echoes an earlier description in 4:15: "For we do not have a high priest who is unable to sympathize with our weaknesses, but we have one who in every respect has been tested as we are, yet without sin."

And just as the high priest doesn't grab for the office but receives it upon God's call, so Christ did not appoint himself. His office came with his baptism: "You are my Son, today I have begotten you."

Comparing Jesus to Melchizedek, to be honest, doesn't do much for me. Even testimony to the voice from heaven proclaiming Jesus the begotten Son doesn't necessarily make him such for me.

What makes Jesus my high priest is his willingness to know the life I know. What makes Jesus divine for me is his willingness to be weak as I am weak, vulnerable as I am vulnerable, tested as I am tested. Jesus can be my *high* priest because he has *lowered* himself to identify with me.

Can salvation come without that identification? without sacrifice? Jesus, the high priest, sacrifices himself.

PRAYER: Lord, teach me how to be a priest, bringing you to people and people to you. Amen.

FRIDAY, OCTOBER 20 • Read Hebrews 5:7-10

Nancy Mairs has multiple sclerosis. In a *Christian Century* article entitled "Learning from Suffering" (May 6, 1998; 481), Nancy explains why she will not consider assisted suicide as an option:

> Perhaps because I have embraced a faith with cruci-fixion at its heart, I do not consider suffering an aber-ration or an outrage to be eliminated at any cost, even the cost of my life. It strikes me as intrinsic to the human condition. I don't like it. I'm not asked to like it. I must simply endure in order to learn from it. [Ending my life would] deny me the fullness of expe-rience I believe I am meant to have.

In the garden Jesus prayed "with loud cries and tears" that God spare him the impending suffering. He prayed with "rev-erent submission" to the One able to save him from death. Yet despite Jesus' sonship, God did not spare him from suffering and death. Jesus "learned obedience" through it and became perfect, whole, and complete. For the author of Hebrews, Jesus' suffering is what qualifies Jesus to be our high priest, able to bring God to us and us to God.

In a culture that worships avoidance of suffering, we can-not believe that suffering can teach us anything worth know-ing. Yet these two persons witness to what we can receive no other way.

Certainly suffering will lead some to anger, bitterness, and despair. But for others, suffering will lead to a fullness of the divine image in which we were created—a fullness that can come no other way.

SUGGESTION FOR MEDITATION: Consider how you've suffered. In what way has your suffering been a curse or a blessing? What have you learned? Give thanks to God.

SATURDAY, OCTOBER 21 • Read Mark 10:35-40

When a child asks, "Will you do one thing for me?" the parents can predict the answer will be no or else the specific request would not have been made. Nevertheless, children play the game, aware that parents rarely issue blank checks. It is worth a try.

James and John have been with Jesus long enough to suspect that their request will not make Jesus happy. They employ the children's strategy: "Teacher, we want you to do for us whatever we ask of you." Their concern focuses on their places in the kingdom when Jesus becomes king.

Jesus is about to enter Jerusalem where his crown will be one of thorns. A cross with its suffering and dying will be Jesus' "glory." Jesus asks the two brothers if they're sure this is what they want. Are they able to follow Jesus all the way and be glorified with him? "We are able," they answer.

James and John don't have a clue either about the nature of Jesus' glory or about what it will require. Jesus is thinking humiliation; they're thinking coronation. Jesus is thinking self-sacrifice; they're thinking self-aggrandizement. Jesus is thinking about being a servant; they're thinking about having servants.

Why do James and John make such a request? Just like us, they have their reasons, don't they? They left the family fishing business when Jesus called them. Their father, Zebedee, probably never could understand why his two sons had left to follow an itinerant preacher. Perhaps James and John think that when Jesus becomes king, they'll sit next to his throne. Maybe then their father will be proud and understand why they did what they did.

PRAYER: Lord, expose the games I play in order to get what I think I need and to prove I'm somebody special. Amen.

SUNDAY, OCTOBER 22 • Read Mark 10:41-45

James and John have sought places of privilege and power beside Jesus. Of course, they misunderstand what Jesus can do for them and what being close to Jesus will bring them. Whatever the consequences, the request itself angers the other disciples. These two brothers betray the spirit of Jesus and sabotage the vision of God's reign that Jesus seeks to realize.

In the reign of God, rank and power have no place. In the way of Jesus, the first become last and the last first. Those considered great will be lowly servants. The powerful will be those who seek solidarity with the powerless. Those who have the most are those who freely give away what they have.

James and John based their request on a vision of "lording it over" others. In God's reign, Jesus models what it means to "lord." He expresses his lordship by giving "his life a ransom for many."

One pays ransom to gain another's release. One becomes expendable for the sake of another. Jesus serves as both lord and ransom. We cannot understand the former without the latter. Jesus puts himself in our place, so we might know how special we are. Seats of power won't prove our specialness—only God can.

I think of those who pay the ransom of self-sacrifice: the husband who devotes every waking hour to the care of his invalid wife; one nation that gives up its land to another for the sake of peace with justice; a wife who repeatedly gives up her career to follow her husband to new church assignments.

PRAYER: Patient God, forgive my efforts to prove how special I am. May I receive the gift Jesus has already given me. Amen.

God's Severe Mercy

October 23–29, 2000 • Michael B. Henderson*

MONDAY, OCTOBER 23 • Read Job 42:1-6

"The church is only one generation away from extinction," the preacher said. I had heard her say the same thing before: "God has no grandchildren, only children"; "You can't live off your grandparents' faith, any more than you can live off the meals they ate." Whatever the phrase, the message was the same. We must develop and experience our faith in God firsthand if we are to find life.

Job discovers the same truth. Although we can never fully plumb the depth of this book, we tend to focus on Job's faithfulness in pain or God's eventual triumph through a faithful person. Yet the Book of Job also conveys a message of God's mercy that brings Job to a full life, a life of shalom, a life of peace and justice.

Sheldon Van Auken described God's mercy as a "severe" mercy; that is, a mercy that is not merely content to forgive and let us continue in our harmful ways but calls and compels us to a life filled with evidence of the reign of God. In today's reading we see that attitude reflected in Job's statement: "My ears had heard of you, but now my eyes have seen you" (NIV).

Job moves from secondhand to firsthand knowledge. And his encounter with the divine calls for a response: "Therefore I push myself aside and turn toward you in humility" (AP).

SUGGESTION FOR MEDITATION: What is your experience of God? Is it firsthand?

---

*Pastor, Bethel United Methodist Church, Oswego, South Carolina; columnist for the South Carolina *United Methodist Advocate*.

TUESDAY, OCTOBER 24 • Read Job 42:10-17

Political historians tell us that in most cases of revolution, when those who were oppressed overthrew the bonds of the oppressors, they took on the characteristics of the oppressors. The Russian revolution leading up to the atrocities of Stalin is a twentieth-century example. The oppression of indigenous peoples in our own country by those only a generation away from European aristocratic dominance comes closer to home.

In Matthew 18 Jesus tells the story of one deeply in debt and virtually owned by his lender. Begging for mercy, he receives forgiveness of his debt. However, he does not forgive the debt another owes him. He has not learned, has not grown from his own experience. The writer of Ephesians states that we struggle against "principalities" and "powers" (6:12, RSV) We struggle not just against evil but against being overcome and seduced by evil.

Job's struggles and loss enable him to know what it is like to be powerless in a hard world. He knows firsthand about having others control your fate. When the tables turn, and Job again rises to a position of wealth and power, his personal experience influences his dealings with others. He sees persons directly related to him caught in a system of oppression—a patriarchal, societal pattern in which only male offspring inherit. Verse 15 states that Job gives both his daughters and his sons an inheritance. Job breaks out of the mold of his day, breaking with tradition to offer a new way of being to others. God's mercy leads Job to implement a just and liberating plan of action. A severe mercy leads Job to grow into a new way of life.

SUGGESTION FOR MEDITATION: **How is God's mercy leading you into a new way of being or acting?**

WEDNESDAY, OCTOBER 25 • Read Psalm 34:1-8

A parishioner in the hospital and I reached the end of our conversation. As we sat quietly, contemplating his long illness, he said, "Well, one thing about being on your back—it sure keeps you looking up to God!"

Although God wants us to grow in faith, God never asks us to be utterly self-dependent. To accomplish great things for God, we must always depend on God's strength and guidance. This psalm reminds us that only through realization of our weakness can we gain access to the strength of the Holy One. Paul's words echo this thought: "But [God] said to me, 'My grace is sufficient for you, for power is made perfect in weakness.' So, I will boast all the more gladly of my weaknesses, so that the power of Christ may dwell in me" (2 Cor. 12:9).

The psalmist alternates the focus between the weakness of those afflicted and the strength of God. God, in divine mercy, does for us what we cannot do. God rescues us. This severe mercy comes in the midst of pain and fear. Realization of divine protection merits our unending praise.

God's severe mercy wants us to rely on divine strength. The circumstances of our world will give ample opportunity for that. We come to see that in our weakness, God will "pitch a tent" (encamp) around us.

PRAYER: Thank you, God, for hearing the prayers of those who are afflicted and oppressed. Let their cries come before you and let your strength be in them. Amen.

THURSDAY, OCTOBER 26 • Read Psalm 34:19-22

A non-Christian friend once asked, "Why do you Christians keep on believing in a God who loves you? It is apparent from history that this will not keep you from having the same problems that other people have."

Like Job, the psalmist tells us that righteous people will have many troubles. He relates a convergence of two things that should not be in the presence of each other—righteous persons and afflictions. Yet the two occur together, often repeatedly, it seems. Once again, God does for the righteous what only God can do—rescues and protects. Belief in a loving and omnipotent God does not negate the sin in the world or the power of sin to touch our lives. It does not negate the random nature of creation, nor does it immunize us from horrible things.

I live among farmers. Drought happens to those who believe as well as those who do not. Cancer strikes children of faithful parents as well as those of no faith. Random violence cuts down the lives of those who are moral and upright as well as those who live on the other side of the law.

But Yahweh rescues and protects us from ultimate despair. Our redemption comes through "taking refuge" in the One who has become available to us. A severe mercy causes us to run to the only place of real refuge.

PRAYER: Great God of mercy, may I take refuge in you, for you are my strength and shield. Let despair not conquer, but let your hope indwell all your people. Amen.

FRIDAY, OCTOBER 27 • Read Hebrews 7:23-28

Van Eyck's painting the *Adoration of the Lamb* pictures a lamb standing on the altar of God very much alive but with a flow of blood coming from its heart and running into a chalice. The lamb represents Christ, "the lamb of God who takes away the sin of the world." The lamb standing on the altar shows One who constantly intercedes on our behalf. And the flow of blood says grace may be free, but it is never cheap. It always costs something.

The sacrificial system of the Temple offered a way for fallen humanity to become reconnected with the perfect divinity. Priests made sacrifices on behalf of individuals and the corporate body to show that humanity's fallen nature is such that something must die to restore us to our original state. Echoes of the warning from Genesis, "In the day that you eat of [the tree] you shall die" (2:17), come to us through the sacrifices made in the Temple. Instead of our death, though, something else was substituted.

If written after the destruction of the Temple in 70 A.D., Hebrews and its author may be pointing out to Jewish Christians that Jesus himself has replaced the sacrificial system. With the destruction of the Temple, persons might come to an understanding that the Temple is no longer necessary. Christ's self-offering is the perfect sacrifice and one that Christ continues to make as he intercedes for us.

SUGGESTION FOR MEDITATION: In what ways does Christ intercede for you? How does that intercession make a difference in your life?

SATURDAY, OCTOBER 28 • Read Mark 10:46-52

At first the question Jesus poses to the blind man, "What do you want me to do for you?" seems superfluous. Jesus is a healer. Already he has healed another blind person, a paralyzed man, a demoniac, a sick girl, and has done many other miracles. His reputation has gone ahead of him. It seems obvious that a blind man would want his sight. So why the question, "What do you want me to do for you"?

Bartimaeus cries out for mercy. We may translate the word *mercy* more accurately as "pity" or "compassion." An expression of one's pity or compassion might be alms, a few coins in the cup of a blind person. It might be a meal that helps Bartimaeus get through the day or a blanket for the night. But the true quality of mercy is not a bandage for temporary relief but the movement through growth toward wholeness.

And so Jesus' question confronts us as it does Bartimaeus. What do we actually want Jesus to do for us? For Bartimaeus, to receive sight would require that he give up begging and blaming. Restored sight would require that he release the familiar and move on to a new and more responsible lifestyle.

If Bartimaeus had answered, "A few coins," he would have had an easier day, but his life would not have changed. Jesus' confrontational question encourages Bartimaeus to take a deeper look at his life, to evaluate where he is and where he would like to be.

Perhaps Bartimaeus wanted pity; but when Jesus asks him the life-changing question, Bartimaeus grows in self-understanding. He asks for sight; he receives true mercy.

PRAYER: O God, look beneath my words and see my true needs. By the power of your Holy Spirit, confront me with the basic questions of life, so that I may grow in faith and become more Christlike each day. In Christ's name I ask this. Amen.

SUNDAY, OCTOBER 29 • Read Mark 10:46-52

God's mercy entails an aspect of discipleship: It always calls for a response. When Bartimaeus received his sight, he had several options in terms of response. He could have thanked Jesus very much, gone home, and started a new life with family and friends. He could have gone to the Temple, proclaimed the great deed that had been done for him, and become something of a celebrity. He could have spent lots of time contemplating this miracle of God and exploring new sight. Or he could respond in the way that Mark records—follow Jesus.

The mercy of God calls us to follow Jesus on the way. In Mark's Gospel, the way leads to Jerusalem and Jesus' entry into passion, death, and, eventually, resurrection. Bartimaeus asked for mercy, received sight, and chose to follow Jesus wherever that road would lead.

God's severe mercy calls us to nothing less. It calls us to wholeness; to shalom; to justice, righteousness, and peace. Jesus' miracles enabled the recipients to follow him, to give praise to God, and to serve others. The miracles never solely benefited the individual. Have you received mercy? How did you respond?

PRAYER: Lord Christ, for all the miracles you have performed in me, for healing of body, mind, spirit, and relationship, I give you thanks. Give me now the willingness to follow you, wherever the way may lead. Amen.

Surely There Is a Future

October 30–November 5, 2000 • *Glen V. Wiberg**

MONDAY, OCTOBER 30 • **Read Ruth 1:1-18**

In the worst of times, hope so often enters through the back-door of history in the least likely places and people. Take Bethlehem, for instance, not as "house of bread" or "How still we see thee lie" but Bethlehem as place of famine. Against this backdrop the storyteller introduces the family of Elime-lech: his wife Naomi and their two sons who, because of fam-ine, become refugees in a foreign land.

After ten years of dislocation in Moab with the loss of spouse and sons, Naomi rises—heroic, wounded, and digni-fied, a pillar of strength for her two daughters-in-law, Orpah and Ruth. In a moving scene awash with tears, Naomi announ-ces her decision to return home. She blesses her daughters-in-law and counsels each to return to her mother's house.

Orpah chooses to return to her own people in Moab, but Ruth clings to Naomi and states that she will go with Naomi to Bethlehem. With Ruth's decision, things will never be the same again—not for an aging woman, for a youthful Ruth, or for the shape of history itself. Ruth chooses love over security, covenant loyalty over ethnic ties, daring risk over playing it safe. And greater things beyond anything either can imagine await in the wings.

Where lies hope for the future if not in the risk-takers, the saints who though not perfect become life-givers, the harbin-gers of hope in the worst of times? And things can never be the same again.

SUGGESTION FOR MEDITATION: **Name those persons who have been life-givers for you, and consider how they have given you hope.**

---

*Pastor Emeritus, Salem Covenant Church (a member congregation of The Evangelical Covenant Church), New Brighton, Minnesota.

TUESDAY, OCTOBER 31 • Read Psalm 146

Singing and praising are an act of hope in the worship of God and often an act of open defiance of the enemy, the empire, or the forces of oppression and death. "Do not put your trust in princes, in mortals, in whom there is no help....Happy are those whose help is the God of Jacob." One observes that while exuberant praise often comes spontaneously from children, it may take a lifetime for adults—or at least those living through enough complexity if not pain—to know where hope and trust lie.

Psalm 146 speaks to the danger in American Christianity of a triumphalism that denies pain and, in so doing, makes praise false and unreal. But biblical faith never glosses over pain, not even in defiance of God. The psalm names those in the ranks of the marginalized—prisoners, the blind, the oppressed, the stranger, orphans and widows, and also the righteous. Here in exuberant praise the community remembers its history, making connections with the Exodus, with rescue and confirmation of promise keeping and covenant keeping. Strong verbs appear in Exodus 2:23-25. God *heard*. God *remembered*. God *looked*. God *took notice*.

Singing and praising as an act of hope come not by denial nor by an optimism that says things are better than they are nor even by a natural capacity for joy but by knowing that God pays attention and comes to the aid of the weak, the lowly, the distressed and grieving, the stranger, and the righteous too. The enthroned King of all the universe and of all the generations "keeps faith forever; who executes justice for the oppressed; who gives food to the hungry" and "sets the prisoners free." So hallelujah!

SUGGESTION FOR MEDITATION: **Read the words to the hymn, "I'll Praise My Maker While I've Breath."**

WEDNESDAY, NOVEMBER 1 • Read Isaiah 25:6-9

ALL SAINTS' DAY

Today is a day for all the saints just like us, as one theologian says, "members of a great host of uncanonized and unhaloed and fortunately yet unmartyred."* This festival in the church year invites us to think large, at least as large as the prophet in today's reading. Wedged in between oracles of judgment we find the mind-blowing vision of a great day coming when people from east and west, north and south will stream in—not to Mount Sinai, a place of holy terror, but to Mount Zion, the place of mystery, protection, harmony, and peace.

But Mount Zion is more than place, more than the seat of David. It symbolizes a homecoming to God's extravagant banquet table and a feast beyond comparison for its richness of food and drink. In Zion there are no supersaints—only those who find consolation, life, and joy never known before. The Lord will remove the shroud cast over all peoples. Could that shroud be our blindness to the glory of God or the fear of judgment now lifted by grace? At any rate, in Zion there will be no more mourning or tears, no more shame or guilt, and no more death, for "he will swallow up death forever."

Little wonder that the citizens of this new city find their ultimate joy in confessing and praising the only true Lord and Savior for which they have longed, the faithful God of the covenant from generation to generation who sits enthroned on Mount Zion. In the words from *The Book of Common Prayer* (Episcopal): "Therefore with Angels and Archangels, and with all the company of heaven, we laud and magnify thy glorious Name; evermore praising thee." Surely there is a future.

SUGGESTION FOR MEDITATION: Consider the thoughts of hymn writer Fred Pratt Green, who enjoins us to rejoice in the saints every day because "a world without saints forgets how to praise."

---

*Carl E. Braaten, *The Whole Counsel of God*.

319

THURSDAY, NOVEMBER 2 • Read Hebrews 9:11-14

Two tents stand in stark contrast—the old tent and the new. Acting as tour guide of the old (Heb. 9:1-10), the writer points out the sacred appointments in the Holy Place: lampstand, table, and bread. Then he lifts the curtain into the Holy of Holies, which is off-limits except when the high priest enters once a year on the Day of Atonement. Here he permits us to look into the forbidden depths—gold dazzles our eyes. We see the altar, the Ark, the jar of manna, Aaron's rod, and the two tablets of the Decalogue—objects dense with symbolism and mystery. According to a rabbinic tradition, if the high priest should drop dead of a heart attack inside the Holy of Holies, no one can go in to retrieve the corpse. So the high priest enters with a rope tied around his leg. The rules are clear, so beware of trespassing!

The new tent provides a startling contrast—no curtains, no gold, no barriers, yet described as "greater and perfect." The new tent is a Person, "a high priest of the good things that have come." His death tears the curtain of the Holy of Holies from top to bottom, thereby opening up a "new and living way" through the curtain of his flesh (10:20). The offering is Christ himself, his outpoured life obtaining eternal redemption and inaugurating a new and "better hope through which we approach God" (7:18). Now God's children, sinners all, may enter the Holy of Holies without a rope around their legs. The barriers are down, and we are welcomed into the innermost courts of God's house to touch the Holy and be touched.

SUGGESTION FOR MEDITATION: **Am I living in the old tent of "dead works" or religious busyness or in the new tent where the worship of the living God consists in responding to the needs of others?**

FRIDAY, NOVEMBER 3 • Read John 11:32-37

"After great pain, a formal feeling comes." The poet Emily Dickinson rightly describes the day after the death of a loved one as a day for "the sweeping up the heart, and putting love away." One feels something of this ceremonial grief in the way the storyteller describes Jesus' arrival in Bethany where his friend Lazarus has died.

Both sisters greet Jesus in the same way, rebuking his delay—Martha first on the road, then Mary later. "If you had been here, my brother would not have died." Both feel the same in heart as anyone who has lost a family member or friend—the great pain turns into formal complaint. Who has not suffered in some similar grievous loss the absence of God?

But the scene awash with tears takes us from the human side of things deeper into the story where hope and comfort lie. Mary weeps and those with her, but Jesus also weeps, entering into the loss and pain of his Bethany friends as one who has also lost a friend. People standing around say, "See how he loved him!"

There is more in Jesus' tears, however: a shudder, a deeper disturbance if not anger at illness and death, a great pain in facing the power of evil he came to destroy. His way to the tomb of Lazarus is also the way to his own death on the cross, where as Author of life he takes on himself the whole kingdom of death and evil. In both his tears and his shudder, Jesus enters into our human losses and grief but with the promise of resurrection and life eternal here and now. "Surely there is a future, and your hope will not be cut off" (Prov. 23:18).

SUGGESTION FOR MEDITATION: Name and reflect on other occasions in the Gospels where Jesus wept.

SATURDAY, NOVEMBER 4 • Read John 11:38-44

For the storyteller/theologian the story of a dead man brought back to life is as much our story as it is the story of Lazarus. And indeed we are Lazarus. The crisis the story creates in the disciples or Martha and Mary or those standing on the sidelines is not whether they will believe the story but whether they will believe him who is the resurrection and the life. "Those who believe in me...will never die. Do you believe this?" (11:25-26).

"Take away the stone"—whatever keeps us captive in the tomb of anxiety or guilt, shame or alienation. However strong the protests of a Martha, however ill-smelling our sleep of death, allow the light of Christ to expose whatever has congealed the habits of the soul and kept us immobile, rigid. Such an exposure prepares us to hear the quickening voice.

Then with the stone lifted, Jesus prays for us so that we may believe in the Sender and the One sent. He calls out "Father"—not simply a child's word *Abba*. With this word *Father*, Jesus invokes Israel's God who, having acted in the Exodus and return from exile, is acting now in the works and words of Jesus himself, challenging the domain of death.

So Jesus cries out with a loud voice, "Lazarus, come out!" And the dead man comes out, now alive. If only that stone be lifted and taken away, the voice of the Lord that awakens the dead will reach and make alive whatever is dead in us. "Very truly, I tell you, the hour is coming, and is now here, when the dead will hear the voice of the Son of God, and those who hear will live" (5:25). With the dead raised, the sinner forgiven and set free from the graveclothes of the old life, surely there is a future and a hope!

SUGGESTION FOR MEDITATION: **Put yourself in Martha's place in the story. How do you respond to Jesus' question: "Do you believe this?"**

SUNDAY, NOVEMBER 5 • Read Revelation 21:1-6*a*

The promise of newness runs as a subterranean stream through the whole of the New Testament: new covenant, new song, new commandment, new creation, new life, new wine, and in the last book of the Bible, new Jerusalem, new heaven, and new earth. But then in today's reading there is an added promise true and worthy of trust: "See, I am making all things new."

Biblical newness, however, does not mean novelty, something newly invented or newly made—like a brand-new car or a brand-new house or brand-new clothes. If newness is something tied to the temporal, then newness would soon be no longer new. Cars eventually wear out or break down; houses become old and stand in need of repair; clothes go out of style only to be replaced by the latest fashion. Such temporal newness is always threatened by obsolescence and death.

The promise of newness given by the One sitting on the throne is quite different. It is qualitative, which means the promise of newness partakes of a vitality that, like a spring of water, is perennially fresh. Yet it does not set aside the old or reject the continuities of the past. The New Covenant would not have been possible without the Old, nor the new wine without the ancient vineyards and the toil of other hands. And the New Jerusalem does not descend from heaven into a vacuum but as a gift descending upon the old and creating out of it something new.

Today Christ offers us the gift of newness and then adds as if to make us strong and believing, "It is done! I am the Alpha and the Omega, the beginning and the end. To the thirsty I will give water as a gift from the spring of the water of life. Those who conquer will inherit these things, and I will be their God and they will be my children" (21:6-7).

SUGGESTION FOR MEDITATION: **Reflect on the different ways Christ makes all things new in your relationships to others.**

Circles of Blessing

November 6–12, 2000 • Bill Barnes*

MONDAY, NOVEMBER 6 • Read Ruth 3:1-5

At first glance, Naomi's suggestions to Ruth seem a bit daring, even dangerous. But nothing in the text detracts from a genuine concern for her loyal and compassionate Moabite daughter-in-law who, like Naomi, is a widow. Both women face all the uncertainties and hardships of widowhood in their time and place.

As our population ages, as researchers develop medical techniques that further foster longevity for the elderly, few families will be spared the agony of nursing home choices. But today's text reverses the normal concern: Here the older Naomi attempts to secure and fulfill Ruth's future.

Yet do not most of us spend time and invest resources to benefit loved ones who will survive us? We do so through financial planning. The concern expresses itself collectively as well as privately. We will work together to insure the soundness of Social Security for the decades ahead of us. And we will continue to press for health care coverage for the children of the working poor and others left out of our current system of coverage. Compassion is collective as well as individual.

Naomi has many reasons to be self-centered and self-pitying. But she exercises great love in planning for Ruth's future and well-being. Perhaps Naomi helps us care, focus, and plan for the younger as well as the older generation.

PRAYER: Dear God, let Naomi's spirit of remarkable compassion and follow-through be in me. In my own time and place, fill me and make me a good steward in the healing of creation. Amen.

---

*Retired United Methodist pastor; lead organizer for Tying Nashville Together, affiliate of Industrial Areas Foundation; coordinator for Shalom Zones, Tennessee Conference of The United Methodist Church; living in Nashville, Tennessee.

TUESDAY, NOVEMBER 7 • Read Ruth 4:13-17

If you tell the story of King David, Israel's most celebrated ruler, and if you describe his ancestry, you have to include a foreign woman, a Moabite named Ruth. Through her selfless devotion, Ruth became an indispensable link in the succession. In Matthew 1, the genealogy finally includes Jesus.

When we read Ezra and Nehemiah, we face a post–exilic attitude of nationalistic exclusiveness ("put away foreign wives"). Ruth and Jonah exemplify the inclusive, universal yearnings of Israel. If we want a story that reflects the way foreigners, outsiders, and immigrants can profoundly bless the life of a welcoming nation, Ruth is a perfect choice.

I pastored a congregation for thirty years in Nashville, Tennessee. Because of the church building's proximity to Vanderbilt University and Scarritt Bennett College, families from Africa, Asia, Latin America, Australia, and the South Sea Islands enriched our congregational life!

Having lived in the same city all of my life, I have found that the recent influx of God's children from all parts of the world has wondrously diversified our city's languages, food choices, labor force, and religious traditions. Life is more and more like a wonderful stew into which all the varied ingredients, without surrendering discrete identity, blend into one another and produce a delicious result.

All about us, as in Israel's history, we hear sounds of resentment, fear, nationalism, exclusiveness. But this passage from Ruth reminds us to approach diversity with anticipation, not fear; with thanksgiving, not competitiveness; with hospitality, not separation.

Rejoice in the simple beauty of Ruth 4:13-17. Let it glow in your heart and mind, creating initiatives of welcome and hospitality. The promise is one of blessing.

PRAYER: Fill me, O God, with a heart and arms that enfold and embrace, so that I too may receive your blessing! Amen.

WEDNESDAY, NOVEMBER 8 • Read Psalm 127

"Unless the Lord builds the house, those who build it labor in vain." The psalmist does not depict Yahweh as a contractor ready to receive our blueprint for a new house. Rather, the psalmist insists that the occupants of the house welcome and invite the presence and guidance of the gracious Creator. Is this a "ho hum" observation, or does the verse have intense relevance for us as households today?

The horror of child and spousal abuse occurs more often than not within houses where families dwell. Our living rooms become dumps where media violence pours into the eyes and ears of family members. We easily allow the gods of violence and consumerism to shape the life of our households. Is the daily life of your household being formed by the God of grace and compassion?

Have you ever staged a house blessing to remind and strengthen the presence and will of Yahweh? Many times I have held the hands of celebrants as we have weaved in and out of the rooms of a newly occupied house. The faith community sings and prays that in that place the sovereignty of Yahweh will continue to hold sway.

Grace at mealtimes that serves as honest, hopeful, and healing communication comes center stage. All present will share in financial decisions and the setting of priorities. The building that the Lord does in a house is ongoing and daily as hearts and minds open anew to One who creates "all things new."

Clearly the words of the psalmist admonish us to take stock. Is the Lord continuing to build our house? Do we daily open doors of discipline through which we invite the Lord of life? The wonderful promise is not only one of willing entrance but of blessed result. Thanks be to God.

PRAYER: Show me new ways, O God, whereby I may receive you daily into my household, so that you may fulfill your will to bless

THURSDAY, NOVEMBER 9 • **Read Psalm 127:1b-2**

"Unless the Lord guards the city, the guard keeps watch in vain." Today's passage admonishes us to be vessels of God's gracious, watchful care in the life of the city. In scripture the city is a creature of God with life-giving intentions of the Creator. The Bible begins in a garden and concludes in a holy city. Jesus breaks down and cries as he approaches Jerusalem, for the city has so tragically resisted the will of God for its life. We may conclude that God loves the city and actively yearns for its conversion and fulfillment as a place of shalom, peace, blessing, unity.

We can easily picture Jesus breaking into tears as he approaches one of our large urban areas. His heart would break over the daily experience of children growing up in large public housing complexes created by political decision-making processes. The familiar scene—crime, drugs, violence, gunshots in the night, paralyzing fear—all but numbs us. If we as disciples begin by sharing Jesus' compassion and tears, we go on to our own versions of clearing the Temple of exploitative economic systems through sustained involvement in the urban process of priority setting and resource distribution.

The psalmist speaks of God's being the guiding presence in the city. Affordable housing, living wage jobs, adequate transportation systems, Jubilee redistribution—these take unity, prayer, tears, obedience, organization, and resilience; maybe even some Good Fridays and Easters. The psalmist beams truth at us: Without God's presence and power shaping our houses and cities, only tragedy awaits us. What might this mean for your life as you work with God for the healing of a fallen Creation, both private and public?

PRAYER: Connect me, O God, to your active compassion for all cities. Make me faithful to see that your presence and power shape and build them to the blessing of all the inhabitants. Amen.

FRIDAY, NOVEMBER 10 • Read Hebrews 9:24-28

The writer of Hebrews provides a wonderful description of Christian faith. Something momentous has happened through Christ. Coming out of the life, death, resurrection, and ascension of Jesus is a marvelous conviction for the writer. He says, in effect, that the risen, triumphant Lord is now in the presence of the creator God. Jesus, in that presence, expresses the same healing grace for us that he lived out in his earthly ministry. In other words, in his transformed state, Jesus continues to promote our healing actively. That truth is dramatized in Jesus once for all.

In the Christ event we discover that we too can live and die in trust and anticipation. What God has done for us in Christ means that we shall encounter the fullness of that grace in the future. And we shall meet Christ, not as a dreadful accuser but as one who will complete his vocation to perfect us in love. So we "are eagerly waiting for him."

But the "once for all" nature of Christ's work doesn't leave us with nothing to do. To live daily with trust and anticipation, set in a history replete with horror, injustice, and cruelty, we must exercise all possible sources of "spiritual income," including the daily disciplines of prayer and scripture reading. That "spiritual income," which will keep faith and hope alive and growing, will also come through active pursuit of justice, through acts of forgiveness and reconciliation. Faithfulness will replace and replenish weakened or elusive faith. Like the writer, we will be able to receive the grace of Christ and persevere in trust and anticipation, confident that Christ will come to us again in fullness and clarity and, above all, in grace and power. Hallelujah!

PRAYER: Thank you, dear God, for that burst of saving grace in Jesus' death and resurrection. Open me daily to your sources of spiritual income, so that my living may continue to express what I understand of Christ until I see Jesus face to face. Amen.

SATURDAY, NOVEMBER 11 • Read Mark 12:38-40

Jesus is painfully aware that we who compete and consume and worry anxiously about ourselves may wear more than one face. In our self-identity, do we live our lives as chameleons and weather vanes or do we live faithfully, aware of the sovereignty and will of a gracious creator God? All of us are subject to Jesus' scrutiny and judgment, for we all know the disorienting power of duplicity.

I read about a Nazi commandant of a concentration camp during World War II. Daily the acid clouds of smoke rose into the sky, signaling the burning of Jews during the Holocaust. He organized and oversaw cruelty of a type and scale that surpasses imagination. Yet at the end of the day, this German officer went home to his family where the members of the household moved sanctimoniously through a meal blessing in the hallowed tradition of their Christian denomination. This scenario seems—and is—pathological, evil, beyond sanity. While the chasm between public and private may seem much smaller for us, we constantly struggle for greater integrity.

Jesus describes the appearance of pillars of the community who, like a hungry dog going for a bone, frantically desire admiration, respect, and honor. But their public image conceals their greedy and evil exploitation of defenseless widows. As we turn inward, we see reflections of ourselves in Jesus' words as we obey the contradictory wills of so many gods. Increased integrity and the consequent peace of mind wait for greater diligence in prayer on our part, for honest self-criticism and a calling up of the gifts of the Spirit offered by God. Let us open our clenched fists to receive the blessings of community, scripture, devotional discipline. We not only will be blessed but will become more of a blessing to this broken world.

PRAYER: Come, Holy Spirit. Lead me out of the dizzying pantheon of gods I serve and lead me into the integrity and peace of serving the one true God of justice and healing. Amen.

SUNDAY, NOVEMBER 12 • Read Mark 12:41-44

Dietrich Bonhoeffer wrote about "cheap grace," grace without serious cost, grace without a cross, cosmetic sharing and blessing not deeply felt. Charity also can be either cheap or costly. We can contribute without feeling the impact on our checkbooks or credit cards. A rabbinic saying reminds us: "The rich are willing to throw coins over the wall to the poor on the other side. But the rich do not wish to tear down the wall." We willingly share our money "off the top" and maybe even a little volunteer time. But we avoid long-term exposure to or lasting relationships with the disadvantaged of our cities or communities. Charity is fine as long as it leaves the givers in control. Jesus sits, watches, and then teaches his disciples about his observation. The poor widow's sacrifice genuinely foreshadows one who gives all on a merciless cross in the consummate expression of *costly* grace.

Years ago one of the little girls (call her "Annie") from the nearby "projects" attended the church's afterschool program. The mother of her single-parent household struggled with alcoholism (a struggle she finally won). Annie's mother lived a miserable life—especially in light of the poverty and addiction she faced daily. One afternoon before the program began, Annie knocked on my office door. When I opened the door, she handed me a surprisingly heavy small paper sack. The sack contained pennies she had accumulated over months. She wanted to contribute to the church's afterschool program, for which she thanked God. I held back tears until she left. Today, some twenty years later, Annie is a full-time member of the church staff and directs its children's ministries program. God is still in the Easter business, transforming the widow's mite or sacks of pennies into concentric circles of blessing. I thank God for Jesus' truth and story. Believe it and do likewise!

PRAYER: Use me, O God, to confirm your power to translate even small but costly sacrifices into joyful blessings for many. Amen.

Once for All

November 13–19, 2000 • Kate Heichler*

MONDAY, NOVEMBER 13 • Read 1 Samuel 1:4-11

I have a friend who says, "You can always get what you don't want." In today's story Hannah's wanting consumes her. She wants a child—not a bad thing to want. She has much: the genuine love of her husband, an undivided portion in the feast. But what she most wants, she lacks. She expresses a sense that God has forgotten her. When have you felt like that?

Hannah's rival serves as a constant reminder of Hannah's failure. Isn't it often true that when we fix our longing on something, we almost always begin to compare ourselves with others? When we focus on what we don't have, we can easily view God as the One Who Withholds rather than as the Giver of Life.

What do you feel you must have—without which you are inconsolable? What demand do you make of the Lord?

Year after year Hannah becomes increasingly depressed, weeping and not eating. Only when Hannah comes to the end of her rope does she pour out her heart to the Lord in the temple. What if we learned to go to God sooner—at our first awareness of an area of pain? before we let it take over and dominate the landscape of our life? before we let it poison our relationships? before we become clinically depressed or habitually miserable or both?

SUGGESTION FOR MEDITATION: Focus on this verse; ask the Spirit to reveal where this truth resides in your life: "Lord, you are my allotted portion and my cup; / you maintain my boundaries: / the lines fall for me in pleasant places; / I am well content with my inheritance" (Ps. 16:5-6, REB).

---

*Episcopal writer and longtime member of Grace Church in New York City; currently a student at Yale Divinity School.

TUESDAY, NOVEMBER 14 • Read 1 Samuel 1:12-20

Hannah prays to the Lord in the intimacy of a relationship with God. When Eli misdiagnoses her problem and acts on his judgment without checking the facts, Hannah responds to him in a self-assured manner. She knows herself to be a deeply troubled woman. She confesses her heartbrokenness.

A broken heart does not function in the same way as one that is intact. But who of us has a heart that is intact?

Hannah pours out her soul to the Lord, praying out of her great grief and anguish. She serves as a model to us of *where* to take our troubles. More than that, she models *how* to take our troubles to the Lord; Hannah invites us to speak to God out of the depths of our grief and misery. We don't have to put on a shiny face for the Lord; in fact, the Lord will make our faces shine. Like Hannah, we may bring all our troubles, heart-breaks, disappointments, grievances—righteous and other-wise—angers, and sorrows to the Lord who hears, remembers, and heals us.

Eli's answer to Hannah goes beyond simply a polite bene-diction; it is a promise. It is the word from God. Eli "words" her healing and restoration with the authority the Lord grants him. And Hannah believes his word. She walks by faith. She goes and eats; her face is no longer downcast. She has not yet received what she has asked, but she believes and proceeds expectantly. And soon she is expecting.

Jesus says, "Whatever you ask for in prayer, believe that you have received it and it will be yours" (Mark 11:24, REB).

SUGGESTION FOR MEDITATION: Consider praying like Hannah about your needs:

> **I have set the Lord before me at all times:**
> **with him at my right hand I cannot be shaken.**
> **Therefore my heart is glad and my spirit rejoices,**
> **my body too rests unafraid. (Ps. 16:8-9, REB)**

Wednesday, November 15 • Read Hebrews 10:11-18

Do you know anyone who participates in a recurring pattern of behavior, repeating steps in relationships, in work, in ministry time and time again, hoping that this time the outcome will be different? Like the sacrifices once offered in the Temple, these patterns cannot accomplish what they purpose.

We read today that Christ did accomplish his work. His effective sacrifice broke the pattern of repeated ritual. The good news is that his atoning sacrifice covers our sins. We need only trust and believe in the sufficiency of his sacrifice. The only sacrifice God wants from us, we are told, is "a broken spirit; a broken and contrite heart" (Ps. 51:17, NIV).

Today's passage says, "So by one offering he has perfected for ever those who are consecrated by it" (REB). This is a radical promise: We, who have been consecrated by Christ's sacrifice in the shedding of his own blood, have been perfected, made holy forever. Holiness is not ours to grasp or earn but has been conferred on us by the sacrifice of Jesus Christ for our sins.

God continually invites us to offer our contrite hearts in repentance and to bring our griefs and sorrows to the Lord, as did Hannah. But there is nothing we can do and nothing we must do to earn forgiveness. That has been granted by the new covenant into which we enter by confessing Jesus as Lord.

SUGGESTION FOR PRAYER: **Call to mind some of the times you have received forgiveness from God and other people. Make this verse your prayer:**

> You will not abandon me to Sheol
> or suffer your faithful servant to see the pit.
> You will show me the path of life;
> in your presence is the fullness of joy. (Ps. 16:10-11, REB)

THURSDAY, NOVEMBER 16 • Read Hebrews 10:19-25

I have always feared being left out, not included. The good news for me—and you—is that God welcomes us at all times and in all places into God's presence, the throne of grace. The shed blood of the perfect and sufficient priest has accomplished once for all what the shed blood of animal sacrifices could not. At Jesus' crucifixion "the curtain of the temple was torn in two from top to bottom" (Mark 15:38, REB), thus opening the way into the Holy of Holies, God's dwelling place, once for all.

Beyond the great promise of forgiveness, today's passage assures us of the great promise of access: "For through [Christ] we both alike have access to the Father in the one Spirit" (Eph. 2:18, REB). Today's passage invites us to make our approach "in sincerity of heart and the full assurance of faith" (REB). Full assurance? A sincere heart? Who of us can say we possess those? How can we confess our hope firmly and unswervingly? What about our experiences of disappointment?

The writer of Hebrews says, "The giver of the promise is to be trusted" (REB). Can we take that step to trust God? Hannah finally did. Faith is a decision of the will as well as an act of the heart.

We have received access to the One who can be trusted. Can we bring to God our burdens and sorrows and joys? Let us encourage one another to trust the Giver of the promise "all the more because we see the day of the Lord drawing near" (REB).

SUGGESTION FOR MEDITATION: How has God encouraged your trust? Meditate on this verse until it becomes your prayer:

I have said to the Lord, "You are my Lord;
from you alone comes the good I enjoy.
All my delight is in the noble ones,
the godly in the land." (Ps. 16:2-3, REB)

FRIDAY, NOVEMBER 17 • Read Mark 13:1-8

We sure are proud of our buildings. Starting with the tower of Babel, we like to build them high and show them off. Have you ever built something that you're really proud of? a house? a business? a relationship? a ministry?

The Temple really impresses the disciples. More than a great building, the Temple is a monument, the visible heritage of the house of David. And here is the Son of David prophesying its destruction.

How can a building made of such huge stones ever fall down? How can an institution like the Temple, with its layers of priests and councils and sacrifices and vendors and beggars, ever fall? Religious life centers in this particular building. The disciples have every reason to believe that Jesus will overturn everything related to their religion that has become lifeless and corrupt.

But Jesus has set in motion a much more radical revolution. No longer do we believe that God dwells in a building, in an inner sanctum behind a veil, accessible only to the high priest once a year. Now Jeremiah's prophecy of a new covenant comes to fulfillment in Jesus, the great high priest whose sacrifice is accomplished. Now God's law will be set within us, written in our hearts.

Before Jesus leaves the disciples, he promises the gift of the Holy Spirit, the "Counselor to be with you forever—the Spirit of truth" (John 14:16-17, NIV).

The Spirit will write God's law on our hearts as we allow, as we learn to listen to God's promptings, asking for guidance, comfort, and faith.

SUGGESTION FOR PRAYER: **Invite the Holy Spirit into your heart anew. Pray for the faith to believe these words:**

I shall bless the Lord who has given me counsel:
in the night he imparts wisdom to my inmost being.
(Ps. 16:7, REB)

SATURDAY, NOVEMBER 18 • Read Mark 13:1-8

Who among us doesn't like to have inside information? When is an event going to happen? How are we going to know? How will we protect ourselves? How can we control the future? We think that by knowing the person at the top, we have access to saving information. Certainly Jesus' disciples think that. "What will be the sign?" they ask.

Not knowing unsettles us, especially if the structures of our lives seem to be crumbling—unrest in our government, decay in our social fabric, squabbling in our churches. Wars, famines, and disasters are mercifully far from our country most of the time, but they surround us in the world.

It takes radical trust to follow and not know. Anxiety can make us susceptible to being misled. We can follow when we trust the leader, when we trust, in our case, the One who knows all things. "For the giver of the promise is to be trusted" (Heb. 10:23, REB). Wars and natural disasters do not signal the end, though they may seem like the end to us. The end is the beginning: the birth of the new age of the kingdom of heaven. "If we hope for something we do not yet see, then we look forward to it eagerly and with patience" (Rom. 8:25, REB).

We have access to the source of all knowledge, though we don't always have the language to understand the information. We are called to trust and to believe expectantly. The end is in the hands of the Author of the beginning, the One who is the Alpha and the Omega, the way, the truth, and the life.

PRAYER: Pray these verses in trust:

You will show me the path of life;
in your presence is the fullness of joy,
at your right hand are pleasures for evermore.
(Ps. 16:11, REB)

SUNDAY, NOVEMBER 19 • Read Psalm 16

This psalm serves as our Sunday devotion to help us digest the rich food we have taken in through our readings this week.

Psalm 16 is a prayer for safekeeping and a psalm of trust. It invites us to take refuge in the Lord when we don't get what we want, when the tumult around us causes fear. We can rest because we trust in the Lord, knowing that God will not abandon us to death and the powers of hell. We affirm God's eternity of love and rest. "I pray…that you may know what is the hope to which he calls you, how rich and glorious is the share he offers you among his people in their inheritance, and how vast are the resources of his power open to us who have faith" (Eph. 1:18-19, REB).

SUGGESTION FOR MEDITATION: First, make yourself comfortable and ask to be brought into God's presence. When settled, bring to mind those things that your heart most desires, not judging them but bringing them to the surface. Bring to mind those things you most fear, which are often connected to the things you most want. Bring to mind the sorrows you carry. Take your time.

Now lay your desires, your fears, and your sorrows before you. Behind you is the Lord. In your imagination—or in your chair if you want to enact this exercise physically—turn yourself around 180 degrees, so that now the Lord is before you. And where are your sorrows, fears, and desires? They are behind you. They become the Lord's problems now. God's eye rests upon them and upon you. Your eye now contemplates the "only good," the source of your healing and delight.

Practice this exercise when your preoccupation with problems or desires overwhelms you. Turn toward God and say with the psalmist, "Keep me, God, for in you have I found refuge…. / I have set the Lord before me at all times: / with him at my right hand I cannot be shaken." (Ps. 16:1, 8, REB)

Gratitude

November 20–26, 2000 • Robert C. Liebold*

MONDAY, NOVEMBER 20 • Read Revelation 1:4b-8

The coming Christ

"'I am the Alpha and the Omega,' says the Lord God, who is and who was and who is to come, the Almighty." In seminary I considered the Revelation to John to be the most confusing book of the New Testament—and I still do!

The need to understand Revelation's apocalyptic predictions often makes for frustrating reading. John's vision and style of writing lend themselves to differing interpretations. A New Testament professor relieved my need to decipher its message by suggesting that the purpose of Revelation is not to know the calendar secrets of Christ's coming but to offer gratitude for what God is doing in the coming of Christ—to experience awe and wonder in the works of God.

Gratitude for the advent (coming) of Christ—past, present, and future comings—results from trust in Jesus. Knowing Jesus who has come, born in Bethlehem and born in my heart, instills in my heart a gratitude for his coming. In the midst of what is often a frightening and changing world, I am able to trust in Christ's future comings, knowing that Jesus who has come "is the same yesterday and today and forever" (Heb. 13:8). Jesus, the "Alpha and the Omega" (the first and last letters in the Greek alphabet), has promised to be with me at the beginning and at the end of all life.

SUGGESTION FOR MEDITATION: As you begin this Thanksgiving week of gratitude, sit quietly and consider the comings of Jesus in your life.

---

*Director of Wellspring Institute for Spiritual Growth; United Methodist pastor in the New York Annual Conference; husband of Ilse and father of John and Mary.

TUESDAY, NOVEMBER 21 • Read Psalm 132:1-18

Sacred places

Read verses 1-5 again and hear David's determination and passion to find a sacred place for the Lord, "a dwelling place for the Mighty One." One might ask whether God needs a place to dwell. Perhaps it's God's people who yearn for a sacred place to dwell in God's presence.

Willoughby Lake in the Northeast Kingdom of Vermont has been such a sacred place for me since childhood. In the setting of the Green Mountains, Willoughby offers a resting place for the soul; it invites me to soak in the goodness of God. Here I have felt the sacredness and nearness of Christ.

In the heart a hunger exists for places of rest in sacred presence, and with gratitude and joy we thank God for dwelling with us. Sacred places vary in nature and location. For you it may be a stroll along the beach, worship in the local church, time alone in solitude and silence, a small-group gathering for prayer and searching the scriptures, coming apart for retreat, Christian conversation with a spiritual director, playing with your children. So many are the places of sacred rest that sometimes we experience ourselves soaking in God's presence without realizing that we're even wet.

Gratitude for God's sacred places affords us an intentional moment to ponder the comings of Christ. Psalm 132 expresses the hunger to identify such places in our lives and our need to experience God there. We do not seek the sacred place in order to experience God, thereby limiting God to that place; rather, God's presence makes the place sacred. And, in that sacred place, we are promised a resting place with God forevermore.

SUGGESTION FOR MEDITATION: **In what sacred places do you experience the coming of Christ?**

WEDNESDAY, NOVEMBER 22 • Read 1 Timothy 2:1-7

God's people

First Timothy 2:1-3 urgently directs us to pray with an attitude of gratitude for everyone, especially "for kings and all who are in high positions." Entering a neighboring pastor's office during Thanksgiving week, I found him writing a series of thanksgiving letters, including one to his dentist. With a genuine sense of gratitude, he remembered all his dentist had done for him. My friend's letter reminded me of the gift of thanks-*receiving*. It is so energizing to be appreciated. The gift of gratitude invites us into the saving grace of God's goodness.

Perhaps these verses direct us to remember the "kings and all who are in high positions," because we easily overlook these persons. Often those in positions of authority and leadership endure our criticisms but receive little of our encouragement. And perhaps we unconsciously assume that those in high positions have no need of our sustaining prayer and thanksgiving.

Sometimes a high position of authority carries with it the illusion of control and of no need for God. Paul's instruction to Timothy suggests that our prayers serve as a means of grace for persons in position of power, enabling effective leadership. In gratitude for these persons, we remember that even the powerful are powerless without God. For Christ Jesus is the "one mediator between God and [all] humankind." No one, no matter how powerful, stands outside the need for encouragement and prayer.

First Timothy urges us to approach one another with prayer and thanksgiving. When we offer the gift of gratitude and encouragement, we open ourselves and those we approach to the saving knowledge of Christ Jesus.

SUGGESTION FOR MEDITATION: To whom is God calling you to offer the gift of gratitude and thanksgiving?

THURSDAY, NOVEMBER 23 • **Read Psalm 126**

THANKSGIVING DAY

A harvest of thanksgiving

"We were like those who dream," writes the psalmist. On this day, when we in the United States celebrate Thanksgiving, do you hear the joyful laughter of the Israelites—those once exiled from the Promised Land who now shout with joy in the fulfillment of their dreams? God has restored the fortunes of Zion, and the people shout with joy for a harvest of thanksgiving. It's like a dream—too good to be truly happening: "I must be dreaming!"

The restoration of Zion causes laughter, shouts of joy, praises to the Lord. It is the harvest of thanksgiving for which the people have waited, hoped, and dreamed. Their vision is now fulfilled. But the harvest was costly, coming at the expense of tears and weeping. Often our tears reveal the inner intensity with which we desire the dream.

God has filled our heart with a dream. It comes as a gift, and, like the Israelites, we are energized by that vision. We feel the passion for its fulfillment, like streams of life-giving water in the desert that enliven and quench the inner desires of the heart. We know the harvest will not come easily; yet as people of faith, we dare to hope in the harvest of thanksgiving: the day when God will fulfill the dream. That fulfillment will bring overwhelming gratitude for God's gift. "Then, our mouth [will be] filled with laughter, and our tongue with shouts of joy."

On this Thanksgiving Day ponder the harvest of thanksgiving. What is the dream of your heart's inner desires? Commit your way to the unfolding of God's will.

"Take delight in the LORD,
and he will give you the desires of your heart." (Ps. 37:4)

BREATH PRAYER: Come, Lord Jesus, let your will unfold in me.

FRIDAY, NOVEMBER 24 • Read Joel 2:21-27

Healing and restoration

Yesterday we expressed our gratitude for a harvest of thanksgiving. Joel 2:21-27 is God's promise following Israel's shaming, through the complete desolation of the harvest. Joel describes a plague of locusts that completely decimates the crops of the field and humiliates the soul of Zion. "Be dismayed, you farmers, wail, you vinedressers / ...surely, joy withers away among the people"(Joel 1:11, 12). Even the animals and the land are in despair: "How the animals groan! ...Even the wild animals cry to you because the watercourses are dried up, / and fire has devoured the pastures of the wilderness" (Joel 1:18, 20).

Some time ago I talked with a clergy member of my conference who has been the target of some viciousness in her congregation. She feels like an abused pastor and compares herself to an abused spouse, somehow feeling she deserves it. She perceives that she has no options or choices and feels powerless to do anything about it. In her despair I sense the hopelessness and anguish of Israel: completely helpless and powerless to end the vicious attack. Malicious attacks humiliate and generate shame in child or adult. And they are life-draining, sapping joy and gladness from the heart.

In the midst of their despair, the people cry out to God. With fasting, weeping, and mourning, the heart of the people returns to the Lord. Overwhelmed and powerless, the nation looks to the One who is all powerful. God responds with a promise of healing and complete restoration that extends to the whole creation: to the soil of the earth, to the animals of the field, to the crops of the land, and to the children of Zion. How do we respond to this promise? With nothing less than our gratitude to and rejoicing in the Lord our God.

BREATH PRAYER: Come, Lord Jesus, let me rest in you.

SATURDAY, NOVEMBER 25 • **Read 2 Samuel 23:1-7**

Spiritual leadership

When one makes a deathbed statement, others should listen. In 1791 John Wesley, age 88 and near death, weakly sings a favorite hymn: "I'll praise my Maker while I've breath; and when my voice is lost in death, praise shall employ my nobler powers." * In his life and death, John Wesley reflects a discerning spirit, guiding the formation of a people called Methodist.

Second Samuel notes the last words of David, king of Israel, acclaiming David as one through whom God speaks, who rules over people justly. Like John Wesley, King David has served as a spiritual leader, discerning the way of the Lord. Neither is perfect, having human faults, sins, and limitations, yet God speaks through John Wesley and King David. The spirit of the Lord resides in each, unfolding the will of God. Wesley and David have a passion for God and a vision for leading God's people.

Samuel describes David as ruling in the fear of God "like the light of morning, like the sun rising on a cloudless morning." In a time and place that lighted the darkness through star and moonlight and the oil lamp, people yearned for and welcomed the morning sun. Darkness is often frightening. Consider a ship in the darkness of a storm, a ship seeking safe harbor through the aid of a lighthouse. David's leadership offered spiritual guidance in an often terrifying and puzzling world for the nation of Israel. Today we offer gratitude for spiritual leaders in the life of the church who, like navigators on a ship, provide direction in the discerning of God's unfolding will.

SUGGESTION FOR MEDITATION: **Who are the spiritual leaders in the life of your church? In gratitude thank God for them.**

The United Methodist Hymnal, #60.

SUNDAY, NOVEMBER 26 • Read John 18:33-38

THE REIGN OF CHRIST SUNDAY

The truth of Christ Jesus

In a volatile and politically unstable land, Pilate has to feel vulnerable on that day when confronted with Jesus, King of the Jews. Pilate questions Jesus' identity, as we all must, answering not as others tell us but as we discern in our own heart. Considering Jesus as king suggests our submission to a ruler and, through Jesus, submitting ourselves to God's will.

In a moment of weariness, Pilate asks Jesus, "What is truth?" Is it even possible to discern the truth of Jesus? Earlier in John's Gospel, Thomas asks Jesus, "How can we know the way?" (14:5) and Jesus replies, "I am the way, and the truth, and the life" (14:6). Through Jesus we come to know the truth of God. John's Gospel repeatedly places us in a state of vulnerability by asking, "Who is Jesus?" "Who do you say that I am?" Jesus asks of all his disciples.

The approaching Advent season calls us again to that question in the hymn:

> What child is this who, laid to rest, on Mary's lap is
> sleeping?
> Whom angels greet with anthems sweet, while shep-
> herds watch are keeping?
> This, this is Christ the King, whom shepherds guard
> and angels sing.
> Haste, haste to bring him laud, the babe, the son of
> Mary.

SUGGESTION FOR MEDITATION: Who is Jesus for you? In gratitude thank God for the truth of Christ Jesus.

In Those Days...

November 27–December 3, 2000 • *J. Paul Womack**

MONDAY, NOVEMBER 27 • Read Jeremiah 33:14-15

The stories I remember from childhood usually began, "Once upon a time." Whether read or told, these stories provided narratives during my childhood that gave me moral meaning and a sense of what living was all about: adventure, honor, self-reliance, chivalry, the victory of good over evil. These stories of past times offered me guidance and values for the present. Now at the cusp of the new century, Christian people of faith once again remember that they can turn to the scriptures for stories of moral meaning that provide direction and guidance, stories that encourage us to love God and neighbor.

Yet Christians need more than moral guidance or a sense of life's patterns to live with an advent spirit of confidence and expectation. We also need hope. So we look in scripture for those stories that generate this necessary hope to sustain us when the future seems uncertain and frightening.

God's promises for the future form Jeremiah's faith. In prophecy after prophecy, Jeremiah offers God's promises. And what God promises is nothing less than a new beginning for all of creation.

Those who would bind themselves to God will discover not only moral guidance in the scriptures but hope and promise as well. In this season we may remember Advents past and wonder, *When? How long?* Or we can reclaim Jeremiah's own hope—"In those days...."

PRAYER: Come, Lord Jesus, not simply as a remembered story but as the very hope of the morrow. By your grace bring salvation to your people. Amen.

---

*Clergy member, Western New York Conference of The United Methodist Church; copastor of Covenant United Methodist Church, Rochester, New York.

TUESDAY, NOVEMBER 28 • Read Jeremiah 33:15-16

Hide-and-seek was a game for lazy summer evenings. From a tried and true place where we could hide but could not stay we would scurry, often with screams and yelps, to avoid the one hunting us and to seek the safety of "home." Since we could not dwell forever in our hiding place, "home" offered us the promise of total safety.

Life often imitates this childhood game. We sometimes feel the need to hide, to be in a secure place. Yet even in our hiding we are hunted, hunted by our sins and guilt, hunted by our fears, hunted by our real and imagined failures. We also know that ultimately our hiding place is not secure. The safe boundaries collapse, and we must move into the open, darting this way and that to evade the hunter and reach the safety of home.

Jeremiah promises that in the days to come we will be found by a Savior, a hunter, who will draw us into the safety of our home. Evade, dodge, hide as we will, we will also be found, Jeremiah exclaims. To our surprise Jeremiah adds that we will find "at home," in the presence of the hunter, respite, forgiveness, and renewal for our souls. In those days we will no longer call God the hunter or the seeker, but we will call God by a new name: God our righteousness, God our safety, God our Savior.

PRAYER: Lord Jesus, in this game of hide-and-seek, we hide and you seek. Free us from our fears of discovery, that we may turn to you in hope this Advent season. Amen.

WEDNESDAY, NOVEMBER 29 • Read Psalm 25:1-10

High above the Valley of the Shadow, located in an area of stark beauty and natural danger and situated about halfway between Jerusalem and Jericho, pilgrims can take a deeply rutted road off the main highway. After carefully easing their way along this narrow roadway, they can park their vehicles and follow an even narrower path up a rocky hill. Beyond the crest an astounding view stretches before them.

On various hilltops pilgrims can see small crosses that mark the spots where monks lived out their hermetic existence. Down below the hills and across the narrow gully known as the Valley of the Shadow is St. George's Monastery, which perches precariously on a cliff. Despite the stunning view, the path itself can intimidate people.

Recently on a trip one group member seemed reluctant to make the trek. Our guide said to him, "You must trust the path." In this Advent season we would do well to remember the faith of the many who have walked ahead of us. They too knew the anxieties, the dangers, and the fears associated with any first-time journey.

We take many journeys in our lives: from infancy to childhood to adolescence to adulthood to old age to death and to resurrection. Each transition can appear frightening, unclear, and intimidating. But the communion of saints who go before us learned to trust the path. We too, following after them, can learn to trust the path. If we set out and willingly risk the walk, we will reach a scene of great beauty and astounding confidence.

PRAYER: Lord Jesus, to you I lift up my soul. Receive its hopes and its fears; teach me your paths. In you I will trust. Amen.

THURSDAY, NOVEMBER 30 • Read 1 Thessalonians 3:9-13

Like so many in our global culture, I live far from family and friends. It is not easy to be so far away. I miss many important family rituals and passages, making the opportunities to be present for family gatherings all the more important. One critical affirmation that comes from being part of a family is the value and esteem we gain. Those who do not experience a sense of being valued and validated by those closest to them often experience a great deficit of meaning and self-esteem. Our personal sense of worth comes not only from our immediate family but from our extended family of friends and neighbors.

Saint Paul gained a powerful sense of his own value from his extended family in Thessalonica. They greeted him warmly, welcoming both his physical presence and his spiritual guidance, which makes Paul feel doubly pleased that he has spent his life as an apostle. Not only is Paul confident of his work on behalf of Jesus Christ, but those persons with whom he preaches and teaches also affirm his vocation.

We can interpret Paul's words of joy and his desire to restore their faith as a kind of presumption, or we can sense in his openness of expression a confidence in knowing he has the wisdom of the gospel to offer, a wisdom they have accepted appreciatively from him in the past.

In this holy season of Advent, as we prepare to be with friends and families, what gifts of faith will we offer those nearest to us? With our physical presence, our words of appreciation, our obvious joy in being together, can we restore or sustain the faith of our family and friends?

PRAYER: Lord Jesus, draw me close in heart and body to family and friends this season. Draw me close for the sake of my joy and the joy of those I love. Amen.

FRIDAY, DECEMBER 1 • Read 1 Thessalonians 3:9

In our most reflective and introspective moments, what generates feelings of deep gratitude within us? Do we think about acts of kindness that have come our way, the moments when others have shared themselves with us in a generous fashion? Do we think about those who taught us in school, those who guided us in Scouts or Sunday school or youth fellowship? Do we remember our mentors with gratitude? Do we remember when a word or deed broke covenant or strained relationship, and do we recall with a sense of renewal the times we have received forgiveness?

Indeed, do we gratefully acknowledge the liberation and the freedom from guilt or shame that those who have loved us, taught us, forgiven us, affirmed us, or just stood by us have engendered? Have we been open in heart, soul, and mind to those who would offer us grace? Paul expresses his gratitude for "all the joy" received from his extended family in Thessalonica. "All the joy" is his way of referring to the cumulative effects of a lifetime of giving and receiving, of Christ's overcoming Paul's initial resistance to Christ's blessings and to life in Christian community. This joy goes beyond simply an emotional response to extraordinary events but finds its root in everyday routine.

Look around this season at the common and the ordinary, which the glitter and the finery may eclipse for a moment, and see the things that can evoke gratitude and joy. Look for the grace of good in the everyday.

PRAYER: Lord Jesus, how prone I am to forget the creating and creative word of God that sustains all life, including my own. Enable me this day to be grateful for the ordinary, the common, and the usual and not to misplace that gratitude in the rushing energies of this season. Amen.

SATURDAY, DECEMBER 2 • Read Luke 21:25-28

Several years ago I stood on the top of a sand dune and peered across the flat desert terrain into the land of those who were, for the moment, defined by the press and the Congress and the commanders of the army as the enemy. I, and those in a small medical unit to which I was attached as chaplain, would go there in a few days. We would go as part of an army with tanks and planes to do battle with the enemy. Our medical mission was to provide succor for those who would be injured in the fighting to come.

We were uneasy. People *do* faint from fear and foreboding of what is coming upon the world. The powers of the earth may indeed shake the powers of heaven.

I wondered how Jesus could ever suggest that such times, frightful as they are, can also be times of redemption. Yet, without once diminishing the horror of warfare or illness or any of the thousand afflictions that can assault the human body and its spiritual center, redemption does occur in those horrific times. We medical missioners found God in the midst of the invasion, in the small deeds of mercy, kindness, and healing that occurred. We found God in the many ways we sustained one another in the midst of our fears and tears. We also found God's presence in the touch of our doctors and nurses and medical personnel who reached out to the enemy. If we could not make the enemy our friends, we at least could care for them with generosity of heart, spirit, and medical supplies.

We learned an invaluable lesson: Redemption does not always mean we are "saved" or rescued by another; it can mean that in the midst of trials and tribulations, we can be gracious and kind. We can depict the God of Jesus: slow to anger and abounding in steadfast mercy to all the generations.

PRAYER: Lord Jesus, you call for alertness to the signs of your coming. Enable me to see your presence in others and in the gentle acts of compassion I can offer. Amen.

SUNDAY, DECEMBER 3 • Read Luke 21:29-36

FIRST SUNDAY OF ADVENT

Having faith can mean many things. Having faith can imply doctrine and content of belief. Having faith can refer to *how* one believes or with what one believes. Having faith can refer to the attitude brought to belief and life.

I've often thought one analogy to having faith is how one has a body. Having a body can be a matter of having a big, short, thin, or expansive body. Having a body can refer to how one thinks about the body as durable, necessary, attractive, or less so. Having a body can refer to how one treats the body. In this last scenario, all across the country we find "health clubs" designed to shape, firm up, mold, sustain, and nurture the body.

Can our congregations be health clubs for faith? Might a congregation be a place where we shape up, firm up, define, mold, and energize our faith? Apparently Jesus acknowledged a hard truth about faith: It takes strength to have faith. Or perhaps Jesus would say, "It takes faith to have faith." Therefore, "be on guard" to watch over your faith. Exercise your faith through prayer, worship, and deeds of mercy so that your faith will not dissipate under the onslaught of the worries of this life.

Having faith can mean doing those things that keep our attitude toward life and belief vibrant and strong; having faith can mean doing those things that keep hope alive, which maintains the practice of random acts of kindness and enables love to be the pattern of our relating to our neighbor.

PRAYER: **Lord Jesus, provide me with family, friends, and experiences that nurture my faith and keep me strong to stand with you. Amen.**

The Day of the Lord

December 4–10, 2000 • Barbara Brown Taylor*

MONDAY, DECEMBER 4 • Read Malachi 3:1-2

All of this week's scripture writers proclaim the coming day of the Lord, which they believe is right around the corner. From our vantage point two thousand years later, reading their writings is like finding an ancient message in a bottle. "God will arrive any minute!" it reads, written on parchment so old it crumbles in the hand. Did we miss something? Or has God decided not to come?

If the world were in better shape, such questions might lose their urgency. The problem comes when we try to match up a just and sovereign God with a corrupt and unstable world. According to the logic of faith, the world would not be in such a state if God were fully present. The suffering of the present time indicates that a vast chasm still exists between the human and the divine.

"Where is the God of justice?" (Mal. 2:17). That is what the people of Israel want to know. Malachi gives them a double-edged answer. The Lord they seek is imminent, he says, but the day of the Lord's coming will confound their expectations. They can forget the catered reception and the ticker-tape parade. When God finally arrives, no one's knees will hold. The divine presence will turn out to be more than anyone bargained for, especially when God says, "Where is the God of justice? Right here. Now where are the people of justice? Where are the people I chose to bring justice to the earth?"

SUGGESTION FOR MEDITATION: While you await the arrival of the God of justice, how will you prepare the way?

---

*An Episcopal priest in the diocese of Atlanta. The author of seven books and numerous articles; Butman Professor of Religion at Piedmont College in Demorest, Georgia.

TUESDAY, DECEMBER 5 • Read Malachi 3:3-4

A friend recently underwent open-heart surgery to replace four clogged arteries. A week later he said he felt like a plucked, gutted chicken. He had stitches in his legs where borrowed veins had been removed. He had staples in his chest where his flesh had been tugged back together over his broken sternum. He had needle bruises on every available patch of skin. He hurt from the top of his head to his ankles, he said. He did not ever want to go through anything like that again.

As my friend complained, his pink cheeks turned red. A week earlier his circulation had been so poor that his skin was the color of beeswax. Now his face shone as his heart pumped fresh blood through newly opened arteries. As much as he hurt, he was still kicking. He had been invited back to life, and the pain was part of his initiation fee.

According to Malachi, the day of the Lord has something in common with open-heart surgery. It too will hurt while it heals as God reaches into our clogged lifelines and pulls out the trash. We may feel the pain on many levels, since this surgery involves every aspect of our lives. Our lopsided economy, our partisan political system, our talk-show culture, and our desiccated religion are all the color of beeswax. Their only hope of regaining their color will involve some fearful cutting and breaking.

Meanwhile Malachi's prophecy gives us a way to interpret the hurt. While others may understand it as divine punishment (or worse, as evidence there is no God), we may endure it as divine medicine. As invasive and painful as it may be, the refiner's fire invites us back to life.

SUGGESTION FOR MEDITATION: Remember a truly painful passage of your life. How did that time work to open you up?

WEDNESDAY, DECEMBER 6 • Read Luke 1:68-75

Instead of a psalm we have a canticle this week, one of three such songs Luke records. The singer is John the Baptist's father, Zechariah, who has been mute since the day the angel Gabriel first told him his wife Elizabeth would bear a child. The old couple had been waiting a long time for that news. To tell the truth, they had almost given up on ever hearing it, which may explain Zechariah's surprise when the word finally comes.

It is the most important day of Zechariah's life to date. When he and the other priests report for duty at the Temple in Jerusalem, they cast lots to determine their roles. Zechariah wins the prize. He alone will enter the sanctuary to burn incense on the altar while the people pray outside. No priest may serve in this position twice in his lifetime; some priests never get to burn incense on the altar at all.

Inside the sanctuary, Zechariah gets the scare of his life when an angel appears to him. What does Zechariah expect? Maybe with his strong focus on the task at hand he forgets whose living room he is in. At any rate he asks one question too many, and Gabriel puts a gag order on him for nine months. Is the gag order a penalty? Or is it a gift from God—a quiet time during which praise grows inside him at the same rate a baby grows inside his wife?

Eight days after the child's birth, Zechariah's tongue is loosed. The first words out of his mouth center not on his own good fortune but on the blessedness of God.

SUGGESTION FOR MEDITATION: **What place does silence have in your life? See what you can discover about the connection between your silence and God's speech.**

THURSDAY, DECEMBER 7 • Read Luke 1:76-79

Zechariah first sings about the blessedness of God. Under the circumstances, his praise might well have concerned what God has done in his life, but it does not. It concerns what God has done for Israel. By raising up a savior to rescue the people from their enemies, God has kept an ancient promise. Those who have waited since the days of Abraham are about to see their dreams come true. How? Zechariah does not know. He speaks under the inspiration of the Holy Spirit, who is famously stingy with practical details.

In the second part of the song, Zechariah focuses on his own child. An ordinary father might have worked up some lyrics about a son who would grow up to look, talk, and think just like him, but Zechariah is no ordinary father. He knows that he is not singing the song. The song sings him. As he listens to the song, he learns who his son will become.

In both parts of the song, Zechariah proclaims ideas he has no way of proving. He reports in the past tense events that have not yet happened, and he predicts a pretty grand future for his own child while he is at it. Any realist in the room could have laughed him right out of his reverie. "Says who, Zechariah? Have you been getting enough sleep? The first few weeks are always the worst. Once you get used to that baby, things will settle down."

In general no prophet gets respect until the prophecy comes true. Both Zechariah's silence and his speech are given by God. His song survives because he is willing to open his mouth.

SUGGESTION FOR MEDITATION: **What song are you not singing because it sounds too far-fetched? Invite the Holy Spirit to sing it with you.**

FRIDAY, DECEMBER 8 • **Read Philippians 1:3-11**

The church at Philippi is particularly dear to Paul's heart. Located in a Roman colony in Macedonia, it represents his first church effort in Europe. The Philippians have showed their gratitude by supporting Paul financially throughout his ministry. Because of their financial support and the fact that the church often has faced persecution as he did, Paul considers the members at Philippi to be full partners in the sharing of the gospel.

Paul writes the letter to the Philippians from jail. He wants to strengthen their confidence in God's providence and to encourage them to stand fast in the faith. No matter what happens to them, he assures them that God will finish the good work begun among them. When the day of Christ comes—and Paul believes it to be coming soon—they will be ready.

While the letter has no date, Paul, writing in the middle of the first century, praises the Philippians for sticking with him "from the first day until now" (Phil. 1:5). Since Paul's entire ministry lasted no more than thirty years, he is talking about a period of time even shorter than that. Before the edges of his letter turn brown, he is dead.

What kind of letter would Paul write to those who still look for the day of Christ? "From the first day until now" has stretched from less than thirty years to almost two thousand. Paul's letters continue to speak as if they were written yesterday. That enduring quality is one reason we find them in the Bible; his writing spoke to the Philippians and speaks to us today. "I am confident of this, that the one who began a good work among you will bring it to completion by the day of Jesus Christ."

SUGGESTION FOR MEDITATION: **What have you anticipated for a long time? Where does your hope come from?**

SATURDAY, DECEMBER 9 • Read Philippians 1:3-11

Paul knows we cannot manufacture righteousness on our own. It is God who has begun a good work in us and God who will bring it to completion. Nonetheless, we still make choices that affect the outcome of the work. Like dancers in God's arms, we may choose to go with or against God's lead. We may turn the dance into a tug-of-war if we like, stepping on toes and wrenching ankles. Or we may tune ourselves to the movement of our partner, until the two of us move as one.

A few years ago an inventor made a lot of money by manufacturing bracelets with *WWJD* on them. The letters stood for "What Would Jesus Do?" and the bracelets served as daily reminders that none of us dances alone. It's amazing how rapidly those letters simplify seemingly complex situations.

Should I give that beggar a quarter even though I may undercut community services and facilitate his staying on the street? *WWJD*? Should I invest in a company that is a proven winner even though I know its products are made in Asian sweat shops? *WWJD*? In most cases those letters bypass the cerebrum and go straight to the heart. The answers they evoke often surprise us. Living each day in the compassion of Christ Jesus makes it easier to know what to do.

Paul does not recommend that we sit down and study the dance steps or otherwise cogitate our way through the decisions before us. Instead he prays that we will overflow with love. Being in step with God is where knowledge and insight come from, he says—not from the cerebrum but from the heart.

SUGGESTION FOR MEDITATION: **What kind of dance are you dancing with God? a waltz? a tango? Close your eyes and feel God leading you.**

SUNDAY, DECEMBER 10 • Read Luke 3:1-6

SECOND SUNDAY OF ADVENT

Luke roots the story of John the Baptist in history by telling us who was in charge of what at that time. The list includes the Roman emperor, the Roman governor of Judea, the Idumaean ruler of Galilee and his brother who ruled parts of Syria. It ends with a little-known ruler of Abilene, a territory northwest of Damascus, and two of the high priests in Jerusalem. At first reading the list seems a tedious prologue to John's ministry, full of obscure names that are hard to pronounce. Luke has a good reason for including it, however, one that goes straight to the heart of his Gospel.

If we were to spread out a map of the world in ancient days and stick red pins in the locations where the powerful governed, we would have a canvas that stretched from Jerusalem to Rome. It would include Judeans, Syrians, Greeks, and Romans. It would include the most powerful military leader on earth, as well as the most powerful religious leaders in Judaism and all the people who lived under their rule.

Luke's point is that the story he is about to tell applies to all of the above. It is not a local story about a Hebrew charismatic who founded a new sect of Judaism. It is a universal story about a divine savior who came to change the world. The last line of Isaiah's prophecy is Luke's theme sentence: "And all flesh shall see the salvation of God."

Before the church ever existed, the gospel was given to all people. To this day the church exists for those who do not belong to it.

SUGGESTION FOR MEDITATION: **In what ways do you attempt to possess Jesus? To whom do you think Jesus belongs, and what must they do to belong to him? Try doing what God did: Give Jesus freely to the whole world.**

Spiritual Ethics

December 11–17, 2000 • Robert Roth*

MONDAY, DECEMBER 11 • Read Zephaniah 3:14-20

Ours is a culture of celebrity and scandal, where movie, television, and rock stars function almost as gods for people. So we wonder: *How can we help sustain the ancient yet contemporary ethics of love?* The spiritual roots of enduring values can seem like a fading story. Newspapers read as if major events occur with God far away. How can we promote the call of compassion without recognizing God's involvement always and everywhere?

The prophet Zephaniah notes his culture's drifting toward Assyrian notions of many gods and arrogant domination. He could turn to fear and shallow moralizing. Yet he focuses on spiritually grounded relationships, because the Lord "will renew you in his love." No other-worldly escape here. No, the prophet faces his culture and begins the serious, creative work of discerning God's involvement and purpose. Zephaniah confronts Babylon-inspired "pop culture" and declares that the Lord "will save the lame and gather the outcast," not in pitying condescension for the forgotten but to "change their shame into praise and renown in all the earth."

"Renown in All the Earth"—sounds like another made-for-TV miniseries about the rich and famous! Do we not also have spiritualities that sustain caste systems blind to the poor and oppressed? The prophet's word is fresh today. In a diverse and changing time, core values of love and connectedness integrate and redeem—even the "outcasts."

SUGGESTION FOR MEDITATION: Read your newspaper today as a spiritual document. Where do you see God's hand moving in the great events?

---

*Writer and clergy member of the West Michigan Annual Conference of The United Methodist Church; living in East Lansing, Michigan.

TUESDAY, DECEMBER 12 • Read Isaiah 12:2-4

Four years ago and eighteen years into my marriage, I fell in love. Most days my wife, Pat, was understanding; some days she was not. She knew that unlike any other time in my life music filled the air. You see, I had fallen in love with jazz.

I started small—listening to a little gypsy guitar music one week and some blazing Latin jazz the next. Soon I purchased "new" (circa 1959) bebop CDs and albums of older (Ella Fitzgerald) and newer (Diana Krall) vocal jazz. The more I learned, the more I discovered how little I knew. My delight with one amazing flavor led me to taste three or four more. *There is no end to it*, I thought, *and it's all good!*

In these four years, I have sometimes wondered how this music could have always been in my world without my really hearing it. The faithful encounter a similar though much larger question: How can God's voice be speaking in much of what happens all around us without our stopping more often to hear it?

Isaiah heard God. Isaiah heard God's voice and witnessed the movement of God's hand as it gathered together the remnants of Israel and Judah. In the hearing Isaiah received a call to speak and act in new and ethical ways and invited the people to be prepared to make known God's "deeds among the nations." Isaiah listened to a world ringing with God's purposes, and it was music to his ears.

SUGGESTION FOR MEDITATION: While listening to some music that helps you reconnect spiritually—gospel music, contemporary Christian, jazz, classical—reflect on an issue of your time and its place in the long process of salvation history (the history of God's saving action).

WEDNESDAY, DECEMBER 13 • Read Isaiah 12:5-6

The recollection of our being made in God's image evokes new possibilities and broadens our horizons. However, our attempts to make God in *our* image greatly limit the options by minimizing our concepts about God and stifling our experiences of God. Our surroundings differ radically from the theonomous cultures of the ancients that melded together the sacred and the secular.

Isaiah 12:1-6, a song of thanksgiving, falls appropriately after the prophecy in chapter 11 about the return of the exiles —an envisioning of restoration. While our cultural divide between sacred and secular is vast, we too often feel that we are in exile. We too find ourselves desiring restoration, a return to what we knew. Perhaps we would more often sing praises to the Lord with the prophet Isaiah if we could but see, as he so clearly does, that "great in [our] midst is the Holy One of Israel." Linking an awareness of our place in sacred creation with God's active place in our history invites a desire to do the right thing. In God's image and by God's side, we seek creative goodness, the imaginative creation of good things.

Our cognizance of holiness in our midst brings both judgment and salvation. Christian ethics, those broad principles inspired by our prayerful connection to God's great causes, can flower in Christian morality. God "has done gloriously" as Isaiah proclaims. In that knowledge, who wouldn't want to do his or her small, glorious part?

Yes, Isaiah's song rings forth into a world brimming with holy people, places, and things if we can but see God in our midst.

SUGGESTION FOR MEDITATION: **Sit before a living thing (a houseplant will do, as will a sleeping baby) and consider where God "has done gloriously" in your midst.**

Thursday, December 14 • Read Luke 3:7-9

John the Baptist sure can peel the smiley face right off church complacency. In a few harsh words John confronts us with wrath and repentance, cutting down and burning up. John announces that God expects action right now. Holy, redemptive, fruitful action—or else.

John urgently warns of the wrath to come. Because God will change the world forever through the coming Christ, it will not be enough to avoid exceptionally bad actions by hanging out with the religious crowd. Decisions have to be made. Lives have to be offered. Gifts have to be shared. A world awaits its redemption to its original glory.

Just as Jesus will soon demonstrate a preferential option for the poor and rejected, John redirects the focus from institutional self-reliance to the earthy fruit bearing of a spiritual movement. Get caught up in the spirit of Christ, John demands, and live accordingly. Make a wide turn to God's way and witness the fruits.

Perhaps we see the Baptist as a wild man because we find such comfort in our sleepy "good enough" behaviors. Appropriately rejecting the self-righteously judgmental, we had best reflect on where judgment is to be found—before the ax falls.

PRAYER: God both of grace and judgment, in my quest for a loving heart and an open mind, help me discern where you "draw the line" and where I must too. Amen.

FRIDAY, DECEMBER 15 • Read Philippians 4:4-7

Friends tell us, "You've got nothing to worry about" when we mention anxiety about a new job, a final exam, or a medical uncertainty. I'm often tempted to snap back, "That's easy for *you* to say!" Their compassion feels too routine and their response too rote. In contrast Paul, who is already in jail and is being threatened with worse, writes, "Do not worry about anything." The advice doesn't appear all that easy for him to give.

Paul advocates gentleness, peace, and thanksgiving to the Philippians who are coming under fire for their faintness. Paul is writing from his jail cell, so his situation seems worse than theirs. Or is it? Through his experience of the Lord's sustaining nearness, Paul models the living out of a faith not defined by circumstances but by the empowering peace of Christ.

Many great moral treatises have taken the form of letters from prison. While others despaired, from a prison bunk Nelson Mandela wrote his vision of the liberation and reconciliation that would one day come to South Africa. Amidst calls for violence, Martin Luther King Jr. wrote a nonviolent "Letter from the Birmingham Jail." Dietrich Bonhoeffer's *Letters and Papers from Prison* (published posthumously) bore witness to courage before the onslaught of terror. Like Paul's epistle, these writings reflect the mind of Christ and a peace that passses understanding.

SUGGESTION FOR MEDITATION: **In the form of a letter to God, journal your hopes and desires regarding the faithful living of your next year of life.**

SATURDAY, DECEMBER 16 • Read Luke 3:10-14

When my eldest aunt passed away last year, I inherited forty volumes of my grandfather's journals, most from the first half of this century. As I read through these journals, I am developing a closeness to a grandfather I knew only as he was quite elderly and significantly diminished by the aging process. He and I share the distinction of being ordained pastors. I used to think the similarities just about ended there. Though labels restrict humanity, here is the shorthand: Grandpa was a "rural southern evangelical"; I am a "cosmopolitan northern liberal."

As I become better acquainted with Grandpa through his writings, a surprising revelation emerges. Theology and politics aside (no small chore!), Grandpa and I share a fairly similar ethical outlook of sharing wealth, pursuing justice, and advocating for the safety and security of all people—actions rooted in the spirit of Christ.

Admittedly I find parts of Grandpa's doctrinal convictions repugnant. However, in his correspondence with a "brother" on Kentucky's death row in 1935, I discovered the depth of his compassion, faith, and love. His depth of character inspires me from beginning to end.

Is the leap from the spirit of Christ into the grist of social ethics too great without the aid of theology and politics? Or is this leap the only way we get there most days?

SUGGESTION FOR MEDITATION: **Survey the clothes in your closet and the balance in your bank account, inviting Christ's presence for the inventory.**

SUNDAY, DECEMBER 17 • **Read Luke 3:15-18**

THIRD SUNDAY OF ADVENT

John the Baptist may not have all the answers as we look toward a new millenium, but his awe and humility before the majesty of God in Jesus Christ are appropriate for any period of human time. In these four verses, John emphasizes the greatness of the One to come in several ways: While John baptizes with water, the Messiah will baptize with the Holy Spirit and fire. John does not feel worthy to serve in the capacity of a slave to untie the thong of the sandal of the coming One who will bring salvation for those who repent and judgment for those who do not.

So John "proclaimed the good news to the people." If John is Proverbs, then Jesus is Ecclesiastes. That is, John suggests wonderfully moral rules for living, but encountering Jesus brings an awareness that God is ultimately in charge. What's the good news for the new millennium?

Though the Y2K computer problem fades away, we continue to struggle with a Y2K spiritual problem: spiritual amnesia and the ethical grogginess it elicits. No, all is not right in this world. The good news is that God is making things right in ways we sometimes find mysterious and shocking. And we can help. Because of God's greatness, grace abounds. After all, what is a mere millenium in the eye of God?

We cannot fault ourselves too much for getting excited at the notion of a new century and a new millenium. May we get even more thrilled at the prospect of the coming of the Messiah. The coming millenium has encouraged the saving of newspaper articles, magazines, and memorabilia. The coming of Christ will inspire the saving of lives. Shalom to all at Christmas, whatever the millenium.

SUGGESTION FOR MEDITATION: **List ten things you hope to do in 2001 to affirm the importance of spiritual ethics in your daily life.**

A Holy Waiting

December 18–24, 2000 • Marjorie Hewitt Suchocki*

MONDAY, DECEMBER 18 • Read Isaiah 9:2-7

Who can read these verses from Isaiah or hear such texts read aloud in Advent without at the same time hearing the echoes of Handel's great *Messiah*? We feel in our souls the thrill of the music, the awe-filled expectation, and the triumphant cry: "A child is born!" Advent and Christmas rolled into one! And our spirits experience the exultation of the Spirit.

But between the announcement of the light to come and the wondrous birth of the child is the middle word: God will break the yokes that bind us, the staffs that burden us, the rods that oppress us! The instruments of war's bloodshed shall be burned like fuel for a fire. Then the child is born!

Don't these verses offer direction for how we wait during this Advent season and during the long advent that is our lives? Waiting for God requires that we discern the yokes, the staffs, and rods that bind us and bow us down. Waiting for God requires that we judge such burdens in the light of Christ. Waiting for God suggests that we work for peace. Advent is an active waiting; we participate in the works of God within ourselves and within our world. While waiting for Advent, we give ourselves up to God's use for goodness.

This text promises that in our very doing, Advent is fulfilled. The wonderful child is born—in us for the world.

PRAYER: O God of all my waiting, teach me the way of waiting. Teach me to discern the yokes and the staffs and the rods in whatever form their binding may take. And make me your instrument for their breaking so that I may know the breaking in of your peace. Even so, come, Lord Jesus! Amen.

---

*Author; Ingraham Professor of Theology at Claremont School of Theology, Claremont, California.

TUESDAY, DECEMBER 19 • Read Micah 5:2-5*a*

Does it not seem strange that we wait for One who always is? Usually waiting speaks of that which is to come, not that which is past or present. But this text from Micah instructs Bethlehem to wait now, in the present. Bethlehem is to wait for One who will come in the future, even though that One's origin is from "long ago" in the past—indeed from the "days of eternity."

What are these days of eternity? Does eternity have days? Is not eternity the opposite of time? What then is the sense of this text, this forthcoming event that bespeaks an eternal "is" that nonetheless existed "long ago"?

These verses remind me of another text that states, "'You are my God.' My times are in your hand" (Ps. 31:14-15). We live out our "time" in days and discover that God's own eternity encompasses our days. God is our future—the One for whom we wait; but God is also our past—the One who has created us and called us into being. God is our present, the One who surrounds us in grace and in mercy and in righteousness.

This God who is our future, our past, and our encompassing present is the triune God. We Christians read the text to see already the foretold incarnation of God for our good. But think! If this incarnate One is none other than God who is eternal, then that coming Incarnation is from the "days of eternity." While occurring in time, the Incarnation involves far more than time. The Incarnation spans all our times. Thus we wait for it as our future, trust in it as our past, and rejoice unspeakably in it as our present. Advent brings God's eternity into our time.

PRAYER: God of our future, deepen our hope and expectation; God of our past, deepen our trust and our confidence; God of our present, deepen our faithfulness and watchfulness. God of all our times, deepen our love. Amen.

WEDNESDAY, DECEMBER 20 • Read Psalm 80:1-7

What a comfort to pray with the psalmist in our times of waiting! Waiting is not always easy, whether we wait for good things or sorrowful things. Sometimes complaint fills our waiting. Were we to pour out our impatience, our anxiety, our agony without these psalms, we might have cause to fear. How dare we complain to the Lord God of hosts, the Creator of all the universe! Should not our prayers be more, well, holy?

But these psalms witness to the wonder that we as human beings may come to God with our complaints. God calls us to honesty in prayer, to pray as we really are, not as we think we ought to be. Encouraged by the psalmist, we dare to bring our prayers to God, even when those prayers express our worst feelings. Like the psalmist we cast our cares on God, knowing that God cares for us.

But consider the last line in today's text: "Make your face shine upon us, that we may be saved" (NIV). The prayer of complaint is at the same time a prayer of trust. The psalmist's prayer first teaches that we may bring our complaints to God, and second that we can do so in trust. We shall be saved.

PRAYER: Ah, Lord God of the universe and all that is in it, teach me to cast my cares on you when the waiting is hard. By the power of your Spirit may I, like the psalmist, pour out my complaint in trust. And in your great love cause your face to shine upon me, and I shall be saved. Amen.

THURSDAY, DECEMBER 21 • Read Titus 2:11-14

We live between the "glories"! The text tells us that God's grace already has appeared, bringing salvation to all through the coming of God with us in Jesus Christ. Surely we witness the glory of God in Christ's birth, for doesn't the text say that the angels sang "glory" to God at Christ's birth? And was not every work of Christ also his glory? The entirety of incarnation is the glory of God.

But the text from Titus speaks of a future glory, telling us that we are to look for "the blessed hope and the manifestation of the glory of our great God and Savior, Jesus Christ." Thus Advent would seem to be a time between the glories, looking back on the one and forward to the other.

But to explain God's grace in this way seems to rob the present of any splendor. If we are between the glories, what is there for us now? I suggest that the text almost laughingly tells us what we have now. With eyes to see, we can find yet another form of glory in the text that fits these "times between the times."

Do you see it? Christ Jesus "gave himself for us that he might...purify for himself a people of his own who are zealous for good deeds." We belong to the One who redeemed us! Belonging to him, we are purified for the sake of continuing his ministry in our zeal for good works. Good works belong to the time between the glories, but these works also bespeak the glory of God who is all goodness. Let us do good and glorify God!

PRAYER: God of grace and God of glory, how I thank you for this grace and glory! May your grace empower me for works that tell your glory to all the world! Amen.

FRIDAY, DECEMBER 22 • **Read Hebrews 10:5-10**

Jesus takes away the old system of sacrifices for sin in order to establish a new way: his own embodiment. "A body you have prepared for me"! And Jesus' embodiment is for God's sake: "I have come to do your will, O God."

Christmas is never far from the cross, which is why we so often symbolically take the trunk of our church Christmas tree and fashion it into the cross of Good Friday, God's Friday. The body prepared for Jesus at Christmas is offered up for us, once for all. Christmas, Good Friday, and Easter are all of a piece.

To what end? The writer of our text proclaims that end results in a new law. And we recall Jeremiah's new covenant in which God writes upon our hearts and minds. We who identify with Christ are to live as Christ lived. We are to put on his righteousness "to do your will, O God."

What is God's will for you, for me? It will vary according to circumstances, but it will always reflect Christ and his righteousness; it will always share God's love; it will always witness to the living new covenant established by Christ to which the Holy Spirit bears witness. Thanks be to God.

PRAYER: As we look toward Christmas, O God, keep me mindful of your Friday, keep me mindful of Easter. Because of Christ's sacrifice, clothe me in your righteousness that I may discern and do your will. Amen.

SATURDAY, DECEMBER 23 • Read Luke 1:39-55

Oh, the exultation of Elizabeth and her babe and of Mary herself in their own time of Advent! How they waited! The joy of God's Coming One fills Elizabeth with the Holy Spirit, and Elizabeth responds by blessing Mary and the child she bears. Are we Elizabeth? God comes to us in so many ways—in the outpouring of God's love on us through others, in opportunities for loving service, in the wonder of the Lord's Supper! Shall we open ourselves to the fullness of God's Spirit and continuously anticipate God's coming?

Verse 41 tells us that Elizabeth's babe leaps in her womb at the sound of Mary's greeting. Are we that babe? At the announced coming of our Lord, do we leap into new possibilities and undreamed-of expectations? Do we feel the constrictions of our own narrowness as measured by his greatness? Do we joyously break out of our small boundaries into his expansive love?

And Mary! How her soul exalts the Lord; what a song she sings, and how its beauty still echoes through the ages! Are we Mary? Do we sing a new song, exulting in God's own exaltation in every work of justice? Do we proclaim God's justice by feeding the hungry and lifting up the humble in the living mercy of God?

Be exultant! Christ comes! Bless God, leap for joy, and sing God's justice!

PRAYER: O God whose mercy is upon generation after generation, fill my spirit with the joy of your Spirit! Grant me the gift of joyous expectation, seeing your coming in a million ways and responding with blessing, with leaping, and with joy! Amen.

SUNDAY, DECEMBER 24 • Read Luke 2:1-20

CHRISTMAS EVE

Hush, he comes, this tiny one.
Small and lowly born, no bigger than a manger,
in the darkness of night.
Hush for this lowly one,
hush for this holy one, hush.

Courage, you frightened ones!
Angels announce his coming, his birth!
Dare to find this one so small
who fills the heavens with light;
dare to find this one so low,
whom angels know. Courage!

See, there are signs.
Was ever it told that God's own self
would lie within a baby, cradled by a manger?
Who could fashion such a sign,
save God's own self?
See the sign, strengthen your hearts,
and hush to find him there, God's own self with us.
And oh, the terrible, wonderful truth:
God who is with us is *for* us! See!

PRAYER: Jesus, shall I find you? Do you still come to us clothed in the flesh of the unexpected? Jesus, shall I find courage in all my dark nights, knowing that you are my very light? Jesus, can I feel your peace in my soul? Shall I hush the noisiness of swaggering hatred and open myself to the quiet joy of you? Oh, give me eyes to see you in hiddenness, to be bold for you and to be quiet in reverent awe at the mystery of your majesty, which is mercy. Even so, come, Lord Jesus. Amen.

Clothed with Christ

December 25–31, 2000 • Sue Joiner*

MONDAY, DECEMBER 25 • Read Psalm 98; John 1:1-14

CHRISTMAS DAY

Christ is born—let the world burst into song! The music of Christmas beckons us to celebrate the miracle of this day. Familiar carols have been playing in the mall for the last few months, but today is what they sing about—the miracle of the Christ child. The psalmist calls us to "sing...a new song." Every song that is sung on this day becomes new. All earth sings to express the joy of Christ's birth.

We are called to join the song (both ancient and new) of this day. When we sing, we prepare our hearts to receive God's amazing gift—the One who makes all things new.

What were Mary and Joseph singing? What were the angels and shepherds singing? What were the animals singing? Did others join the song?

Now comes our turn to join in—to sing the miracle of this day. No longer do we listen as appreciative observers. Today we sing as people of faith, "O come, let us adore him." The words remind us that the Christ born many years ago is once again born among us. Today we pause to wonder at the miracle in our midst as the tune wells up from deep inside until we can no longer contain the notes, and they fill the air, "Joy to the world, the Lord is come!"

Christ is born! God's song has entered the world, and we become part of that song as we sing it once more.

PRAYER: O God, creator of all music, call forth the song until all creation sings the miracle of this day! Amen.

---

*Pastor, Monroe United Methodist Church, Monroe, Oregon.

TUESDAY, DECEMBER 26 • Read Colossians 3:12-17

Christmas has come and gone—now what? We spend so much energy preparing for Christmas that we often feel disappointed as well as relieved when it is over. There is so much hype, so much buildup that December 26 is often a letdown. Perhaps we can turn quietly to the text today and by doing so, discover a richness that we have not realized before now.

Christmas is over. Now what? Now "clothe yourselves with compassion, kindness, humility, meekness, and patience." Now "bear with one another." Now "forgive each other." Now "clothe yourselves with love." Now "let the peace of Christ rule in your hearts." Now "be thankful." Now "let the word of Christ dwell in you richly." Now "teach and admonish one another in all wisdom." Now "sing psalms, hymns, and spiritual songs to God." Now "do everything in the name of the Lord Jesus."

Christmas is over. We are God's chosen ones, holy and beloved. The scripture calls us to act like it—to live as God's chosen ones. Today is not a letdown; it is a new beginning. It is no small thing to be God's chosen. We have amazing work ahead of us. God's dreams for the world require our participation. These verses picture what God's people look like. As God's people, we clothe ourselves in love and compassion.

Each morning we have the opportunity to choose our attributes for the day. Rather than looking to *Vogue* magazine for advice, it is time to look to Jesus Christ to determine what we will wear today.

SUGGESTION FOR MEDITATION: **How does my life reflect my faith in Christ? With what do I clothe myself today?**

WEDNESDAY, DECEMBER 27 • Read 1 Samuel 2:18-20, 26

It is hard to say who desires to be faithful the most. Hannah longs for a child; far beyond childbearing age, she continues to pray fervently for a child. While she prays for a child, she promises to give the child to God's service.

It may appear that this is another "bargaining" prayer: "If you will just give me an *A* on this test, I promise to be in church every Sunday." How many bargaining prayers have we heard or prayed ourselves? Such prayers arise out of desperation and the wish to escape a current predicament. While we may pray for relief from stressful circumstances, we often forget the prayers later.

Hannah, a woman whose faith runs deep, believes in God's power enough to make a promise she later fulfills without wavering. Her prayer sounds as if it has already been answered. With Samuel's birth, Hannah fulfills her promise and then prays with confidence and joy, "My heart exults in the Lord; / my strength is exalted in my God" (1 Sam. 2:1). Her devotion both to God and to her son is admirable.

Samuel's vocation is determined before he is born. His birth is an answer to Hannah's prayer and clearly signals that God is not bound by human understanding. Samuel grows up in the temple surrounded by signs of the sacred. As a boy, Samuel ministers "before the Lord." Hannah has given Samuel to God's service, which forms him for leadership of the Israelites. Samuel serves attentively and eagerly. Though merely a boy, God's purpose for him is great. Samuel has some difficult days ahead, but he prepares for the future as one consecrated to God.

PRAYER: Lord, stir up in me a desire to serve you. Amen.

THURSDAY, DECEMBER 28 • Read Luke 2:41-52

The New Testament records only one story about Jesus between birth and adulthood—and this is it. I have always wondered about Jesus' childhood. Was he playful or silly? Was he always as serious as he is in this story? We have been told from the beginning about Jesus' uniqueness. In this story Jesus claims his unique relationship to God and gives us a glimpse into his call. At age twelve he seemingly knows his vocation and takes advantage of every opportunity to prepare for it. Jesus' parents have raised him in the temple, but now Jesus begins to claim God's mission for himself. He speaks with such authority that we forget for a moment who is the parent. "Did you not know that I *must* be in my Father's house?" (italics added). At age twelve Jesus clearly knows who and whose he is. Jesus sees the big picture.

Each of our lives has a big picture. In some ways we live it out like putting a puzzle together. Piece by piece our lives take shape until we can look back and see the whole. Jesus had the ability to look ahead and see the whole.

I have watched with interest and, at times, impatience as the pieces of my own life puzzle come together. The puzzle continues to take shape, and in God's hands the journey is exciting.

All pieces at all ages play an important part in the puzzle. Along the way we must deliberately place ourselves in God's presence. We must ask questions and listen for answers so we can claim God's call for our lives. With all the competing claims for our lives, we must make a habit of spending time with God as the puzzle comes together.

SUGGESTION FOR MEDITATION: How am I listening for God's call in my life?

FRIDAY, DECEMBER 29 • Read 1 Samuel 2:26; Luke 2:52

Samuel and Jesus—two boys with unique stories, and God calls each of them to important work. Rather than showing fear or reluctantly embarking on such great vocations, each seems confident in his call. Faith has shaped them both, and they reflect a desire to grow.

I know a ten-year-old girl who loves coming to church every Sunday. She comes alone and arrives half an hour before Sunday school begins. While the building hosts little activity at that time, she simply enjoys being in the presence of the older adults who begin to gather. She carries out her tasks of acolyte and evangelist enthusiastically, eagerly contributing and spreading the word to others.

God's call comes to people of all ages. How do we help the children in our communities hear and understand that call? Both Jesus and Samuel were surrounded by adults who spent time helping them discern God's call and teaching them the stories of faith.

Jesus later said, "Let the little children come to me; do not stop them; for it is to such as these that the kingdom of God belongs" (Mark 10:14). He wants us to know that taking time for children is not simply a good deed; it is fulfilling God's desire for creation. If we focus on our own needs to the point of ignoring the children of our world, we may hinder them from finding their way to the kingdom.

Reaching out to children is the least we can do. Sometimes it is also the most we can do.

PRAYER: Gracious God, open my heart to the children in my midst. Together may we grow in your favor. Amen.

SATURDAY, DECEMBER 30 • Read Psalm 148

How often do we hear an invitation so vast that it includes even sea monsters? No person or part of creation is excluded. When we think of the glory of our Creator, we can do no less than offer our praise. God created us to praise, and the desire to praise resides within each of us. Perhaps the key lies in pausing long enough to savor creation's goodness. For what can we praise God this Christmas season?

Praise God for the miracle of Christ's birth!

Praise God for the wonder of each new morning!

Praise God for the stars that beckon us beyond the bounds of earth!

Praise God for the human heart that does not lose hope!

Praise God for laughter that fills empty spaces!

Praise God who continues to be God in the face of tragedy.

Praise God for quiet moments.

Praise God for daily bread.

Praise God for songs of joy and healing!

Praise God for all of life—for each moment!

Christ is born. What can we do but praise? Praise makes us whole. Praise fills us with awe and wonder and reminds us that life is a miracle. Without praise our days are incomplete. How shall we praise the God of all creation? How shall we praise the miracle of Christ?

Shall we sing in harmony or even a little off-key?

Shall we pray quietly?

Shall we dance as if no one is watching?

Shall we laugh until our sides hurt and the tears flow?

Shall we run with arms outstretched until we are breathless?

Shall we spend this day showing God's love
    to one who is lonely?

Today is a gift. All of life is a gift! Let us praise God!

PRAYER: God of all creation, you amaze me. Free me to praise you all of my days. Amen.

SUNDAY, DECEMBER 31 • Read Colossians 3:12-17

We called ourselves The God Squad, an intramural sports team of people preparing for church-related professions. Proud of our clever name, we wore our t-shirts with confidence. Years later I still have that t-shirt—purple with gold letters—tucked away in a box. It boldly proclaims my identity as a Christian. I do not recall being particularly conscious of my behavior when I wore that shirt, but I should have been.

As a follower of Christ, I find that the most important clothing I choose today is not made of fabric. My words and actions will reveal much more about me than my clothing. Will I choose them as carefully as I choose my clothing? Today gives me an opportunity to show the love of Christ through my attitudes and behavior.

We do not always remember that as Christians we represent Christ in the world. When we were school-age children preparing for a field trip, our leaders always sternly reminded us that our behavior reflected not only on ourselves but also on our school. Our chaperones wanted us to think beyond ourselves before we acted—to realize that we were part of a bigger picture that could be affected by our choices.

My bigger picture is one titled "the kingdom of God." While I am only a small part of that picture, my actions and attitudes affect it more than I realize. What does one wear in the kingdom of God? One wears love—above all, love. Christ is born. Love has come to a hungry, hurting world. Now it is up to us to wear that love at all times.

PRAYER: Gracious God, you loved the world in the life of Christ. Now enable me to love others with boldness. Amen.

The Revised Common Lectionary* for 2000
Year B – Advent / Christmas Year C
(Disciplines Edition)

January 1–2
Jeremiah 31:7-14
Psalm 147:12-20
Ephesians 1:3-14
John 1:10-18

January 3–9
BAPTISM OF THE LORD
Genesis 1:1-5
Psalm 29
Acts 19:1-7
Mark 1:4-11

> **January 6**
> **EPIPHANY,**
> *(These readings may be used for Sunday, January 9.)*
> Isaiah 60:1-6
> Psalm 72:1-7, 10-14
> Ephesians 3:1-12
> Matthew 2:1-12

January 10–16
1 Samuel 3:1-20
Psalm 139:1-6, 13-18
1 Corinthians 6:12-20
John 1:43-51

January 17–23
Jonah 3:1-5, 10
Psalm 62:5-12
1 Corinthians 7:29-31
Mark 1:14-20

January 24–30
Deuteronomy 18:15-20
Psalm 111
1 Corinthians 8:1-13
Mark 1:21-28

January 31–February 6
Isaiah 40:21-31
Psalm 147:1-11, 20c
1 Corinthians 9:16-23
Mark 1:29-39

February 7–13
2 Kings 5:1-14
Psalm 30
1 Corinthians 9:24-27
Mark 1:40-45

February 14–20
Isaiah 43:18-25
Psalm 41
2 Corinthians 1:18-22
Mark 2:1-12

February 21–27
Hosea 2:14-20
Psalm 103:1-13, 22
2 Corinthians 3:1-6
Mark 2:13-22

February 28–March 5
TRANSFIGURATION
2 Kings 2:1-12
Psalm 50:1-6
2 Corinthians 4:3-6
Mark 9:2-9

   March 8
   ASH WEDNESDAY
   Joel 2:1-2, 12-17
    (*or* Isaiah 58:1-12)
   Psalm 51:1-17
   2 Corinthians
    5:20*b*–6:10
   Matthew 6:1-6, 16-21

March 6–12
FIRST SUNDAY IN LENT
Genesis 9:8-17
Psalm 25:1-10
1 Peter 3:18-22
Mark 1:9-15

March 13–19
SECOND SUNDAY IN LENT
Genesis 17:1-7, 15-16
Psalm 22:23-31
Romans 4:13-25
Mark 8:31-38 (*or* Mark
 9:2-9)

March 20–26
THIRD SUNDAY IN LENT
Exodus 20:1-17
Psalm 19
1 Corinthians 1:18-25
John 2:13-22

March 27–April 2
FOURTH SUNDAY IN LENT
Numbers 21:4-9
Psalm 107:1-3, 17-22
Ephesians 2:1-10
John 3:14-21

April 3–9
FIFTH SUNDAY IN LENT
Jeremiah 31:31-34
Psalm 51:1-12
 (*or* Psalm 119:9-16)
Hebrews 5:5-10
John 12:20-33

April 10–16
PASSION/PALM SUNDAY

Liturgy of the Palms
Mark 11:1-11
  (*or* John 12:12-16)
Psalm 118:1-2, 19-29

Liturgy of the Passion
Isaiah 50:4-9a
Psalm 31:9-16
Philippians 2:5-11
Mark 14:1–15:47
  (*or* Mark 15:1-47)

April 17–23
HOLY WEEK
Acts 10:34-43
Psalm 118:1-2, 14-24
1 Corinthians 15:1-11
John 20:1-18
 (*or* Mark 16:1-8)

HOLY MONDAY
Isaiah 42:1-9; John
  12:1-11

HOLY TUESDAY
Isaiah 49:1-7; John
  12:20-36

HOLY WEDNESDAY
Psalm 70; John 13:21-32

MAUNDY THURSDAY
Exodus 12:1-14;
Psalm 116:1-2, 12-19;
  John 13:1-17, 31*b*-35

GOOD FRIDAY
Isaiah 52:13–53:12;
  Psalm 22; Hebrews
  10:16-25; John
  18:1–19:42

HOLY SATURDAY
Job 14:1-14; Psalm 31:1-
  4, 15-16; Matthew
  27:57-66 *or* John
  19:38-42

April 24–30
Acts 4:32-35
Psalm 133
1 John 1:1–2:2
John 20:19-31

May 1–7
Acts 3:12-19
Psalm 4
1 John 3:1-7
Luke 24:36*b*-48

May 8–14
Acts 4:5-12
Psalm 23
1 John 3:16-24
John 10:11-18

May 15–21
Acts 8:26-40
Psalm 22:25-31
1 John 4:7-21
John 15:1-8

May 22–28
Acts 10:44-48
Psalm 98
1 John 5:1-6
John 15:9-17

May 29–June 4
Acts 1:15-17, 21-26
Psalm 1
1 John 5:9-13
John 17:6-19

June 1
ASCENSION DAY,
Acts 1:1-11
Psalm 47 or Psalm 93
Ephesians 1:15-23
Luke 24:44-53

June 5–11
PENTECOST
Acts 2:1-21
Psalm 104:24-34, 35*b*
Romans 8:22-27
John 15:26-27; 16:4*b*-15

June 12–18
TRINITY
Isaiah 6:1-8
Psalm 29
Romans 8:12-17
John 3:1-17

June 19–25
1 Samuel 17:1*a*, 4-11,
  19-23, 32-49
Psalm 9:9-20
2 Corinthians 6:1-13
Mark 4:35-41

June 26–July 2
2 Samuel 1:1, 17-27
Psalm 130
2 Corinthians 8:7-15
Mark 5:21-43

July 3–9
2 Samuel 5:1-5, 9-10
Psalm 48
2 Corinthians 12:2-10
Mark 6:1-13

July 10–16
2 Samuel 6:1-5, 12*b*-19
Psalm 24
Ephesians 1:3-14
Mark 6:14-29

July 17–23
2 Samuel 7:1-14a
Psalm 89:20-37
Ephesians 2:11-22
Mark 6:30-34, 53-56

July 24–30
2 Samuel 11:1-15
Psalm 14
Ephesians 3:14-21
John 6:1-21

July 31–August 6
2 Samuel 11:26–12:13a
Psalm 51:1-12
Ephesians 4:1-16
John 6:24-35

August 7–13
2 Samuel 18:5-9, 15, 31-33
Psalm 130
Ephesians 4:25–5:2
John 6:35, 41-51

August 14–20
1 Kings 2:10-12; 3:3-14
Psalm 111
Ephesians 5:15-20
John 6:51-58

August 21–27
1 Kings 8:1, 6, 10-11,
  22-30, 41-43
Psalm 84
Ephesians 6:10-20
John 6:56-69

August 28–September 3
Song of Solomon 2:8-13
Psalm 45:1-2, 6-9
James 1:17-27
Mark 7:1-8, 14-15, 21-23

September 4–10
Proverbs 22:1-2, 8-9, 22-23
Psalm 125
James 2:1-17
Mark 7:24-37

September 11–17
Proverbs 1:20-33
Psalm 19
James 3:1-12
Mark 8:27-38

September 18–24
Proverbs 31:10-31
Psalm 1
  (or Jeremiah 11:18-20)
James 3:13–4:3, 7-8a
Mark 9:30-37

September 25–October 1
Esther 7:1-6, 9-10; 9:20-22
Psalm 124
James 5:13-20
Mark 9:38-50

October 2–8
Job 1:1; 2:1-10
Psalm 26
Hebrews 1:1-4; 2:5-12
Mark 10:2-16

October 9–15
Job 23:1-9, 16-17
Psalm 22:1-15
Hebrews 4:12-16
Mark 10:17-31

October 9
THANKSGIVING DAY, CANADA
Joel 2:21-27
Psalm 126
1 Timothy 2:1-7
Matthew 6:25-33

October 16–22
Job 38:1-7, 34-41
Psalm 104:1-9, 24, 35c
Hebrews 5:1-10
Mark 10:35-45

October 23–29
Job 42:1-6, 10-17
Psalm 34:1-8, 19-22
Hebrews 7:23-28
Mark 10:46-52

October 30–November 5
Ruth 1:1-18
Psalm 146
Hebrews 9:11-14
Mark 12:28-34

November 1
ALL SAINTS DAY
Isaiah 25:6-9
Psalm 24
Revelation 21:1-6a
John 11:32-44

November 6–12
Ruth 3:1-5; 4:13-17
Psalm 127
Hebrews 9:24-28
Mark 12:38-44

November 13–19
1 Samuel 1:4-20
Psalm 16
Hebrews 10:11-25
Mark 13:1-8

November 20–26
THE REIGN OF CHRIST
2 Samuel 23:1-7
Psalm 132:1-18
  (or Daniel 7:9-10, 13-14)
Revelation 1:4b-8
John 18:33-37

November 23
THANKSGIVING DAY, USA
Joel 2:21-27
Psalm 126
1 Timothy 2:1-7
Matthew 6:25-33

November 27–December 3
FIRST SUNDAY OF ADVENT
Jeremiah 33:14-16
Psalm 25:1-10
1 Thessalonians 3:9-13
Luke 21:25-36

December 4–10
SECOND SUNDAY OF ADVENT
Malachi 3:1-4
Luke 1:68-79
Philippians 1:3-11
Luke 3:1-6

December 11–17
THIRD SUNDAY OF ADVENT
Zephaniah 3:14-20
Isaiah 12:2-6
Philippians 4:4-7
Luke 3:7-18

December 18–24
FOURTH SUNDAY OF ADVENT
Micah 5:2-5a
Luke 1:47-55
  (*or* Psalm 80:1-7)
Hebrews 10:5-10
Luke 1:39-55

> **December 24**
> **CHRISTMAS EVE**
> Isaiah 9:2-7
> Psalm 96
> Titus 2:11-14
> Luke 2:1-20

> **December 25**
> **CHRISTMAS DAY**
> Isaiah 52:7-10
> Psalm 98
> Hebrews 1:1-12
> John 1:1-14

December 25–31
FIRST SUNDAY AFTER CHRISTMAS
1 Samuel 2:18-20, 26
Psalm 148
Colossians 3:12-17
Luke 2:41-52

❦ 2000 ❦

JANUARY

S	M	T	W	T	F	S
						1
2	3	4	5	6	7	8
9	10	11	12	13	14	15
16	17	18	19	20	21	22
23	24	25	26	27	28	29
30	31					

FEBRUARY

S	M	T	W	T	F	S
		1	2	3	4	5
6	7	8	9	10	11	12
13	14	15	16	17	18	19
20	21	22	23	24	25	26
27	28	29				

MARCH

S	M	T	W	T	F	S
			1	2	3	4
5	6	7	8	9	10	11
12	13	14	15	16	17	18
19	20	21	22	23	24	25
26	27	28	29	30	31	

APRIL

S	M	T	W	T	F	S
						1
2	3	4	5	6	7	8
9	10	11	12	13	14	15
16	17	18	19	20	21	22
23	24	25	26	27	28	29
30						

MAY

S	M	T	W	T	F	S
	1	2	3	4	5	6
7	8	9	10	11	12	13
14	15	16	17	18	19	20
21	22	23	24	25	26	27
28	29	30	31			

JUNE

S	M	T	W	T	F	S
				1	2	3
4	5	6	7	8	9	10
11	12	13	14	15	16	17
18	19	20	21	22	23	24
25	26	27	28	29	30	

JULY

S	M	T	W	T	F	S
						1
2	3	4	5	6	7	8
9	10	11	12	13	14	15
16	17	18	19	20	21	22
23	24	25	26	27	28	29
30	31					

AUGUST

S	M	T	W	T	F	S
		1	2	3	4	5
6	7	8	9	10	11	12
13	14	15	16	17	18	19
20	21	22	23	24	25	26
27	28	29	30	31		

SEPTEMBER

S	M	T	W	T	F	S
					1	2
3	4	5	6	7	8	9
10	11	12	13	14	15	16
17	18	19	20	21	22	23
24	25	26	27	28	29	30

OCTOBER

S	M	T	W	T	F	S
1	2	3	4	5	6	7
8	9	10	11	12	13	14
15	16	17	18	19	20	21
22	23	24	25	26	27	28
29	30	31				

NOVEMBER

S	M	T	W	T	F	S
			1	2	3	4
5	6	7	8	9	10	11
12	13	14	15	16	17	18
19	20	21	22	23	24	25
26	27	28	29	30		

DECEMBER

S	M	T	W	T	F	S
					1	2
3	4	5	6	7	8	9
10	11	12	13	14	15	16
17	18	19	20	21	22	23
24	25	26	27	28	29	30